WINNING NLRB ELECTIONS
Management's Strategy
and
Preventive Programs

CORPORATE LAW AND PRACTICE
Practice Handbook Series
Number 6

WINNING NLRB ELECTIONS
Management's Strategy
and
Preventive Programs

Louis Jackson
Robert Lewis

Tenth Printing

B1-0277
PRACTISING LAW INSTITUTE
New York City

"If you wish in the world to advance,
Your merits you're bound to enhance,
You must stir it and stump it,
And blow your own trumpet,
Or, trust me, you haven't a chance!"

SIR WILLIAM S. GILBERT,
Ruddigore, Act 1.

FOREWORD

This book is a manual for employers who wish to avoid union organization and for the lawyers who represent them. It is a counterpart of guides in existence for organizers and attorneys representing unions. A frankly partisan book, it is one that those on the other side will probably have to reckon with.

Step by step, the authors counsel the employer, starting *before* the union perches on the doorstep, continuing through each phase of organization and counterattack until the ballots are counted and, win or lose, immediately after the vote. Different phases are covered in brief detail, the crystallization of the authors' years of experience reduced to its essence.

The book is profusely illustrated with exhibits from live campaigns. Where a form is needed, it is presented and explained. Finally, for the more sophisticated, there is a meaty appendix, including, among other things, a brief history of the labor movement, the full text of the Labor Management Relations Act, and examples of unfair labor practices upon which 100 NLRB bargaining orders are based.

SELMA ARNOLD
Staff Editor, *Practising Law Institute*

vii

ACKNOWLEDGMENTS

The authors express their appreciation to many of their office staff who have lent their aid in the preparation of this book, and particularly acknowledge the valued research of G. Harrison Darby, Roger S. Kaplan and Peggy L. Braden. To Thomas P. Schnitzler and William A. Krupman, partners of the authors, we are indebted for their encouragement, critique and analysis. Last, but not least, sincerest of thanks to the authors' wives, Sylvia Jackson and Ethel Lewis, for their understanding and cooperation in foregoing the many hours and weekends which this book preempted.

ACKNOWLEDGMENTS

TABLE OF CONTENTS

APPENDICES

LIST OF FACSIMILES

INTRODUCTION

Most employers are not unionized. Many have never had experience with unions. Similarly, only a small percentage of the bar are labor practitioners. When the Practising Law Institute asked us to write this book and requested a statement of what we conceived to be its purpose, we made the following reply:

> It has been our experience in practicing in the field of labor relations law that there is still a substantial number of employers and their counsel who have had limited exposure to union organizational activity. National Labor Relations Board Chairman, Edward B. Miller, in commenting on this phenomenon, concluded that there was a 'real need for the labor bench and bar to continue our efforts to educate the business community as to the basic framework of Federal Labor Law. . . .'

> This, then, is our purpose—to set forth in non-technical language a treatise for both layman and lawyer as a reference guide in the area dealing with union organizing activities. The book is written from the viewpoint of how the attorney may best protect his client's interest, and how the client may best reach his objective of remaining unorganized.

> It is our hope that this book will be of interest to your wide clientele and that it will bring to your remarkable organization additional resources for furthering your contribution to continuing educational efforts.

1

The employer whose employees are not represented by a union can take pride in the fact that he has created the proper human relations climate. In all likelihood, he is an enlightened employer. He is paying fair wages and providing competitive fringe benefits. He places heavy emphasis on good employee relations. He attends to his employees' needs. He communicates with them and provides outlets for their communicating with him. In sum, he is a good employer.

Perhaps he is just lucky. One day his luck may run out. In the pressure of profitmaking he may have overlooked the very people who helped make it possible. He learns that his employees are being solicited for union membership. What should he do? He starts off with a handicap. With a business to run, his interest in labor relations is only part-time, in contrast with the union organizer who works daily at his "trade." It is generally agreed that he should quickly obtain competent advice.

Engaging in a National Labor Relations Board election is not a do-it-yourself enterprise. It is a cooperative effort between employer and lawyer. The attorney's role, of course, is to prevent missteps. As in other areas of the law, counsel does not wait to extricate his client after the trap has snapped. He counsels him in advance. With this is mind, we have set forth the rights and obligations of an employer faced with union organizing. We offer suggestions, drawn from practical experience, for the successful proselytizing of the electorate.

Winning an NLRB election is an admixture of law and psychology. It is a contest for the allegiance of employees. It is a journey into individual and group attitudes. The authors offer this Baedeker to help the uninitiated travel this tortuous road.

CHAPTER I

COUNSELING THE NON-UNION EMPLOYER

Why are some plants a constant beehive of union organizing activity while others enjoy relative freedom from union attention? The answer lies in the employer's personnel relations program. An employer who practices good personnel relations is less likely to be organized.

The essence of preventive labor relations, *i.e.*, avoiding or averting union activity, lies in establishing and maintaining an aggressive employee relations program designed to build employee morale, loyalty and commitment to the goals of the business. Such a program must be initiated long before any signs of union organizing activity and must be maintained with a single-minded dedication. It may well require more management effort and attention than dealing with a union.

The primary objective of a sound personnel program is to contribute to the success and profitability of the business. Lower unit labor costs through greater employee productivity, improved product quality, and reduced absenteeism and turnover are but some of the benefits. Employees benefit too. Working in a healthy, profitable enterprise, they enjoy steady, secure work and regular improvements in wages, fringe benefits and working conditions. A company's non-union status is a by-product of this program.

3

The keystone of a sound personnel program is good employee communications. It plays a decisive role both as a preventive tool and in winning an election. Other elements of the program include:

—Wages and benefits equal to or better than competition.
—Safe, healthy work environment.
—Avenues for resolution of employee complaints.
—Meaningful, interesting work.
—Recognition and incentive for good work performance.
—Opportunity for personal growth and job advancement.
—Respect for the self-esteem and needs of the individual.
—Fair and consistent administration of discipline.
—Written, up-to-date personnel policies.

The challenge for the employer today is to apply these basic concepts in such a way that they become the foundation of a sound employee relations policy. Then, such an employer can truly say to his employees:

Our success as a company is founded on the skill and efforts of our employees.

It is our policy to deal with our employees fairly and honestly and to respect and recognize each as an individual.

It is our opinion that unionization would interfere with this principle of individual treatment, respect and recognition.

It is for this reason that we are opposed to unionization as being against your interest and ours.

STUDYING THE COMPANY

The attorney whose counsel is sought by an unorganized employer needs to know more than labor law. He should have a knowledge of personnel administration and be familiar with the history of labor unions in this country. (See Appendix A for recommended publications dealing with personnel administration and Appendix B for a brief labor history.)

Initially, the attorney should inquire about his client's attitude. Some employers have an inherent dislike for unions. Some are uncertain of their own attitudes. Others are convinced that unionization is inevitable.

If the client holds to the inevitability view, the attorney can show by statistics that unionization is not inevitable. Today, unions are losing almost one-half of all elections.[1*] Furthermore, union membership has not kept pace with the growth of the working forces in this country. Unions report a combined membership of 19.4 million,[2] out of a total workforce of eighty-two million.[3] Twenty-three percent does not add up to "inevitability." The employer who wants to operate without a union has a good chance of accomplishing it.

After ascertaining that his client desires to remain unorganized, the attorney should then study his client as a business organization. The study should be done as a critique and assessment, identifying the employer's faults, and highlighting his deeds. The following checklist may be used:

1. The Principals

2. Plant locations (an on the scene, personal survey is desirable)
   a) Labor supply
   b) Unionization of nearby plants
   c) Community attitudes

3. History of the founding of the business

---

* Footnote references are at the end of each chapter.

4. Nature of business and products, past and present; general financial condition

5. Chart of growth
   a) Number of employees
   b) Distributorships, branches and warehouses
   c) Sales volume
   d) Seasonal fluctuations of business

6. Table of organization

7. Personnel administration
   a) Administrator and staff
   b) Functions performed
   c) Professional quality

8. Supervisory staff
   a) Recruitment and training of supervisors
   b) Extent of involvement in personnel functions

9. Analysis of non-supervisory staff
   a) By job classification
   b) By sex within classifications

10. The employment process
    a) Sources of labor
    b) Employment forms—requisitions, employment applications, medical reports
    c) Job specifications
    d) Interviewing guides
    e) Physical examination
    f) Validated tests
    g) Reference checks
    h) Applicant files
    i) Final approval
    j) Orientation of the new employee
    k) Probationary period and its use

11. Transfers and promotions, upgrading, demotion
    a) General policy, seniority vs. merit
    b) Wage considerations
    c) Job bidding procedures

12. Termination of employment
    a) Review and appeals of discharge cases
    b) Exit interviewing and use of the exit interview
    c) Turnover statistics—analysis of reasons and utilization of the analysis

13. Wages and hours
    a) Applicability of Federal Wage & Hour Laws
    b) Wage and benefit surveys—comparison with employer's own industry and with related local, regional and national wage trends
    c) Wage chart showing rates for all job classifications
    d) Method of payment—cash, check, weekly
    e) Job evaluation and wage progression system
    f) Incentive plans—piece work, day rate, commissions, production standards, time study
    g) Merit reviews
    h) History of general wage increases
    i) Cost of living escalator
    j) Overtime premium pay—daily, weekly, Saturday, Sunday
    k) Overtime distribution procedure
    l) Shift differential
    m) Pay for holidays worked
    n) Reporting and call-in pay, pay for time lost due to weather, power failure, etc.
    o) Rest periods, wash-up time
    p) Deductions for absences and tardiness

14. Physical working conditions
    a) Age of plant and equipment
    b) Housekeeping and sanitation

c) Light, ventilation, dust, heat
d) Noise
e) Employee distribution; comfort of work areas
f) Lunch rooms, rest rooms, drinking fountains, cafeteria services, vending machines
g) Safety provisions and safety committees
h) Provisions for first aid, doctors, nurses
i) Work clothing, safety glasses and shoes, tools, etc.

15. Benefits
   a) Paid holidays
   b) Vacations
   c) Military leave
   d) Jury duty pay
   e) Pension
   f) Clothing allowance
   g) Bereavement pay

16. Leave of Absence
   a) Maternity
   b) Sickness and disability
   c) Personal, educational leave

17. Insurance
   a) Life, accidental death and dismemberment
   b) Sick leave and disability protection
   c) Hospital, surgical and major medical
   d) Dental and other plans
   e) Contributory nature of plans

18. Financial incentives
   a) Profit sharing
   b) Pension
   c) Credit union
   d) Loans
   e) Christmas bonus
   f) Employee savings plan
   g) Tuition contributions and scholarships
   h) Parking privileges

19. Training programs
    a) For supervisors
    b) For non-supervisory employees
    c) Apprenticeship

20. Employee publications and publicity
    a) Employee handbook
    b) House magazine or periodical news sheet; extent of
       employee participation
    c) Letters to employees
    d) Annual reports
    e) Local press releases
    f) Suggestion system, awards

21. Employee interviews and meetings; grievance procedure
    a) Interviews of individual employees; scheduling;
       analysis
    b) Plant-wide or office-wide meetings
    c) Departmental or other group meetings
    d) Formal grievance procedure—steps and final resolution
    e) Informal grievance procedure; personnel involved;
       final resolution
    f) Log of complaints and disposition
    g) Other methods of measuring employee morale

22. Employee activities
    a) Bowling and other sports
    b) Picnics, dances, dinners
    c) Plant tours
    d) Contests

23. Concerning unions and union activity
    a) Extent of unionization in company
    b) Current collective bargaining agreements—part of plant
       involved, other locations involved
    c) Present activity—handbilling, calls at homes, letters,
       in-plant activity

d) Election petitions pending
e) Charges of unfair labor practices pending
f) Outstanding court decrees or judgments arising out of prior and current labor union activities
g) History of prior union organizing
h) Extent of organization in employer's industry; unions involved

This profile will be an invaluable tool in counseling the employer. It will be helpful in preparing for hearings before the NLRB. It will be a source of reference in advising on responses to union communications to employees. This analysis also may reveal areas of weakness which may be the source of employee discontent and, thus, points of attack by the union. It can point up areas for improvement.

Lest one dismiss the undertaking as too arduous or detailed, consider what the Office & Professional Employees International Union prescribes as preparation for the organizer's background. Its publication, *Now Let's Get Out and Organize*,[4] lists the following items:

1. Location of the plant or office.
2. The product or service given.
3. The entrances and exits used.
4. A floor plan of the office.
5. Restaurants where employees eat.
6. Taverns employees frequent.
7. Mode of transportation used.
8. Location of parking lots.
9. Number of employees involved.
10. Number of shifts.
11. Female-male ratio.
12. Starting and quitting times.
13. What is the wage structure?
14. When are employees paid?
15. Do they get a bonus?
16. Shift premiums.

17. Overtime practices.
18. Vacation entitlement.
19. Pension plan.
20. Sick and accident policy.
21. Group insurance plan.
22. Hospitalization.
23. Surgical plan.
24. Major medical plan.
25. Cost of above to employees.
26. How is overtime distributed?
27. Is seniority followed?
28. What is promotional policy?
29. How can employees transfer in job?
30. Leave of absence policy.
31. Layoff practice.
32. Recall procedures.
33. Disciplinary procedures.
34. Financial condition of company.
35. Are they near bankruptcy?
36. Are they economically vulnerable?
37. When is the peak business cycle?
38. Tactics of company toward unions.
39. Are the plant workers organized?
40. Have they had strikes there?
41. Do they have a good contract?
42. Will they cooperate with you?
43. Is there a bowling league?
44. Is there a company magazine?
45. Is there an employees' manual?

An in-depth study of a company is a standard operating procedure for most unions.   The AFL-CIO *Guidebook for Union Organizers* encourages organizers to conduct such a survey prior to contacting any employees.[5]   It is ironic that the diligent organizer may do so good a job that, in certain respects, he gets to know the company better than its own management.   Employer's counsel should do at least as thorough a job.

LABOR-MANAGEMENT RELATIONS ACT

An employer seeking advice in the field of labor-management relations will, in most instances, come within the jurisdiction of the National Labor Relations Board.[6] The statute law which applies to such employers is the Labor-Management Relations Act of 1947, as amended.[7] (The full text of the Act is reproduced as Appendix C.)

The Act's Findings and Policies state that there is an "inequality of bargaining power between employees who do not possess full freedom of association" and "employers."[8] This inequality, it was found, affected the flow of commerce, and tended to aggravate recurrent business depressions, by depressing wage rates and the purchasing power of wage earners.[9]

It therefore was declared to be the policy of the United States to eliminate the causes of obstructions to the free flow of commerce by:

> encouraging the practice and procedure of collective bargaining and by protecting the exercise by workers of full freedom of association, self-organization and designation of representatives of their own choosing. . . .[10]

This statement of policy often is used by unions to encourage organization. (See Facsimile No. 1, page 13.) Often omitted in such communications, however, is the statutory pronouncement of the equal right of employees to refrain from collective bargaining and self-organization.[11]

Thus an employee has the right to partake in collective activities or refrain therefrom. How do employees implement this right? What is the role of the union? May an employer seek to dissuade his employees from unionization? We begin our study.

FACSIMILE No. 1

NOTES TO CHAPTER I

1. In the fiscal year ending June 30, 1970, unions lost 44% of Board-conducted elections. 35 NLRB Ann. Rep. 15 (1970).

2. U. S. Dep't of Labor, Bureau of Labor Statistics, *Directory of National & International Labor Unions and Employee Associations* (1971), as reported in 78 LRR 56.

3. 1970 BNA Lab. Rel. Yearbook 388.

4. Office & Professional Employees Int'l Union, AFL-CIO-CLC, *Now Let's Get Out and Organize* 5-6.

5. Indus. Union Dep't, AFL-CIO, *A Guidebook for Union Organizers* 4-5 (Pub. No. 42, Sept. 1961).

6. The labor relations of federal employees, airlines and railroads are separately regulated. Exec. Order No. 11,491, 3 C.F.R. 510 (1971) (federal employees). Railway Labor Act, 45 U.S.C. §§ 151-163, 181-188 (1964) (airlines and railroads). The agricultural industry is at the present unregulated. Labor Management Relations Act § 101.2(3), 29 U.S.C. § 152(3) (1964). Labor relations of state and municipal employees is regulated by state law. For example, New York's Public Employees' Fair Employment Act (Taylor Law), N. Y. Civil Service Law §§ 200 *et seq.* (McKinney Supp. 1970).

7. Labor Management Relations Act, 1947, 29 U.S.C. §§ 151-168 (1964), *amending* National Labor Relations Act, ch. 372, 49 Stat. 449 (1935) (hereinafter cited as LMRA).

8. LMRA § 101.1, 29 U.S.C. § 151 (1964).

9. *Id.* These findings were carried over from the original Act.

10. *Id.* This policy was discussed recently in United Aircraft Corp., 192 NLRB No. 62, 77 LRRM 1785, 1791 (1971).

11. LMRA § 101.7, 29 U.S.C. § 157 (1964).

CHAPTER II

INVESTIGATING THE UNION

The AFL-CIO views "a campaign to organize a union [as] a contest between labor and management. . . ."[1]

As in any contest, one must know his opposition. Familiarity with labor history helps to understand unions' present day motivations and their *modus operandi*. Appendix B briefly summarizes this history.

There are current facts to be ascertained. How is the union structured? How strong are its finances? What is its reputation? Is it prone to strike when recognition is denied? Who are its officers and what are its policies?

The union will spend a great deal of time obtaining detailed information about the company it seeks to organize. The employer should know equally as much about the union. Some of the specific areas he should investigate include the following:

1. Name and address of union
2. Names and titles of officers
3. Bylaws and constitution
4. Financial status
5. Salaries, expense accounts and criminal records, if any, of officers and staff
6. Record of strikes: economic, sympathetic, or in contract violation

       7. History of boycott activities, either self-initiated or
          in support of other unions
       8. Strike funds
       9. Record of unfair labor practices

What are some of the sources for this information? The following are commonly known materials.

SOURCE MATERIAL

Newspapers such as *The New York Times* and *The Wall Street Journal;* magazines such as *Business Week, Newsweek* and *Time Magazine* and a number of newsclipping services can be utilized.[2]

The labor press is an important source. Most international unions have their own newspaper or magazine publication, for which they accept subscriptions. The New York Public Library receives copies of most of these publications.[3]

Trade publications often provide insight into union activity and results of union elections in the particular industry. The Fairchild Publishing Company is an example.[4]

Employer associations such as the U.S. Chamber of Commerce, the Industrial Management Council and the Commerce and Industry Association in New York, also provide source material. Virtually any industry association can provide a treasure chest of information.

The NLRB publishes a variety of reports. It issues weekly summaries of decisions and directions of election, dismissals of petitions, and other miscellaneous actions. It also publishes a monthly summary of election results, classified by industry, with names of company and union involved and the votes cast.[5]

In addition it publishes an annual report, which summarizes its decisions for the preceding fiscal year and provides charts and statistics of its activities. The full texts of NLRB decisions are available upon request.[6] Trial Examiners' decisions in unfair labor practice proceedings also may be obtained.[7]

The Bureau of Labor Statistics of the U.S. Department of Labor, has many publications available for purchase.

State Departments of Labor often provide relevant material. For example, New York publishes a record of strikes, citing such valuable information as the length of the strike, the issues involved and the terms of settlement.[8]

Labor law services. The most frequently used are the Bureau of National Affairs,[9] Commerce Clearing House[10] and Prentice-Hall.[11] These publications can be found in most bar association and law school libraries and in some court and public libraries.[12]

Directories are valuable reference tools. The U.S. Department of Labor, Bureau of Labor Statistics, publishes the *Directory of National & International Labor Unions*, listing all national and international unions.[13] The New York State Department of Labor, Division of Research and Statistics, publishes the *Directory of Labor Organizations in New York State*,[14] listing the names, addresses and officers of labor organizations located within the state. The New York City Office of Collective Bargaining publishes the *Directory of New York City Public Employee Organizations*, listing the names, addresses, phone numbers, officers and publications of public employee organizations.[15]

The employer newly confronted with a unionization drive should also undertake a prompt survey of what the union will try to sell his employees. A visit with other employers who have jousted or have contracts with the same union will often be helpful.

STRUCTURE AND FINANCES

The Labor-Management Reporting and Disclosure Act of 1959,[16] requires labor organizations to file reports with the U.S. Department of Labor.

One report must be filed within ninety days after the date when the union first becomes subject to the Act.[17] This filing is not repeated. It is submitted on Form LM-1, the "Labor Organization Information Report."

This report contains the names and titles of the union's officers, fees, and dues. The union is required to designate certain parts of its constitution and bylaws, and to summarize particular matters such as qualifications for membership, levying of assessments, meetings, audits, selection of stewards and officers and strike authorization procedures.[18] (See Facsimile No. 2, pages 20-21.)

The LMRDA requires labor organizations to file annually Form LM-2, known as the "Labor Organization Annual Report."[19] It is essentially a financial report. It itemizes such matters as salaries of the union's officers and employees, car and other expense allowances, receipts from fines and assessments, and disbursements for such items as strike benefits.

Employees rarely have the opportunity to see these reports. Employers may disseminate information extracted from them. (See Chapter VII, pages 135, 142.)

Upon filing a report, the union is assigned a reporting number. These numbers are compiled in the *Register of Reporting Labor Organizations* published by the U.S. Department of Labor, Labor Management Services Administration. It is an alphabetical listing by state of the labor organizations which have filed reports under the reporting provisions of the LMRDA. An employer who desires to examine or obtain a copy of a report may do so at any of the twenty-four offices of the U.S. Department of Labor's Office of Labor-Management and Welfare-Pension Reports. (See Appendix D for a listing of the area offices.)

In the event that the area office does not have the particular union's report or lacks some information, such as the union's constitution and bylaws, it may be available at the U.S. Department of Labor, Office of Labor-Management and Welfare-Pension Reports, Publications Department, 8701 Georgia Avenue, Silver Spring, Maryland 20910. The full name and address of the union involved and its reporting number are required. Copies of documents are available at 25 cents per page.

Under the Welfare and Pension Plans Disclosure Act,[20] administrators of welfare and pension benefit plans are required to file Forms D-1 and D-2 with the Office of Labor-Management and Welfare-Pension Reports in Washington.[21] This law applies to all plans, both union and employer, and to plans jointly established by unions and employers.

A study of these reports will enable the employer to make a comparison of his plans with those propagandized by the union. This information can be supplemented by study of union contracts, where available.

FACSIMILE No. 2

| U.S. DEPARTMENT OF LABOR
OFFICE OF LABOR-MANAGEMENT
AND WELFARE-PENSION REPORTS
WASHINGTON, D.C. 20210 | LABOR ORGANIZATION INFORMATION REPORT
Act of September 14, 1959, Public Law 86-257
Form LM-1
(Revised 1967)
FILE TWO COPIES | Form approved.
Bureau of the Budget No. 44-R1124. |

DO NOT USE THIS SPACE

READ INSTRUCTIONS CAREFULLY BEFORE PREPARING REPORT

1 Name of labor organization (Include local number and affiliation, if any.)

Mailing address (Where official mail should be sent to the union.)

Number and Street:

| City | County | State | ZIP Code |

| Records necessary to verify this report are kept at (check box) |
| □ Address in Item 1. |
| □ Address in Item 2. |

Section 201(a) of the Labor-Management Reporting and Disclosure Act of 1959 requires that a report of the following information be filed with the Secretary of Labor by each labor organization subject to the Act within 90 days after the labor organization becomes subject to this Act. A report of any changes in the information reported below must be filed annually with the Secretary at the time of filing of the annual financial report required by section 201(b) of the Act.

2. Address of principal office, if different from address in Item 1

3. Any other address or addresses at which records necessary to verify this report are kept

4. (a) Indicate type of labor organization by a check in the applicable box:

    (1) □ Local   (2) □ National or International   (3) □ Other (Describe) ....

    (b) Are you affiliated with or chartered by a National or International Union or National Federation?
    If YES, give name of such organization(s)   □ Yes   □ No

5. Enter the month and day on which the fiscal year of the reporting labor organization ends ....

6. List the names and titles of your present officers. (For definition of officers, see instructions.)

7. List fees and dues required:

| | | IF MORE THAN ONE RATE APPLIES, ENTER | |
		Minimum	Maximum
(a) Initiation fee or fees required from new members . . . . $............		$............	$............
(b) Fee or fees required from transferred members . . . . $............		$............	$............
(c) Fees required for work permits . . . . . $............ per (Year, mo., etc.)		$............ per	$............ per
(d) Regular dues or fees or other periodic payments required to remain a member of the reporting labor organization . $............ per		$............ per	$............ per

8. The Act requires every labor organization to adopt, and to file with this report a copy of, a constitution and bylaws—that is the basic written rules governing the organization.

Please identify below the documents filed with this report to fulfill the above requirement.

....

....

FACSIMILE No. 2

9. The Act requires detailed statements showing the provisions made and procedures followed with respect to each of the items listed below.

Please either (1) show in the proper column where a detailed statement on the particular item can be found in the documents submitted under question 8, or (2) attach such a detailed statement and identify the attachment in the proper column below.

ITEM	PAGE AND SECTION OR PARAGRAPH NUMBER OF CONSTITUTION OR BYLAWS	IDENTIFICATION OF OTHER DETAILED STATEMENT ATTACHED
(a) Qualifications for or restrictions on membership		
(b) Levying of assessments		
(c) Participation in insurance or other benefit plans		
(d) Authorization for disbursement of labor organization funds		
(e) Audit of labor organization financial transactions		
(f) The calling of regular and special meetings		
(g) (1) The selection of officers and stewards and of any representatives to other bodies composed of labor organizations' representatives		
(2) Give specific statement of the manner in which each officer was elected, appointed, or otherwise selected:		
(h) Discipline or removal of officers or agents for breaches of their trust		
(i) Impositions of fines, suspensions, and expulsions of members including the grounds for such action and any provisions made for notice, hearing, judgment on the evidence, and appeal procedures		
(j) Authorization for bargaining demands		
(k) Ratification of contract terms		
(l) Authorization for strikes		
(m) Issuance of work permits		

Under section 209(d) of the Labor-Management Reporting and Disclosure Act of 1959, each individual required to sign this report is personally responsible for the filing of such report and for any statement therein which he knows to be false.

Records providing in sufficient detail the necessary basic information and data from which the reports and other documents filed may be verified, explained or clarified, and checked for accuracy and completeness must be maintained and kept available for examination for at least 5 years after the date of filing the report. These records include vouchers, worksheets, receipts, and applicable resolutions.

Each of the undersigned, duly authorized officials of the above labor organization, declares, under the applicable penalties of law,* that all of the information submitted herewith (including the information contained in any accompanying documents) has been examined by him and is to the best of his knowledge and belief, true, correct, and complete.

Signed at ....   Signed at ....
            (City and State)   (City and State)

this .... day of ...., 19.......   this .... day of ...., 19.......

....
        (Signature)   (Signature)

(Title—President (or corresponding principal officer if there is no president))   (Title—Secretary (or corresponding principal officer if there is no secretary))

*See section on "Penalties" in accompanying instructions.

HOW UNIONS ORGANIZE

A union commences an organizing campaign by assigning an individual to the company. He may have any one of a number of titles: organizer, business agent or field representative. He is a professional. If the union is successful, he may be the person with whom the employer will have to negotiate the contract.

It has been said that an ideal organizer is part missionary, part salesman, part politician, part counselor, part teacher, part psychologist and part lawyer.[22] As to the latter, he may be more knowledgeable concerning NLRB procedures than many a general practitioner.

A union looks for the following attributes in a good organizer: attractive appearance, initiative, judgment, leadership, speaking ability, loyalty, personality, sincerity, patience, adaptability and imagination.[23] This picture is not of an ordinary man of ordinary qualities and capabilities. He should never be underestimated. But why has he been assigned to "this" company?

The company may be the target because disgruntled employees have sought help from the union. An employer who wonders "why me?" may be the victim of his own shortcomings.

The company may have been chosen, not because of employee discontent, but because it has been selected by the union. Often there is pressure on unions from organized employers to work on the unorganized so as to remove alleged economic differences.

Generally, there is nothing "personal" about the organizer's interest in a company. As a professional, he looks upon his task objectively—to organize employees. His deep commitment to the union cause will not lead him into vendettas. Of course, if there is a history of unfair labor practices which thwarted past organizational attempts, feelings may run high. In the normal case, however, objective considerations predominate.

ORGANIZING TECHNIQUES

Some unions begin organizing by soliciting their present membership for assistance. District 65 of the National Council of Distributive Workers uses this technique:

> The main job before us is to halt the drop in '65 employment, which saps the strength of the union. This we can only do by organizing additional shops. Newly organized shops increase our membership, add to our strength and provide additional job opportunities for our members. We, therefore, must find a way quickly, immediately to revive organization.
>
>   ✿   ✿   ✿
>
> In each Local each steward will have an assignment to organize the shop next door, in the same building, on the same block or, in a few cases, a block or two away.[24]

A similar program was instituted by the IUE in Philadelphia. (See Facsimile No. 3, page 24.) Another method used is to contact card signers from previous unsuccessful campaigns. (See Facsimile No. 4, page 25.) Some unions take a mail survey as the initial step to organizing. (See Facsimile No. 5, page 26.)

The most common technique used by unions is to pass out literature at the plant gate, with little or no prior employee contact. This literature, commonly referred to as handbills, usually will have an authorization card attached or included, to be detached, filled in and returned. (See Facsimile No. 6, page 27.) The extent of employee response will influence further efforts.

FACSIMILE No. 3

INTERNATIONAL UNION OF ELECTRICAL,

RADIO & MACHINE WORKERS,

ROOM 711, 4 NORTH 11th STREET

PHILADELPHIA 7, PA. — PHONE: WAlnut 5-7435

TO ALL LOCAL UNION MEMBERS

Dear Sir and Brother:

We are certain that you, a trade unionist in one of our most progressive and militant IUE unions, know the necessity for a relentless, unending effort to organize the unorganized. Successful organizational activity is particularly needed in the Philadelphia Metropolitan area.

New plants are rapidly springing up and old established plants continue to operate without a union, with company unions, or under UE contracts. Many of these plants are competitive with our own plants. The great majority are paying minimum rates. They have the serious effects of making it tougher for us to better our own contracts and are making it increasingly more difficult to protect and maintain our present standards. These plants also present many opportunities for your company's present customers to transfer their business elsewhere, with disastrous effect upon employment in your own shop.

In this day and age of atomic energy, automation and new electronic developments, a trade unionist cannot afford to "make like an ostrich". We must take a good look at these unorganized plants, recognize the threat they represent to our security and well-being, and resolve to do something about the problem.

One of the easiest ways to assist in organizational work is to give the name, address and phone number of your relatives, friends, neighbors or others whom you know to be employed at any unorganized, company-union or UE plant. We also need the full name and address of the plant and type of product(s) manufactured.

We would be more than happy to have an indication from you, as an individual, of your willingness to contribute some of your nonworking time to assist in organizational work. Please send us your name and address if you are interested.

FACSIMILE No. 4

Oil, Chemical and Atomic Workers
International Union

H. J. McCLAIN, DIRECTOR
DISTRICT NO. 7

COLONIAL SAVINGS & LOAN BLDG.
4740 WEST 55TH STREET
SUITE 2-D
OAK LAWN, ILLINOIS 60453

TO: LAST YEAR'S CARD SIGNERS

At this time I would like to make inquiry as to your interest in joining O.C.A.W. to have full job protection. In the news media we read and hear where more and more people are becoming unemployed. This trend seems to have continued for some time, without prospect of improving. Without Union security you have no guarantee of job layoff by seniority. Join today and make your future and your family's welfare more secure.

Remember, all the benefits you now receive will be retained. O. C. A. W. will strive to better your present benefits, seek better wages and improve your working conditions. May I request that you join us today. As an International Representative, I know that O.C.A.W. can and will do a job for you. We must have your help to bring organization about.

Most sincerely yours,

FACSIMILE No. 5

TO ALL EMPLOYEES

GREETINGS FROM THE WESTERN CONFERENCE OF PRINTING SPECIALTIES AND
PAPER PRODUCTS UNION.

WE HAVE BEEN ASKED BY SOME OF THE EMPLOYEES TO HELP YOU ORGANIZE
YOUR PLANT INTO THE UNION.

AT THIS TIME THE UNION IS GOING TO TAKE A SURVEY OF THE EMPLOYEES
TO FIND OUT THE INTEREST IN FORMING A UNION. ITS BEEN BROUGHT
TO OUR ATTENTION BY SOME OF THE EMPLOYEES THAT THE PLANT IS IN NEED
OF A UNION NOW MORE THAN EVER. OUR UNION HAS A NEW ORGANIZING
PROGRAM TO HELP YOU. ALSO MANY NEW PROGRAMS FOR OUR UNION MEMBERS.

ENCLOSED IS A SELF ADDRESSED ENVELOPE. PLEASE ANSWER AND MAIL
THE FORM BACK TO US.

THIS FORM IS CONFIDENTIAL!

1.   ARE YOU STILL EMPLOYED?
2.   WOULD YOU BE INTERESTED IN SOMEONE CALLING ON YOU IN
        THE PRIVACY OF YOUR HOME TO EXPLAIN THE UNION AND ITS
        BENEFITS TO YOU?

YES   ☐   NO   ☐

3.   DO YOU THINK YOU NEED A UNION?
4.   DO YOU THINK YOUR FELLOW EMPLOYEES NEED A UNION?

NAME _____

ADDRESS _____

PHONE NO. _____

YOUR TYPE OF WORK _____

YOUR SHIFT _____ STARTING TIME _____

FACSIMILE No. 6

OCAW

Oil, Chemical and Atomic Workers International Union, AFL-CIO

The democratic way to:

- **Better jobs**
- **Secure future**
- **Higher wages**
- **Orderly advancement**
- **Improved working conditions**
- **Old age protection**
- **Fair treatment**

In a union that is controlled and operated by and for its members.

To build a better future for yourself and your fellow employees, fill in, sign and mail this membership application in the attached envelope.

THE OIL, CHEMICAL AND ATOMIC WORKERS
INTERNATIONAL UNION, AFL-CIO
– AUTHORIZATION –

Name _____ Phone No. _____
PLEASE PRINT
Address _____ City _____

Name of Company _____ Location _____

Department _____ Shift Hr's. _____

I hereby designate and authorize the Oil, Chemical and Atomic Workers International Union, AFL-CIO, as my collective bargaining representative in respect to rates of pay, wages, hours of employment, and other terms and conditions of employment. I also hereby authorize said union to request recognition from my employer as my bargaining agent for said purposes.

Date _____ Signature _____

Another organizing method is through the Trojan horse technique, or, more colloquially, the use of a "plant." [25] The procedure is simple. A union sponsored individual applies for a job. If employed, he becomes assimilated. Within a short time, after careful conversations and weighing of responses, the "plant" builds up a cadre of sympathetic employees. They are then introduced to the union organizer. He takes it from there.

RECRUITING IN-PLANT LEADERS

"The organizer has two immediate objectives when he makes his first contacts with workers," states the *AFL-CIO Guidebook*.[26] "He is looking for leadership for his campaign and information about the specific problems and complaints of the employees." [27]

The Office & Professional Employees International Union advises the organizer that, in seeking potential leadership, he should look for persons who can command the respect of their fellow employees. In his search for in-plant leadership, he is advised to avoid "soreheads" and "gripers."

The organizer is a practical man. He does not need to manufacture or fabricate issues. Those which he has not learned about through his survey he will readily discover in conversations with employees.

The OPEIU manual states:

> The basic technique should be an attentive ear to the needs of the people and develop the language of how —through a Union Contract— they can achieve job security, job opportunity, wage increases, fringe benefits and improved working conditions.[28]

The organizer begins. He meets with a few key people in bars, restaurants, or in their homes. He molds a cadre. He keeps a "low profile." Usually, at this point, the employer is not aware of the meetings.

The organizer's success is the measure of the employer's failure. If he convinces, not the complainers or the chronically dissatisfied, but the conscientious workers, there is fertile ground for unionization.

Having developed a cadre, the organizer now seeks to enlarge it. The small group is encouraged to solicit fellow workers. They attempt to obtain signatures on cards which give the union authority to act as their representative in collective bargaining. The solicitation takes place in restrooms, locker rooms, lounges or lunchrooms, and sometimes in work areas.

At this point, the employer may become aware that there is organizational activity in his plant. An employee who has been solicited may inform his supervisor. There may be other evidence: furtive glances and hushed conversations which had not occurred before; small group huddles which break up in silence on the approach of the supervisor; an upsurge in lack of cooperation to the point of insubordination and insurgency; an increase in gripes; a decrease in quality of work; an increase in lateness and absenteeism; dawdling in the lunchroom and restrooms; growing aggressiveness; reluctance or outright refusal to work overtime.

THE ORGANIZER SURFACES

The union organizer will now come out in the open. He will engage in handbilling at the plant gate, using the type of handbill reproduced in Facsimile No. 7, page 30, or any of numerous different types.

The "questionnaire" (see Facsimile No. 8, pages 31-32) is a particularly good technique. By asking employees to state what they think they should be paid, what they should receive in hospitalization and pension benefits, and whether or not they would like to see other improvements (the answers to which, of course, are affirmative), the union has conditioned the employees to believe that all they desire will be attained.

FACSIMILE No. 7

SECURITY BOND

The UNITED STEELWORKERS OF AMERICA, AFL-CIO and its 1,200,000 members offer to you this Security Bond. In order to receive dividends from this Bond there is just one important requirement on your part. We ask that you join us in membership with our Great American Union of good men and women just like you.

There isn't one of us, who at one time or another throughout our work-a-day life has not received a dividend from this valuable Bond. The feeling of Security one receives from this Bond in membership with the United Steelworkers of America is immeasurable. It is your Employment Insurance.

The United States Government, the Federal and State Labor Laws are the Trustees of this Security Bond; they protect your Individual Right to be a holder, without prejudice, fear or punishment from your employer. Our Union guards and protects you in your exercise of this reight. The initial act to make this Security Bond redeemable now rests in your hands.

In order to obtain bargaining rights under the law, our union follows the following procedure:

1. You will find attached to this message a white application card that is self-explanatory. Please fill out and sign card.

2. Please enclose this card in the business reply envelope furnished and mail immediately.

3. At an appropriate time after a majority of employees have signed cards authorizing the Union to represent them, we will request that the employer recognize the United Steelworkers of America as your designated collective bargaining agent. If this request is refused, we will take the necessary steps before the Federal Government's National Labor Relations Board to require the employer to bargain with your Union.

4. The Federal Government protects your right to belong to our Union and to urge others to belong, and Federal law makes it illegal for the company to discipline employees or to treat them differently because they have joined or campaigned for the Union.

5. Many of your co-workers want to exercise this legal right that will give them their own Union contract, covering and improving rates of pay, hours of work, and all other conditions of employment, in contract form, signed by the company officials.

If you haven't done so as yet, won't you join with them now by sending in your signed card. It won't cost you one cent now or until a contract has been signed. This contract will be negotiated and approved by you and your co-workers, IN YOUR OWN LOCAL UNION. All Inquiries and Information are Confidential.

FACSIMILE No. 8

Q U E S T I O N N A I R E

☐   WHAT DO YOU WANT IN YOUR UNION CONTRACT?

☐   WHAT DO YOU THINK ABOUT UNIONS GENERALLY?

☐   WHAT IS YOUR OPINION ABOUT THIS ORGANIZING CAMPAIGN?

We need the answers to these questions from both, those who favor the union, and those who oppose it. When a majority of employees vote for the union in an N.L.R.B. election, the union then becomes the exclusive representative of all employees in the voting unit regardless of whether they have joined the union or not.

To fulfill this responsibility it is necessary that we know what goals you expect to achieve. To negotiate a contract for you we have to know where you stand today and where you want to go.

The following questionnaire is designed to give us some of these answers. Everyone is urged to complete the questionnaire and mail it in the enclosed envelope as soon as possible. The average time required to complete this form is less than 15 minutes.

INDIVIDUAL, QUESTIONNAIRING WILL BE KEPT CONFIDENTIAL

SECTION I

This section is designed to tell us where you stand today and give us an idea of how much your insurance and pension will cost. We have to know where you are so that we may better understand how to get you where you want to go when we negotiate your union contract.

1. Date_____
2. Store Name and No._____
3. ☐ Male   ☐ Female
4. Your birth date_____
5. Your marital status: Married
                           Single
                           Divorced
6. Number of dependent children living with you?_____
7. Ages of dependent children living with you?_____
8. Is your job the only income in your household?
        ☐ Yes   ☐ No
9. Do you consider your income essential to your household?
        ☐ Yes   ☐ No
10. What is your present rate of pay?_____
    (If on commission explain)_____
11. What is your length of service with your company?___Years___Mos.
12. What is your department name and number?_____
13. How many employees work in your department?_____
14. What is your job classification?_____
15. How many hours are you normally scheduled to work each week?
    _____

16. Are you covered by your company's hospitalization plan?
        ☐ Yes   ☐ No

FACSIMILE No. 8

17. Are you covered by your company's pension plan?
    ☐ Yes   ☐ No

SECTION II

This section is designed to tell us what you expect to achieve
through the negotiation of your union contract. A union's
existence is based on the achievements of goals for its members.
In this section we are asking you what those goals should be.
If you wish to comment further about your contract, please jot
down any thoughts you might have on this subject and return them
with this questionnaire.

1. What hourly rate of pay or what rate of commission should
    you receive under your Union Contract?_____

2. Do you think that your contract should have a strong seniority
    clause? ☐ Yes   ☐ No

3. Do you think that your contract should have a strong job secu-
    rity clause and require that your company submit proof to the
    union for any disciplinary action taken against you?
    ☐ Yes   ☐ No

4. Do you think that any disciplinary action taken by the company
    against you should be subject to a ruling by an impartial umpire?
    ☐ Yes   ☐ No

5. How much Life Insurance should you have where you work?_____

6. Should your hospitalization pay the full cost when you or your
    dependents are hospitalized?
    ☐ Yes   ☐ No

7. (a) How much sick pay should you receive when you are unable
        to work?_____

    (b) How long should your sick pay continue?_____

8. Should your Health and Welfare Plan include dental care?

        ☐ Yes   ☐ No

9. Should your Health and Welfare Plan include prescription benefits?
    ☐ Yes   ☐ No

10. How much pension should you receive?

THE ORGANIZATIONAL MEETING

As the campaign progresses, the organizer will openly announce organizational meetings and seek to obtain additional signed authorization cards. Group selling of this sort has produced very tangible results. Most such meetings follow the same format. The following testimony by a union organizer at an NLRB hearing describes a typical meeting:

Q. Can you tell us to the best of your recollection all that you told the employees at that time?

A. I'll try. I introduced myself and my associate and described what we do and what our jobs were with the International Union, and why we were here—why we were in town, that we were in town because some people from the plant had contacted us through another source stating that they wanted organization.

I then described the nature of our organization, because I didn't think they were familiar with us that much, and I described our organization, what we do, what we stand for and so forth. I then proceeded to point out the benefits derived by joining a labor organization such as ours.

I pointed out the difference in wages, working conditions, fringe benefits, such as pensions, health and welfare amongst other things, that we have these and have enjoyed these things for years in other areas where workers were organized; that this was solely brought about through union organizations for the purpose of dealing collectively with the Employer rather than on an individual basis.

I pointed out the advantage of collective bargaining as against individuals going into or appealing to the company for a wage increase or for other things that they may think they might need.

I then described that in order to represent the employees, we would have to have authorization cards.

And authorization cards were passed out amongst the group and we read the authorization card out and why we needed them, that in order to represent a group of employees, we must be authorized first by the employees through a signed card; that after we secure these cards, we would contact the company for recognition. I told them that I would do that immediately after the meeting. We then collected the cards and we received thirty-one out of thirty-two—thirty-one cards out of the thirty-two people that were at the meeting.

After the meeting was completed, we gave some additional cards to the several people that were there and they were to contact those that were not there and ask them to sign cards.

Q. About how long did this meeting last?

A. Oh, I would say about an hour and a half.

Q. Were any questions asked?

A. Yes.

Q. Can you tell us briefly what answers were made?

A. Well, when they asked us about the Union dues, we told them there wouldn't be any dues collected or paid by anyone until such time that a contract was negotiated and ratified. We told them that there wouldn't be any initiation fees collected from anyone that was there working at the plant at this time, that the initiation fees and dues would be set by the members themselves, and not myself or the International Union.

Sometimes the organizer finds it helpful to "soften up" the object of his affection with a few drinks. In this event, the organizational meeting will occur in the back of a bar where, at the propitious time, the attendees are asked to sign authorization cards.[29] This technique, when employed, is usually successful.

NOTES TO CHAPTER II

1. Brief for AFL-CIO as *amicus curiae* at 14, NLRB v. Wyman-Gordon Co., 394 U.S. 759 (1969).

2. Example of newsclipping services are the A.T.P. (American Trade Press Clipping Bureau), 15 East 26th Street, New York, N. Y.; International Press Clipping Bureau, Inc., 5 Beekman Street, New York, N. Y., and 1868 Columbia Road, N. W., Washington, D. C. 20009. *See also*, "Clipping Bureaus" listing in Yellow Pages of local telephone directory.

3. The New York Public Library's general catalog is located in Room 315 of its main branch at Fifth Avenue and 42nd Street, New York City.

4. Fairchild Publishing Company publishes *Women's Wear Daily, Daily News Record, Home Furnishing Daily, Footwear News, Electronic News,* and *Supermarket News.*

5. To be placed on the NLRB mailing list, write to Division of Information, NLRB, Washington, D. C. 20570, stating an interest in the weekly summary of NLRB cases or the monthly NLRB election report.

6. Specific Labor Board decisions may be obtained from the Division of Information, NLRB, 1717 Pennsylvania Avenue, N.W., Washington, D. C. 20570.

7. Decisions of Trial Examiners may be obtained by writing the Chief Trial Examiner, NLRB, 1717 Pennsylvania Avenue, N. W., Washington, D. C. 20570, or the Director of Information.

8. To be placed on mailing list, write to Labor News Memorandum, New York State Department of Labor, 80 Centre Street, New York, N. Y.

9. Examples of the BNA's services are *Daily Labor Report, White Collar, Retail* and *Construction Labor Reports,* and *Labor Relations Reports.* BNA, upon request and for a nominal fee, will also provide research material on a particular subject, such as a union's strike record; write to: BNA, 1231 25th St., N.W., Washington, D. C.

10. Examples of CCH's services are *Labor Law Guide, Employment Practices Guide,* and *Labor Law Reporter.*

11. Examples of Prentice Hall's services are *Wage and Hour Guide, Industrial Relations Guide, Labor Relations Guide, Policies and Practices (Personnel)* and *Payroll Guide.*

12. The New York Public Library's branch at 5th Avenue and 40th Street contains the BNA and CCH Labor Law Services.

13. Write to U.S. Government Printing Office, Washington, D. C.

14. Write to 80 Centre Street, New York, N. Y. 10013; $2.50 per copy.

15. Write to 250 Broadway, New York, N. Y. 10007.

16. Labor-Management Reporting and Disclosure Act of 1959 (Landrum-Griffin Act), 29 U.S.C. §§ 153, 158-160, 164, 186, 187, 401 *et seq.* (1964) (hereinafter cited as LMRDA).

17. LMRDA § 207(a), 29 U.S.C. § 437(a) (1964).

18. LMRDA § 201(a), 29 U.S.C. § 431(a) (1964).

19. LMRDA § 201(b), 29 U.S.C. § 431(b) (1964).

20. Welfare and Pension Plans Disclosure Act, 29 U.S.C. § 301 *et seq.* (1964).

21. *Id.* at § 5, 29 U.S.C. § 304 (1964).

22. Schlossberg, "Foreword" to S. I. Schlossberg & F. E. Sherman, *Organizing and the Law* at IX (1971).

23. Office & Professional Employees Int'l Union, AFL-CIO-CLC, *Now Let's Get Out And Organize* 3-4.

24. *The Distributive Worker,* August 1971, at 8, cols. 1-2.

25. Reliable Mfg. Co., 13-CA-15,941 (NLRB June 21, 1964); *Central Hardware Co. v. NLRB,* 439 F.2d 1321 (8th Cir. 1971).

26. Industrial Union Dep't, AFL-CIO, *A Guidebook for Union Organizers* 5 (Pub. No. 42, Sept. 1961).

27. *Id.*

28. OPEIU, *supra* note 23, at 2.

29. Morse Chain Co., 175 NLRB No. 98, 71 LRRM 1004 (1969); Mid-State Beverages, 153 NLRB 135, 59 LRRM 1437 (1965).

CHAPTER III

THE EMPLOYER SPEAKS UP

The union campaign is underway. Organizational meetings are being held, union handbills passed out, and authorization cards distributed. Pro-union talk abounds on and off the employer's premises. What shall the employer do now? Should he remain silent for fear that by reacting he is "dignifying" it?

The employer who asserts "Let's not dignify it!" has lost. He must speak up. In this context, silence is not golden. Winning an NLRB election may be an achievement, but a greater achievement is not to have one.

MEANING OF CARD SOLICITATION

By now, a significant aspect of union organizing may have become apparent. In most cases, the employee has not had the benefit of the employer's point of view before signing a card. Yet, if industrial democracy is to be meaningful, the choice which the employee must make—between individual and collective representation—should be an informed one.

Only after hearing both sides, can employees be reasonably certain that their decision is the correct one. "[T]he best test of truth is the power of the thought to get itself accepted in the competition of the market. . . ."[1] The obligation of giving employees the other side of the story falls upon the employer.

Counsel's threshold inquiry natually will be how far his client can go in expressing his views on unions. Can he say whatever he likes? Are there any limitations? The answers will be found in NLRB and court interpretations of Section 8(c) of the Act, the so-called "free speech" provision. This section states:

> The expressing of any views, argument, or opinion, or the dissemination thereof, whether in written, printed, graphic, or visual form, shall not constitute or be evidence of an unfair labor practice under any of the provisions of this Act, if such expression contains no threat of reprisal or force or promise of benefit.[2]

Very simply, the employer may speak freely, as long as he does not attempt to threaten or bribe employees.

To the employer who wants to preserve his non-union status, the expression of "views, argument and opinion" is a command, not merely a statutory permit.

The employee has not heard the employer's position. He may have been told the employer is in favor of the union or not opposed to it. He may not be aware that his employer would view his pro-union activities unsympathetically. It is imperative, therefore, that the employer, in his first communication, state his views and seek to answer the many questions that come to mind.

The employer must react to union organizing promptly. A good place to start is to explain the meaning of the authorization card which the employee is being asked to sign. A timely explanation may be decisive. If he is successful, the union may never reach its intermediate goal of signatures from 30% of the employees.[3]

Or, if it has reached that point, it may never reach the 50% plus one necessary to demand recognition as representative of a majority of the employees.[4]

In regard to card solicitation, misrepresentations abound. The Supreme Court's decision in *NLRB v. Gissel Packing Co.*[5] sanctioned organization by misrepresentation, *i.e.*, the solicitation of cards by union agents who claim that the card's purpose is to obtain a secret ballot election, when in truth, it is only one of the purposes. This unfortunate consequence is discussed at greater length in Appendix E.[6]

To offset the unfairness of this decision, the employer should anticipate union misrepresentations and expose them to his employees. For example, he should advise his employees not to believe the union solicitor who states:

> "You must sign a card to vote."
>
> or
>
> "If you don't sign now, you won't have your job after we win."
>
> or
>
> "It will cost you more if you don't join now."
>
> or
>
> "This card is only to get an election."
>
> or
>
> "This card is only to get more information."

The employer who dispels these false statements assists the employee in making the right decision. He may decide not to sign up at all or at least defer a decision on signing until he hears more.

Another common misrepresentation used by unions is the assertion that the cards signed by employees will remain confidential. Typically, the union states in its literature:

> The cards are strictly confidential. The only people knowing whether you signed a card are yourself, the union, and the NLRB agent. In no event will the Company see, or find out, who signed or did not sign cards.

Employers have replied that cards may be submitted into evidence at an unfair labor practice hearing. (See Facsimile No. 9, page 41.) The Board, however, has held that in the context of other unfair labor practices it is unlawful for an employer to advise employees that cards are not confidential.[7] The courts have disagreed,[8] some vehemently:

> It startles the conscience to deny an employer . . . the right to tell its employees the truth. . . . However unbefitting, verity can never amount to illegality. Yet the Board holds just the opposite.

> Union cards are not confidential material. They are executed *for presentation* to the employer. The remotest possibility of an employee's understanding that his signature is a secret should be dispelled. . . .[9]

Until the question is resolved, an employer should refrain from advising his employees, in *haec verba*, that the cards they sign will not be confidential. However, an employer clearly has the right to discuss the use to which they will be put and the legal consequences of their execution. He may do this in meetings with his employees, individual conversations with them and in home mailings.

We now turn to the various ways in which the employer communicates his views to his employees.

An effective way to explain the significance of card signing to employees is to write to their homes. (See Facsimile No. 9, page 41.) Such letters often are read by the employee's family.

LARGE GROUP MEETINGS

There are many employers who have never spoken to groups of employees. However, just because an employer has never done so before does not mean he should not start now. He must

FACSIMILE No. 9

Dear Fellow Employee:

We have heard that the union is trying to get you to sign cards. Why? As a means of answering this question, we have drawn up a series of questions and answers:

WHAT IS A UNION AUTHORIZATION CARD?

A signed statement from an employee stating that he wants the union to be his collective bargaining agent.

DOES SIGNING A CARD OBLIGATE YOU?

Yes. It is a *legal* statement that you want the union to represent you.

WHAT DOES THE UNION DO WITH THE CARDS IT COLLECTS?

There are two possibilities:

a. If the union gets cards signed by 30% of our people, they can petition the National Labor Relations Board for an election, or

b. If the union gets cards signed by 51% of our people, it will send us a letter asking us to bargain. (It may send copies of the cards in its possession—some unions do.)

IF THE UNION HAS 51% OF THE CARDS AND ASKS THE COMPANY TO BARGAIN, MUST THE COMPANY DO SO?

No.

WHAT CAN THE UNION DO IF THE COMPANY REFUSES TO BARGAIN IN THESE CIRCUMSTANCES?

The union has three possibilities:

1. It can call an immediate strike for recognition.
2. It can request an NLRB election, or
3. It can request the NLRB to count the cards at a public hearing.

We all know what a strike or an election is, but what does "Counting The Cards At a Public Hearing" mean, and how does it work?

Under the card counting procedure, the union gives the cards to the NLRB and accuses the company of an unfair labor practice because it did not bargain with the union.

The Labor Board will hold an "Open Hearing" where employees who signed cards may be subpoenaed by the NLRB or the company to testify. On the witness stand they will be shown the cards, asked to identify them, and be cross-examined concerning the circumstances under which they signed the cards.

The main thing you should realize is that signing a card is a very meaningful thing. It legally assigns a person's right of representation to the union. Nobody should sign a card unless he is willing to accept all the consequences and obligations of such representation.

Very truly yours,

General Manager

not be paralyzed into inaction. It is rather a time to make amends for his prior silence.

A "straight from the shoulder" presentation, well thought out in advance, is best. It is not a time for subtlety. The employer should be factual, reasonable, temperate, instructive and impressive.

A prepared text, though possibly formal, avoids misinterpretations resulting from extemporaneous statements. (See prepared talks to employees in Appendix H.)

One note of caution on group meetings. There is divided opinion as to the desirability of inviting questions from the floor. Experience dictates that it is best to handle such questions by responding that they will be answered individually following the talks. Thus, employee interest is sustained and the employer is afforded an opportunity to answer the questions later and to avoid the embarrassment of being unable to respond to a "shop lawyer's" tough, sometimes prepared questions. More important, it avoids the spontaneous, unprepared response of questionable legality.

Occasionally, a union representative will request an opportunity to reply to the employer's talk. Or, the union may challenge the employer to "debate the issues." Such requests or challenges should be rejected.[10] Unions have their own avenues and methods of proselytizing and responding, such as letters, handbills, meetings and visits to the homes of the employees.

SMALL GROUPS

The expression of "views, argument and opinion" takes on a different dimension in talking with small groups of employees. Such meetings are more intimate and usually more effective. Employees in small groups often speak up and ask questions. An employer speaking to small groups can respond more easily, in contrast with large meetings, where answering questions can be troublesome. A plant personnel manager, often unaccustomed to addressing large groups on controversial subjects, will be more comfortable and therefore more effective with smaller groups.

A major cause of unsatisfactory employee-relations is poor communications. It is a truism in human relations, whether at home or in the plant, that communicating can avoid misunderstanding. Small group meetings provide the means for two-way communications—downward and upward.

They should be a regular part of a personnel program, instituted long before any organizing begins. They are an excellent forum for disseminating information on business related activities of interest to employees. The company's future plans, new products contemplated, sales forecasts and a variety of subjects can be discussed in an informal, class-like atmosphere.

These meetings also provide an opportunity for employees to talk about their job, and to offer housekeeping and safety suggestions. Such meetings also provide a means for explaining company policies and benefit programs and to answer employees' questions about them.

It generally is agreed that meetings with six to ten employees are the most productive. Employees are comfortable in groups of this size. If much smaller, they feel "singled out" and, if much larger, the meetings become unwieldy and inhibit discussion. Employees may be selected by department, or on some other basis, such as alphabetically. Meetings should be limited in duration. If there are matters not quite finished, they can be held over to a later date. Formal minutes are not desirable, but notes should be made of matters which require follow-up.

The selection of the person to lead the meetings merits careful consideration. The group leader preferably should not be from top management. Yet, he must have sufficient stature to gain the employees' confidence. He must be trustworthy, tactful and level-headed. He should know the employees and be familiar with the business. A personnel manager often has these qualifications.

It is essential that the employer's supervisory staff support this program. In explaining it to them the emphasis should be that these meetings will assist them and are not being undertaken as a by-pass. Further support will come about when the group leader takes up problems with the supervisors who are responsible for their solution. Thus the supervisors will become an integral part of the program.

Counsel should review the format for any proposed small group meetings to avoid the possibility that they may be held unlawful. If their purpose is to solicit grievances, and they were first adopted during a union organizing drive, the NLRB will consider them suspect. The Board holds that:

> Where . . . an employer, who has not previously had a practice of soliciting employee grievances or complaints, adopts such a course when unions engage in organizational campaigns seeking to represent employees, we think there is a compelling inference that he is implicitly promising to correct those inequities he discovers as a result of his inquiries. . . .[11]

Where, however, the employer has had group meetings as part of his regular personnel program, and has used such meetings as a forum for broad two-way communications, he will be able to substantiate their propriety, if challenged.[12]

Care must also be taken that the meetings are held in areas where the employees are accustomed to meet and visit. It has been held to be coercive to hold such meetings in the executive suite rather than in a lunch room, training room or employee lounge.[13]

With these proscriptions in mind, such meetings are lawful and an excellent means of communication.

THE INDIVIDUAL EMPLOYEE

Group talks, although important, are no substitute for speaking with the individual employee. Employees want to talk. They should know that someone in management will give them a sympathetic ear. Employees want to feel they will obtain responsive action or adequate explanation for their questions and problems.

It has been said that even ears have walls. Most employers could benefit from a course in effective listening. It is ironic that an employee spends most of his waking hours on the employer's premises, yet a union representative, an utter stranger, can come upon the scene and in a short time know more about the employee than the employer. This result is simple default on the part of the employer. He has not talked to his people. He has not listened.

Employers have always had excuses for not taking time to talk to their employees. They can find time to improve machinery, to devise procedures, and to study new methods, but they fail to allocate time to study the individuals, without whom the machinery, procedures and methods would be useless.

It is often said "I have an open door policy; my door is always open." The employer who states this is sometimes not being frank. Few executives have the time to keep their doors open for people to wander in and out at will. The open door truly exists when employees can freely discuss their problems, on and off the floor, with supervisory and managerial personnel.

Some companies use morale surveys to find out what employees are thinking.[14] The survey's main drawback is that it is necessarily anonymous and therefore provides no way of ascertaining how the individual employee actually feels. Nor does it assure the employee that his ideas are actually reaching his employer. Surveys should not be instituted during an organizing campaign. They have been held to convey an implied promise to remedy grievances if the union is defeated.[15]

A survey is not a substitute for reaching the individual directly. Personal interaction is essential. It can happen only through individual conversations.

Individual employee talks may be structured around scheduled events or certain occasions. Some examples are:

> Change in job duties;
> Change in rate of pay;
> Promotion or transfer;
> Anniversary of employment;
> Award of service pin;
> Scheduling of vacation;
> Return from vacation;
> Explanation of pension rights;
> Change of beneficiary under company insurance policy.

The interviewer may be a supervisor or a personnel assistant, a person who is sincere and a good listener. The employee will talk about himself in relation to his job. He will make suggestions. He will express ideas on how his job can be improved. Who knows this better than he? More often than not, if he voices a complaint, it will involve matters such as work environment and equipment, rather than matters of economics.

These interviews will assist the employer in assessing employee morale. If the talk is centered about employee benefits, it will remind the employee of what he often takes for granted or is not even aware of.

Structured talks about employee benefits and the advantages of working for the company are a form of intramural public relations. Employers advertise to create good will with the public, but they often forget about the good will they can create with their own employees.

In addition to such scheduled talks, the employer will be talking to his employees in normal day to day conversations. Through supervisory contact, he will work for greater understanding with his employees. He will be responsive to their needs. He will take care of their complaints as they arise. He knows that employee loyalty and cooperation cannot be purchased. It must be earned. The way to earn cooperation is through attention. The way to lose it is through inattention.

When an employer overlooks his employees' needs, and complaints are unheeded, frustration sets in. Then, often as a last resort, employees seek union help. The employer who was too busy attending to other matters now takes the time to ascertain the reason his employees sought union representation. Alas, it is often too late. Now, if he seeks out and corrects the grievances, he may run afoul of the law. Two case histories, drawn from NLRB reports, are illustrative.

A manager of a store selling farm machinery received a visit from a representative of the International Association of Machinists. The union agent stated that he had signed cards from 10 out of 15 employees in the service department and showed him the cards. The manager looked at them carefully, acknowledged that the union represented a majority, but declined to recognize the union.

The store manager thereupon phoned his district office and was instructed to find out what grievances the employees had. He spoke to them and was told that they were annoyed because they had to work with defective jacks, bad brakes on a truck, a faulty hydraulic hoist, and a steam vent that did not vent outside the building. A few days later the men had new brakes for the truck, a new hoist, the defects in the jack were corrected, and the steam was vented outside the building.

It was too late. The remedying of the grievances was held unlawful. The NLRB ordered recognition, stating:

> There are few unfair labor practices so effective in cooling employees' enthusiasm for a union than the prompt remedy of the grievances which prompted the employees' union interest in the first place.[16]

In the same vein is the case of a retail manager who received a telegram from a Teamsters' local requesting recognition. He immediately phoned his regional office.

Thereafter, personnel officials visited the store and spoke with individual employees. Among the complaints were poor working facilities, insufficient lighting, a rough table top, unrepaired equipment, and the lack of warm clothing to wear on the dock. The personnel officials advised the employees that they would look into the matter and find out what could be done.

Subsequently, better lighting was installed, the table top surface fixed, the equipment repaired, and protective clothing provided. The NLRB held these actions unlawful.[17]

An employer who follows the policy of communicating with his employees individually, on a daily basis, has the key to good employee relations. He is able to respond to his employees' needs as they arise. He thereby avoids the crises and legal involvements. He thus will have more satisfied employees and consequently better workers.

THE SUPERVISOR

The voice of the employer is heard primarily through his first line supervisor. He interprets company policy to the employee. An employee who likes his supervisor will probably like his employer. An employee who dislikes his supervisor will probably dislike his employer, no matter how well he is paid or how good his fringe benefits. It therefore is important to know what makes one supervisor liked and another disliked.

A good supervisor:

> treats his people as individuals, with respect and dignity, as he would like to be treated.
> knows his people well, their interests, motivations, needs, ambitions, problems.
> keeps his people well-informed.
> resolves all complaints, questions and problems as promptly as possible.
> listens, encourages ideas and suggestions, and follows up.
> maintains reasonable discipline by fair and consistent enforcement of rules of conduct.
> administers all company policies consistently and fairly.

Supervisors are not employees under the Act,[18] and may be excluded from the bargaining unit. They are on the employer's team, and as such can bind him by their acts and statements.[19] Because of their status, the employer may forbid them to partake in union activities.[20] Should they nevertheless support the union, they should be warned and, if necessary, disciplined.[21] Bear in mind, however, that supervisors themselves are individuals, with problems and gripes of their own. If their attitude is not right, then the attitude of the employees they supervise will not be right.

A sound supervisory training program should be instituted long before the start of union organizing. As discussed previously, employees often are troubled by small job-related problems. If these irritations are permitted to fester through lack of attention, they often become a *cause célèbre*. The supervisor who has been trained to attend to employee needs on a daily basis will promptly remedy these irritations. The result will be a better worker and a contribution to overall plant morale.

First line supervisors must know the company's attitude concerning unionization. Too often the supervisor is left guessing that the employer's policy is probably not to have a union, but he is not sure. He has never seen nor heard the policy expressed. It was never told to him.

Similarly, supervisors must be familiar with the employer's fringe benefit and wage administration programs. With effective training and indoctrination, the supervisor is in a better position to communicate the employer's viewpoint. It may well be that the employer's program is better than the standards achieved by the union in other plants. If the supervisor is knowledgeable, he can make the comparison.

Supervisors should be told that they are not merely fighting the employer's battle. They are fighting their own. Supervisors in a unionized plant suffer restrictions on their ability to manage. They are often hamstrung by shop stewards in dealing with employees. Supervisors with experiences in union plants are well aware of these facts, but it may be advisable to remind them.

Face-to-face communications between supervisors and employees supplement an employer's other means of communications. If handled properly, with trained supervisors, it is a most effective method of influencing employee behavior.

NOTES TO CHAPTER III

1. Abrams v. U.S., 250 U.S. 616, 630 (1919) (Holmes, J., dissenting opinion).

2. LMRA § 101.8, 29 U.S.C. § 158(c) (1964). Certain conduct by an employer in a labor relations context is unlawful. There are five general types stated in Section 8(a) of the Act. See Appendix C.

3. NLRB Rules & Regulations §§ 101.17, 101.18, 29 C.F.R. §§ 101.17, 101.18 (1971).

4. LMRA §§ 101.8(a)(5), 101.9(a), 29 U.S.C. §§ 158(a)(5), 159(a) (1964).

5. 395 U.S. 575 (1969). See full text in Appendix F.

6. Lewis, *Gissel Packing: Was The Supreme Court Right?* 56 A.B.A.J. 877 (1970). See Appendix E.

7. J. P. Stevens & Co., 181 NLRB No. 97, 75 LRRM 1371 (1970); Werthan Bag Corp., 167 NLRB 11, 65 LRRM 1732 (1967); Sidles Co., 156 NLRB 457, 462-63, 61 LRRM 1102 (1965); Hobart Bros. Co., 150 NLRB 956, 962-64, 58 LRRM 1220 (1965); Sparton Mfg. Co., 150 NLRB 948, 951-52, 58 LRRM 1223 (1965). *Cf.* Brake Parts Co., 178 NLRB No. 43, 74 LRRM 1068 (1969).

8. NLRB v. Hobart Bros. Co., 372 F.2d 203 (6th Cir. 1967), *denying enforcement to* 150 NLRB 956, 58 LRRM 1220 (1965); NLRB v. Sparton Mfg. Co., 355 F.2d 523 (7th Cir. 1966), *denying enforcement to* 150 NLRB 948, 58 LRRM 1223 (1965).

9. J. P. Stevens & Co. v. NLRB, 441 F.2d 514, 76 LRRM 2804, 2805 (4th Cir. 1971), *denying enforcement in part to* 181 NLRB No. 97, 75 LRRM 1371 (1970), *cert. denied,* __ U.S. __ (No. 70-264, Oct. 12, 1971).

10. There is one exception to an employer's right to deny unions equal time. In a department store which enforces a broad no-solicitation rule (prohibiting solicitation in certain store areas on *non-working time*), the union may effectively request time to reply to such talks on the store's premises. Montgomery Ward & Co., 145 NLRB 846, 55 LRRM 1063 (1964), *enf'd as modified,* 339 F.2d 889 (6th Cir. 1965); Marshall Field & Co., 98 NLRB 88, 29 LRRM 1305 (1952), *modified on other grounds,* 200 F.2d 375 (7th Cir. 1952); May Dep't Stores Co. d/b/a Famous-Barr Co., 59 NLRB 976, 15 LRRM 173 (1944), *enf'd,* 154 F.2d 533 (8th Cir. 1946), *cert. denied,* 329 U.S. 725 (1946).

11. Reliance Elec. Co., 191 NLRB No. 1, 77 LRRM 1327, 1330 (1971).

12. On occasion, a union has successfully challenged a formal arrangement of group meetings as an unlawfully employer sponsored "labor organization" under Sections 2(5) and 8(a)(2) of the Act. NLRB v. Cabot Carbon Co., 360 U.S. 203 (1959). *See also,* NLRB v. Ampex Corp., 442 F.2d 82, 77 LRRM 2072 (7th Cir. 1971), *cert. denied,* __ U.S. __ (No. 71-320, Nov. 9, 1971).

13. Great Atlantic & Pacific Tea Co., 140 NLRB 133, 51 LRRM 1570 (1962); General Shoe Corp. (Marman Bag Plant), 97 NLRB 499, 29 LRRM 1113 (1951).

14. ITT Telecommunications, 183 NLRB No. 115, 74 LRRM 1386 (1970).

15. NLRB v. Tom Wood Pontiac, Inc., __ F.2d __, 77 LRRM 2968 (7th Cir., No. 18778, decided July 23, 1971), *enforcing* 179 NLRB No. 98, 72 LRRM 1494 (1969). Even after an election, surveys have been held unlawful when questions were posed, such as why the employee voted as he did and what he thought of various propaganda devices used by the employer and the union. Cannon Elec. Co., 151 NLRB 1465, 58 LRRM 1629 (1965).

16. Int'l Harvester Co., 170 NLRB No. 134, 68 LRRM 1272 (1968), *reaff'd*, 179 NLRB No. 124, 72 LRRM 1467, 1468 (1969).

17. Sears, Roebuck & Co., 182 NLRB No. 68, 74 LRRM 1150 (1970). The Court of Appeals for the Sixth Circuit, however, disagreed with the Board's holding. __ F.2d __, 78 LRRM 2520 (6th Cir., No. 21010, decided Oct. 13, 1971). The Court relied upon the fact that "supervisory people were in the habit of making frequent inquiries of employees as to how things were going, [and were] alert to discover justified dissatisfaction." 78 LRRM at 2552. Thus, the Court stated that "[w]hat was done by Sears was but a continuance . . . of what had long been its policy of seeking and maintaining good relationships with its employees . . . and were of the same kind . . . conducted at various other stores." 78 LRRM at 2521.

18. LMRA §§ 101.2(3), 101.2(11), 29 U.S.C. §§ 152(3), 152(11) (1964).

19. NLRB v. Link-Belt Co., 311 U.S. 584 (1941); Heinz Co. v. NLRB, 311 U.S. 514 (1941); Int'l Ass'n of Machinists v. NLRB, 311 U.S. 72 (1940).

20. Nat'l Freight, Inc., 154 NLRB 621, 59 LRRM 1789 (1965).

21. Palmer Paper Co., 180 NLRB No. 156, 73 LRRM 1239 (1970). It is unlawful, however, to discharge a supervisor for his refusal to commit an unfair labor practice. Jackson Tile Mfg. Co., 122 NLRB 764, 43 LRRM 1195, *enf'd*, 272 F.2d 181 (5th Cir. 1959); Talladega Cotton Factory, Inc., 106 NLRB 295, 32 LRRM 1479 (1953), *enf'd*, 213 F.2d 209 (5th Cir. 1954).

CHAPTER IV

MANAGEMENT COUNTERATTACK

The employer with the best supervision has the best defense against union incursion. Careful recruitment and training will pay later dividends. During an organizing effort, supervisors should receive more specific instruction on their role—what they may and may not say—and how to answer the questions asked of them. Frequent meetings should be held for this purpose and to critique incidents as they arise.

WHAT SUPERVISORS MAY SAY AND DO

A supervisor should be guided by the following general rule: he may speak freely, but may not threaten, promise, or interrogate. This general principle is illustrated below.

(1) Supervisors may tell employees that the employer neither wants nor needs a union.[1]

(2) They may tell employees that the law gives them the right to refrain from joining a union,[2] and that employees may not be threatened or coerced into joining.[3]

(3) They may tell employees of the benefits which they enjoy and may compare these benefits with those in unionized companies.[4]

(4) They may tell employees that with a union they may have to bring their problems to a shop steward instead of dealing with their supervisor.[5]

(5) They may tell employees of the disadvantages of belonging to a union, such as the payment of dues and initiation fees, the loss of income due to strikes, and the possibility of picket line duty, fines and assessments.[6] They may tell employees that if they engage in an economic strike, they may be permanently replaced and need be reinstated only if an opening occurs.[7]

(6) They may tell employees that a union will always out-promise an employer but can guarantee nothing.[8] They may point out the untruth of statements being made by the union. They may recall events from personal knowledge of unhappy union experiences. They may criticize union officials and cite their arrest records.[9]

(7) Supervisors may tell employees that they do not have to sign authorization cards. They may tell employees that signing a union card is like signing a blank check.[10] They may tell employees that they do not have to speak to union organizers at their homes if they do not desire to do so.[11]

(8) Supervisors may campaign vigorously against the union. They may distribute literature and speak to employees individually or in groups, at the employee's work station, in the employee cafeteria or in other areas where employees are accustomed to being.[12] They may request employees to vote against the union and ask them to tell others to do the same.[13]

(9) Supervisors may continue to operate normally. They need not tolerate insubordination or soldiering on the job. They may continue to discipline and discharge, as warranted by the circumstances.[14]

(10) Supervisors may advise employees that the employer's policies with respect to merit pay adjustments, promotions and transfers will be continued as before.[15]

WHAT SUPERVISORS MAY NOT SAY OR DO

Correlatively, there are acts which supervisors must avoid.

(1) They may not promise employees pay increases, promotions, improved working conditions, additional benefits or special favors, on condition that the employees refuse to join the union or vote against it.[16]

(2) They may not threaten employees with loss of job or reduction in wages, or use threatening or intimidating language calculated to influence an employee in the exercise of his right to support a union.[17]

(3) They must not discriminate against an employee who is taking part in union activities by separating him from other employees; nor may they intentionally assign or transfer employees to undesirable tasks because of their union activities.[18]

(4) They may not threaten to or actually discipline or discharge an employee for soliciting other employees to sign authorization cards or for engaging in other union activity during his non-working time.[19] Lunch periods and coffee breaks are considered non-working time even though the employee may be paid during these periods.[20] Similarly, an employee standing in line, waiting to punch out, is on non-working time.[21] However, even though an employee is on non-working time himself, he may be warned and disciplined if he is interfering with another employee who is at work.[22]

(5) Supervisors may not engage in surveillance of employees attending union meetings or receiving union handbills,[23] or give the impression that employee activities are being watched.[24]

(6) They may not question employees about their prior or present union affiliations, internal union affairs, or union meetings,[25] nor ask an employee whether he has signed a union card.[26] It is not improper, however, for a supervisor to receive such information if an employee volunteers it.

(7) Supervisors may not call employees away from their places of work to their office, or any similar place on the premises where employees are unaccustomed to being, in order to urge them to vote against the union.[27]

(8) They may not ask employees their personal opinions about the union or the feelings of other employees.[28]

(9) Supervisors may not systematically visit the homes of employees to urge them to vote against the union.[29]

(10) They may not solicit or encourage employees to request the return of their authorization cards,[30] or assist them by writing letters to the union or the NLRB.[31] However, they may respond affirmatively to employee questions as to whether they can get their cards back, and advise them, if this is their desire, to contact the person who solicited their signature.[32]

CAVEATS FOR THE ATTORNEY

There are also cautions an attorney should exercise. In the course of advising in this field, the attorney should avoid what is called "persuader activities" on behalf of his client. Examples are addressing a convocation of the employees of his client,[33] making uninvited visits to employees' homes to dissuade them from joining a union,[34] or interrogating individual employees about their union activities (except in preparation for a hearing or trial).[35] Should he engage in such activity, he would be required to file detailed reports with the Department of Labor of his receipts from all employer clients to whom he renders labor relations advice and services.[36]

This is not to suggest an attorney may not advise his client on any and all matters without being required to file a report. Indeed he may, as long as he does not directly or indirectly influence employees in their right to engage in collective activities.[37]

RESPONDING TO UNION HANDBILLS

The AFL-CIO points out the purpose of handbilling is to create an emotional appeal:

> In using publicity, the [union] representative should remember that while his campaign may be based upon facts, he must create an emotional appeal. Words such as 'security,' 'freedom,' 'dignity,' 'fear,' 'equality,' 'justice,' and 'self-respect' have this appeal. *A Guidebook For Union Organizers*, p. 13.

A prompt factual response can dissipate emotional appeal. The simplest way to respond is through the supervisor. Thus, when the union's "handbill of the day" has been passed out at the gate, the on-shift supervisors should be called to a short briefing session to discuss the handbill. The response is agreed upon. Then, handbill in hand, each supervisor is instructed to speak to his employees.

This procedure commends itself because supervision is "brought into the act" and it encourages face-to-face communication with employees. Its main advantage is in timing. The response, usually within an hour of distribution, will be more interesting to employees and will answer the union's propaganda before the appeal has had its intended impact. Where a more detailed response is desired, a written handout may be distributed, preferably by supervision.

A response to a union handbill may also be made through a home mailing. Supervisors should be given copies of the letters their employees will receive prior to mailing. In this manner, they will be prepared to discuss the letter with employees the following day.

Not every union handbill requires written reply. Indeed, it is wrong to do so, because, by its very nature, a response is usually defensive.

Facsimile No. 10, page 59, is an example of a union handbill with which an employer may be confronted. It has a simple message, using stock phrases of union promises.

Tips on how to reply to the handbill follow:

Higher Wages

An employer who has watched the trend of the market place, who regularly reviews his wage scales, who practices a fair wage policy and administers it consistently, should advise employees of those procedures. He can also assert that a union may promise higher wages, but cannot guarantee them. (See Facsimile No. 11, page 60 for an example of a brief reply.)

Better Insurance, Hospital Coverage and Pensions

The union's promise to improve fringe benefits is best answered by recounting what has been done in the past and what is being done in the present. The employer then may allude to what might be expected in the future based upon what has been done in the past.

Seniority

Unions find the promise of absolute seniority easy to sell. It has a pleasing ring to many employees. The longer one is on a job, the stronger, it is alleged, is his hold on the job. Assertions by the employer that seniority has limitations and disadvantages for the newer employee are easily misconstrued against the employer and exploited in union propaganda.

The answer of the employer lies in his own practices. Where it is his practice to give consideration to continuous length of service in layoffs, recall from layoffs, transfers and promotions, and in the application of personnel policies such as vacation preferences, he is well equipped to meet this phase of union propaganda.

FACSIMILE No. 10

YOUR BEST BUY

The stock market is busy. Stock prices are high and dividends are large. But if you're a working man in the metal industry, your best buy is a share (that is, a membership card) in the UNITED STEELWORKERS OF AMERICA.

Your membership in USWA pays constant dividends. It brings higher wages. It increases your security by supplying a fair seniority rule and workable grievance machinery. It protects you against unfair discharge, thus giving you job security. It helps you gain a decent pension for old age. It pays dividends every day in many ways.

HIGHER WAGES
PREMIUM PAY FOR Overtime & HOLIDAYS
BETTER INSURANCE 365 DAYS HOSPITAL COVERAGE
SENIORITY
GRIEVANCE MACHINERY
JOB SECURITY
PENSIONS
UNION STOCK

You get a share in the United Steelworkers of America simply by being a member of the union; you get a share equal to that held by any other member. Every member has the same vote; there are no market manipulators to corner a controlling interest, such as happens with corporation stocks.

FACSIMILE No. 11

Dear Fellow Employee:

     In its handbill this morning, the union promised you "Higher Wages" if you become a union member.

     The union can make promises, but cannot guarantee their fulfillment. Let me remind you of the progress you made during the past year. You have had merit wage increases on a regular basis. You have had a general wage increase.

     These combined wage increases are greater than the increases the union has negotiated in their contracts. These increases were yours without loss of wages due to strikes.

     Our record of progress, not mere promises, has been built without union interference. Let us work together to provide an even better future for all of us.

               Sincerely,

               General Manager

Grievance Machinery

The union's promise of a grievance procedure has surface appeal. It is a promise of formal participation in discussions with employer representatives concerning plant problems and complaints. Some employees may relish the prospect of a hostile confrontation with the "boss" and the thrill of participating in the combat between the union and the employer. They are promised their own representatives (shop stewards) who will speak for them and "protect" them from employer actions.

The union's promise will have little impact where the employer and his supervisory staff practice the policy of promptly considering complaints and problems before they become grievances. Some non-union employers prefer a formalized grievance procedure. An example is set forth in Facsimile No. 12, at page 62.

Job Security

Job security is an attractive shibboleth. Its implication for the employee is that he is promised perpetual tenure, a secured career, and insulation from discharge.

It is an inaccurate premise and promise. A union contract does not give permanency of employment. If a business fails, if there is a business recession, if there is a seasonal drop-off in sales, no union contract can give "job security" in this sense.

The refutation of the union's promise of job security can be an embarrassing one for the employer. To deny the validity of the union's promise is almost to lend credence to the assertion that the employee is subject to termination or layoff.

This forensic trap must be avoided by an exposition of what job security really is. In the first place, it is the securing of a job. It can only be obtained from the employer. The union does not provide it.

FACSIMILE No. 12

GRIEVANCE PROCEDURE

PURPOSE

The objective of the Grievance Procedure is to provide the mech-
anism that will allow employees to bring to the attention of management conditions which the employee feels are unjust or unfair.
The Grievance Procedure will provide an opportunity to clear up
any misunderstandings, to take action to remove causes for legitimate
complaint and to help create sound employee-management relations.
When a condition exists which is felt to be unjust or unfair, the
employee is directed to the following procedure:

PROCEDURE

(1) Step 1: An employee who has a grievance may
present it to his supervisor.   It is desirable
that this be done as soon as possible after the occur-
rence complained of or after the aggrieved employee
may reasonably be presumed to have knowledge of the
matter.   The decision of the supervisor shall be
rendered to the employee promptly, within ten (10)
days from the time the employee present the grievance.

(2) Step 2: In the event the grievance is not settled
under Step 1, the employee may within five (5) working
days from the time the decision is rendered to her (him)
submit the grievance in writing to the Department Manager.
The decision of the Manager will be rendered within
ten (10) working days from the time the employee presents
the grievance to him.

(3) Step 3: If the grievance is not settled in Step 2,
then the employee may request submission of the grievance
to the President, whose decision shall be final.

ASSISTANCE

An employee will be welcomed in seeking the assistance of the personnel
department.   He may also avail himself of the aid of any other active
employee of the company in preparing and presenting his complaint.

AUTHOR'S NOTE:

Some grievance procedures in non-union companies permit
arbitration by a neutral person as the final step.

In the second place, job security is making an employee secure in his job. An employee has job security when he is working for a healthy, growing company, with the assurance of steady work. These concepts may be portrayed through an in-plant poster stating:

JOB SECURITY IS

* Having a place to work

* Having equipment with which to work

* Being an employee every working day

* Having no interruptions in work

* Getting regular pay every pay day

* Enjoying a regular vacation and holidays with pay, and a job to come back to

Let's Put It In Writing

A major point in union propaganda is the promise of a written contract (see Facsimile No. 13, page 64).

A proper response to this assertion is that the employees presently have written statements of policy and benefits in the form of handbooks. The employer's insurance and benefit program, described in booklets, also are written confirmation of benefits. It may be stated that the benefits set forth in these publications have grown and have never been taken away, and that a written contract is therefore unnecessary.

It also may be pointed out that a contract rigidifies conditions, often preventing an employer from making necessary improvements in surroundings, working conditions and operations for the benefit of the employees. The employer may demonstrate that many plants have shriveled and died, embalmed in union contracts.

FACSIMILE No. 13

LET'S PUT IT IN WRITING!
YOU'RE SELLING THE BEST YEARS OF YOUR LIFE ON THE INSTALLMENT PLAN HOUR BY HOUR—DAY BY DAY

You might say that our modern economy is based on the legal contract. When you buy a house, you sign a contract. When you buy a car or refrigerator or TV set on time-payments, you sign a contract. Business men sign contracts, and get the services of lawyers to protect their contracts.

Insurance companies insist upon contracts — can you imagine an insurance man selling a group health plan without getting somebody's signature on a contract?

Unions sign contracts too — and for the best of reasons — to PROTECT WORKERS. You are selling the best years of your life on the installment plan, hour by hour, day by day. You need the same kind of CONTRACT PROTECTION.

Union contracts are negotiated to make sure that the workers gains and benefits will not be taken away from them.

When you are a union member, your union contract assures that you will not be laid off out of line of seniority just because the employer likes somebody else better.

The contract guarantees that you will not be fired without just reason. And it provides, that you can go to a neutral arbitrator and make the company prove that there was a good reason for discharge. The contract guarantees you against pay cuts and provides an orderly system for settling disputes that protects the employees. This system is called "grievance procedure," and is one of the most important parts of a union contract.

Many non-union men and women have good jobs, good pay, good working conditions. But union members have better jobs. Their good wages, good conditions and job security are guaranteed in a written contract signed by the employer.

"Put it in writing" is always good advice. Join our union and get some job security and benefits guaranteed in writing — in your union contract.   ORGANIZING COMMITTEE

REQUEST FOR RECOGNITION

Notwithstanding the employer's efforts to discourage card signing, the union's activities may be successful. One day the employer receives a letter or personal visit from the union representative claiming representation of a majority of employees, and requesting recognition. What should he do?

It is a well-accepted principle that an employer may decline to recognize and bargain with a labor organization upon receiving a demand for recognition.[38] Such an employer must be careful, however, that his actions do not accord the union *de facto* recognition. This is particularly important in the case of a personal visit at the employer's premises, which often comes without prior notice.

REJECTING CARD CHECKS

Frequently, during personal visits, the union representative may offer to prove the union's majority representation by a comparison of the signatures on cards in his possession with employees' signatures appearing on the company's payroll records.

The union representative may suggest that the employer make the comparison in his presence or that it be done by some disinterested third party, such as a clergyman. Caught off guard, the company officer, branch store or plant manager might unwittingly commit the firm to this procedure and thus to recognition of the union. The experience of a retail store manager who looked at union cards under such circumstances has previously been mentioned. Advance counselling will avoid these occurrences.

A union's request for recognition via a "card check" should be rejected and management officers should be so advised. The reason is clear:

(1) If the offer is accepted and the comparison demonstrates that the union has a majority, the NLRB will direct recognition.[39]

(2) If the comparison demonstrates that the union does not have a majority, the employer has gained nothing. The union goes away, only to return another day with more cards.

When a union requests recognition, it should be presumed that the union has procured the signatures of a majority of employees. Most unions, as a matter of policy, will not otherwise seek recognition.[40]

Why do unions follow this course?

First, if recognition is granted, the ensuing bargaining relationship will be lawful because it is founded on majority status.

Second, if recognition is not granted, and the union files a petition for an election, the union's possession of a majority of cards will enhance its likelihood of success.

Third, where recognition is not granted, and the employer reacts by committing serious unfair labor practices, its possession of a majority of cards will enable it to seek a Board order directing the employer to recognize and bargain with it. This latter course was made possible by the Supreme Court's decision in *NLRB v. Gissel Packing Co.*[41]

Infrequently, an employer will recognize a union which does not have majority support. This form of recognition is unlawful. (See Appendix I.)

POLLING EMPLOYEES

Occasionally, an employer's reaction to a union's claim that it represents a majority is to poll the employees for verification.

Unless carefully handled, such a poll is unlawful.[42] The Board has permitted such polls only when "(1) the purpose of the poll is to determine the truth of a union's claim of majority, (2) this purpose is communicated to the employees, (3) assurances against reprisal are given, (4) the employees are polled by secret ballot, and (5) the employer has not engaged in unfair labor practices or otherwise created a coercive atmosphere."[43] The Board tolerates little, if any, deviation from these rules.

An important reason to be cautious of polls is the possibility that it will result in an affirmation of the union't claim. This is tantamount, in the language of the Board, to "independent knowledge" of the union's majority. Such knowledge can result in a bargaining order.[44]

Independent knowledge also has been imputed to an employer when a majority of his employees have engaged in a strike.[45] Some unions will enclose copies of authorization cards in their letter requesting recognition.[46] An examination of these cards has been held to constitute independent knowledge, where it reveals a majority.[47]

DENYING RECOGNITION

There are cogent reasons for the rejection of a union's request for recognition based solely on its claim that it has a majority of employees "signed up." For one thing, the unit sought by the union may not be appropriate.[48] Equally important, the cards may be invalid. Thus, for example:

(a) The employees' signatures may have been forged;[49]

(b) The cards may have been obtained through coercion, e.g., employees may have been told that unless they signed, they would be out of a job once the union got in;[50]

(c) The cards used may be ambiguous, dual-purpose cards;[51]

(d) The cards used may be clear and unambiguous, but the clear language on the cards may have been overcome by the misleading talk of the solicitors;[52]

(e) The cards may be stale, *i.e.*, not considered valid because of passage of time.[53]

These possibilities are sufficient to put an employer on guard against the hasty acceptance of a union's request for recognition based on authorization cards. As one court stated: "Unless the employer is extraordinarily gullible and unimaginative, he will at least suspect unreliability in the cards and their signatures."[54]

Even where the union possesses a valid majority of cards, recognition need not be accorded. The employer may insist on a secret ballot election.[55] Nor will majority status be sufficient by itself to obtain a bargaining order. "[T]he key to the issuance of a bargaining order is the commission of serious unfair labor practices that interfere with the election processes and tend to preclude the holding of a fair election."[56] In the two and one half years since *Gissel*, the NLRB has issued 100 bargaining orders against employers who committed serious unfair labor practices.[57] (See Appendix G for a listing of post-*Gissel* bargaining orders.)

It therefore behooves every employer to avoid the commission of unfair labor practices. Prior cautions relating to the conduct of supervisory personnel, should be studied in this connection.

When a union requests recognition in writing, a written reply should be made. Facsimile No. 14, page 69, is an example.

The rejection of a union's request for recognition often signifies the beginning of a proceeding leading toward an election and, sometimes, litigation. If handled properly, with due caution and attention to the rules, the employer will not have prejudiced his legal position.

FACSIMILE No. 14

Gentlemen:

This is in reply to your letter in which you state that a majority of our employees have authorized your union to represent them, and in which you request that we recognize your union. Since we doubt that you do represent a majority of our employees, we reject your request.

Your offer to establish proof of your majority via a card check is unacceptable. Such a mechanical check of signatures would in no way resolve whether an employee has been coerced into signing a card or signed as a result of misrepresentation as to its purpose.

We believe, as does the United States Supreme Court, that a secret ballot election is the best way to determine whether a union has majority support. Since you have already filed a petition, recognition of your union will await and depend upon the results of the election.

Yours truly,

General Manager

NOTES TO CHAPTER IV

1. LMRA § 101.8(c), 29 U.S.C. § 158(c) (1964).

2. LMRA § 101.7, 29 U.S.C. § 157 (1964).

3. LMRA § 101.8(b)(1), 29 U.S.C. § 158(b)(1) (1964).

4. LMRA § 101.8(c), 29 U.S.C. § 158(c) (1964).

5. D & C Textile Corp., 189 NLRB No. 113, 77 LRRM 1055 (1971); Bostitch Div. of Textron, 176 NLRB No. 47, 71 LRRM 1241 (1969).

6. Essex Wire Corp., 188 NLRB No. 59, 77 LRRM 1016 (1971); Texaco Inc., 178 NLRB No. 72, 72 LRRM 1146 (1969), *enf'd on other grounds,* 436 F.2d 520 (7th Cir. 1971).

7. Cain Co., 190 NLRB No. 24, 77 LRRM 1049 (1971). *See also, Int'l Technovation, Inc.,* 194 NLRB No. 36, 78 LRRM 1515 (1971), wherein the Board held that the employer's statement as to its plans should a strike occur was unobjectionable. The Board stated:

> The contingency plans . . . outlined were to take effect only 'in the event' the Union, during or after bargaining, chose to strike, and constituted a factual, unobjectionable representation of the Employer's right under existing law to carry on its business in the event of a work stoppage. 78 LRRM at 1516.

8. Cain Co., *supra* note 7. *Cf.* Deutsch Co., 178 NLRB No. 95, 72 LRRM 1248, 1250 (1969), where NLRB found objectionable the statement that the employee could gain nothing by voting for the union.

9. Beatrice Food Co., 192 NLRB No. 34, 77 LRRM 1726, 1728 (1971); Olin Conductors, 185 NLRB No. 56, 76 LRRM 1691 (1970); Brewer & Brewer Materials, Inc., 182 NLRB No. 119, 74 LRRM 1215 (1970), *enf'd on other grounds,* 436 F.2d 1383 (6th Cir. 1971); Howard Mfg. Co., 180 NLRB No. 47, 75 LRRM 1515 (1969), *enf'd on other grounds,* 436 F.2d 581 (8th Cir. 1971), *cert. denied,* 402 U.S. 930 (1971). *Cf.* Buddies Supermarkets, Inc., 192 NLRB No. 143, 78 LRRM 1236 (1971) (employer used "wanted" poster showing arrest records of four union organizers—two of whom were not organizers but had similar names).

10. LMRA § 101.8(c), 29 U.S.C. § 158(c) (1964).

11. Ripley Mfg. Co., 144 NLRB 1132, 1140-141, 54 LRRM 1202 (1963).

12. Dempster Bros., 154 NLRB 688, 60 LRRM 1006 (1965).

13. Gary Aircraft Corp., 190 NLRB No. 61, 77 LRRM 1160 (1971).

14. Presto Mfg. Co., 168 NLRB 1073, 67 LRRM 1173 (1968).

15. Deutsch Co., *supra* note 8, at 72 LRRM 1250.

16. United Packing Co., 187 NLRB No. 132, 76 LRRM 1156 (1971); Drives, Inc., 172 NLRB No. 101, 68 LRRM 1428 (1968), *reaff'd,* 179 NLRB No. 88, 72 LRRM 1388 (1969), *enf'd,* 440 F.2d 354, 76 LRRM 2296 (7th Cir. 1971).

17. Zinke's Foods, Inc., 185 NLRB No. 109, 75 LRRM 1211 (1970).

18. Champa Linen Serv., 177 NLRB No. 69, 72 LRRM 1535 (1969), *enf'd,* 437 F.2d 1259 (10th Cir. 1971).

19. Exide Alkaline Battery Div., 177 NLRB No. 99, 71 LRRM 1489 (1969), *enf'd,* 423 F.2d 625 (4th Cir. 1970). A formal, written no-solicitation rule is not required. Universal Packing & Gasket Co., 151 NLRB 1528, 1556, 58 LRRM 1652 (1965), *enf'd,* 379 F.2d 269 (5th Cir. 1967). A valid no-solicitation rule, however, may not be applied discriminatorily. Rogers Mfg. Co., 175 NLRB No. 163, 71 LRRM 1191 (1969)

20. Exide Alkaline Battery Div., *supra* note 19.

21. *Id.*

22. Omni Spectra, Inc., 186 NLRB No. 93, 75 LRRM 1402 (1970), *supplementing* 176 NLRB No. 24, 71 LRRM 1222 (1969); Stoddard-Quirk Mfg. Co., 138 NLRB 615, 51 LRRM 1110 (1962).

23. John S. Barnes Corp., 180 NLRB No. 139, 73 LRRM 1215 (1970), *enf'd,* F.2d ___, 77 LRRM 2372 (D.C. Cir., No. 24021, decided March 11, 1971), *cert. denied,* ___ U.S. ___ (No. 71-98, Oct. 12, 1971); L. C. Ferguson & E. F. Von Seggern d/b/a Shovel Supply Co., 118 NLRB 315, 40 LRRM 1189 (1957); Wright & McGill Co., 102 NLRB 1035, 31 LRRM 1394 (1953)

24. J. J. Kane d/b/a Kane Bag Supply Co., 173 NLRB No. 180, 69 LRRM 1571 (1968), *reaff'd,* 179 NLRB No. 51, 72 LRRM 1323 (1969), *enf'd,* 435 F.2d 1203 (4th Cir. 1970); Rish Equip. Co., 150 NLRB 1185, 58 LRRM 1274 (1965), *enf'd,* 359 F.2d 391 (4th Cir. 1966).

25. John S. Barnes Corp., *supra* note 23.

26. G & A Truck Line, Inc., 168 NLRB 846, 67 LRRM 1084 (1967), *enf'd,* 407 F.2d 120 (6th Cir. 1969).

27. Phelps Dodge Corp., 177 NLRB No. 68, 71 LRRM 1385 (1969); Great Atlantic & Pacific Tea Co., 140 NLRB 133, 51 LRRM 1570 (1962); Nat'l Caterers, 125 NLRB 110, 45 LRRM 1070 (1959); Peoples Drug Stores, Inc., 119 NLRB 634, 41 LRRM 1141 (1957); General Shoe Corp. (Marman Bag Plant), 97 NLRB 499, 29 LRRM 1113 (1951).

28. Atlas Engine Works, Inc., 163 NLRB 486, 495, 64 LRRM 1376 (1967), *enf'd,* 396 F.2d 775 (6th Cir. 1968), *cert. granted,* 395 U.S. 828 (1969), *reaff'd on remand,* 181 NLRB No. 13, 73 LRRM 1276 (1970), *enf'd,* 435 F.2d 558 (6th Cir. 1970).

29. Imperial-Eastman Corp., 139 NLRB 1255, 51 LRRM 1482 (1962); Hurley Co., 130 NLRB 282, 47 LRRM 1293 (1961); F. N. Calderwood, Inc., 124 NLRB 1211, 44 LRRM 1628 (1959); Peoria Plastics Co., 117 NLRB 545, 39 LRRM 1281 (1957). *Cf.* Superior Coach Corp., 175 NLRB No. 32, 70 LRRM 1514 (1969) (no violation of Act, where two supervisors each visited the homes of two employees to persuade them to vote against the union).

30. Taber Instruments, Div. of Teledyne, Inc., 172 NLRB No. 169, 69 LRRM 1069 (1968), *enf'd as modified,* 421 F.2d 642 (2d Cir. 1970), *enf'd in full on rehearing,* 438 F.2d 901, 74 LRRM 2224 (2d Cir. 1970).

31. Deutsch Co., *supra* note 8; Cumberland Shoe Co., 160 NLRB 1256, 63 LRRM 1148 (1966). *Cf.* North American Aviation, Inc., 163 NLRB 863, 65 LRRM 1017 (1967), *enf'd on other grounds,* 389 F.2d 866 (10th Cir. 1968); Clark Control Div. of O. A. Smith Corp., 166 NLRB 266, 65 LRRM 1551 (1967).

32. KDI Precision Prods. Inc., 176 NLRB No. 18, 73 LRRM 1190 (1969), *enf'd on other grounds,* 436 F.2d 385 (6th Cir. 1971).

33. Wirtz v. Fowler, 372 F.2d 333 (5th Cir. 1966), *rev'g* 236 F.Supp. 22 (S.D. Fla. 1964); Douglas v. Wirtz, 353 F.2d 30 (4th Cir. 1965), *vacating* 232 F.Supp. 348 (M.D.N.C. 1964), *cert. denied,* 383 U.S. 909 (1966).

34. Wirtz v. Fowler, *supra* note. 33.

35. *Id.* Such interrogation may also violate § 8(a)(1) of the LMRA, absent appropriate safeguards. *See,* Gerbes Super Mkts., Inc., 176 NLRB No. 1, 71 LRRM 1182 (1969), *enf'd,* 436 F.2d 19 (8th Cir. 1971); Johnnie's Poultry Co., 146 NLRB 770, 55 LRRM 1403 (1964), *enforcement denied on other grounds,* 344 F.2d 617 (8th Cir. 1965).

36. Labor-Management Reporting and Disclosure Act of 1959 (Landrum-Griffin Act) § 203(b), 29 U.S.C. § 433(b) (1964).

37. Loomis, *Employer and Consultant Reporting Requirements,* Symposium On LMRDA 399 (R. Slovenko ed. 1961).

38. NLRB v. Gissel Packing Co., 395 U.S. 575, 591 (1969).

39. Pacific Abrasive Supply Co., 182 NLRB No. 48, 74 LRRM 1113 (1970); Redmond Plastics, Inc., 176 NLRB No. 10, 73 LRRM 1237 (1967), *reaff'd,* 187 NLRB No. 60, 76 LRRM 1035 (1970); Snow & Sons, 134 NLRB 709, 49 LRRM 1228 (1961), *enf'd,* 308 F.2d 687 (9th Cir. 1962).

40. The UAW is an example. See S. I. Schlossberg & F. E. Sherman, *Organizing and the Law* 55 (1971).

41. Gissel, *supra* note 38. Although the Court approved the use of authorization cards by unions to prove their majority status, it conceded that cards were "admittedly inferior" to a secret ballot election. 395 U.S. at 594.

42. Heck's Inc., 171 NLRB No. 112, 68 LRRM 1194 (1968), *reaff'd*, 181 NLRB No. 129, 73 LRRM 1524 (1970); Offner Electronics, Inc., 127 NLRB 991, 46 LRRM 1136 (1960). However, it is the Board's position that this prohibition does not apply to union conducted polls. Lipman Motors, Inc. v. NLRB, __ F.2d __, 78 LRRM 2808, 2811 (2nd Cir., Nos. 35813 and 71-1554, decided Nov. 4, 1971).

43. Struksnes Constr. Co., 165 NLRB 1062, 1063, 65 LRRM 1385 (1967).

44. Sehon Stevenson & Co., 150 NLRB 675, 684-85, 58 LRRM 1156 (1964), *enf'd*, 386 F.2d 551 (4th Cir. 1967).

45. Wilder Mfg. Co., 185 NLRB No. 76, 75 LRRM 1023 (1970). *But see*, Summer & Co., 190 NLRB No. 116, 77 LRRM 1305 (1971).

46. Hart Beverage Co., 170 NLRB No. 58, 68 LRRM 1029 (1968), *remanded*, 414 F.2d 618 (8th Cir. 1969), *reaff'd*, 170 NLRB No. 58, 68 LRRM 1029 (1970).

47. Redmond Plastics, Inc., 187 NLRB No. 60, 76 LRRM 1035 (1970) __, *supplementing* 176 NLRB No. 10, 73 LRRM 1237 (1969); Snow & Sons, *supra* note 39.

48. Decision, Inc., 166 NLRB 464, 65 LRRM 1660 (1967).

49. Reliable Mfg. Co., 13-CA-15, 941 (NLRB June 21, 1964).

50. Clement Bros. Co., 165 NLRB 698, 63 LRRM 1437 (1967).

51. A dual purpose card authorizes a union to file a petition for an election and to represent the signer in collective bargaining. *See* John S. Barnes Corp., *supra* note 23. *See also*, Collins Mining Co., 177 NLRB No. 55, 75 LRRM 1518 (1969), *enf'd on other grounds*, 440 F.2d 1069 (6th Cir. 1971); Silver Fleet, Inc., 174 NLRB No. 141, 70 LRRM 1316 (1969). The Supreme Court, in *Gissel*, did not pass upon the validity of dual-purpose cards. Gissel, *supra* note 38, at 609. For a more detailed discussion of dual-purpose cards and examples of wording on such cards, see Lewis, *The Use and Abuse of Authorization Cards in Determining Union Majority*, 16 Lab. L.J. 434, 439 (July 1965); Krupman, *The Joy Silk Rule—The Courts Weave A New Fabric*, 19 Lab. L.J. 603, 610 (Oct. 1968).

52. As stated by the Supreme Court: ". . . words calculated to direct the signer to disregard and forget the language above his signature." Gissel, *supra* note 38, at 606. *See also*, Eckerd's Mkt., Inc., 183 NLRB

No. 40, 74 LRRM 1319 (1970); Levi Strauss & Co., 172 NLRB No. 57, 68 LRRM 1338 (1966); Cumberland Shoe Corp., 144 NLRB 1268, 54 LRRM 1233 (1963), enf'd, 351 F.2d 917 (6th Cir. 1965).

53. The NLRB generally will not count cards executed more than one year prior to the bargaining request, except in the unusual circumstance of a continuous campaign lasting more than one year, or one that was interrupted by the filing and processing of unfair labor practice charges. Blade-Tribune Publishing Co., 161 NLRB 1512, 63 LRRM 1484 (1966), remanded, __ F.2d __, 71 LRRM 3104 (9th Cir., No. 21860, decided July 14, 1969), rev'd on other grounds, 180 NLRB No. 56, 73 LRRM 1041 (1969); Knickerbocker Plastic Co., 104 NLRB 514, 32 LRRM 1123 (1953), enf'd, 218 F.2d 917 (9th Cir. 1955).

54. NLRB v. S. S. Logan Packing Co., 386 F.2d 562, 566 (4th Cir. 1967), enforcing in part 152 NLRB 421, 59 LRRM 1115 (1965). Similar words of condemnation were used by Circuit Judge Harold Medina: "[T]his 'representation' card business is an abomination." Schwarzenbach-Huber Co. v. NLRB, 408 F.2d 236, 249 (2d Cir. 1969), cert. denied, 396 U.S. 960 (1969).

55. Gissel, supra note 38, at 591.

56. Id. at 594.

57. The 100 bargaining orders issued by the Board do not include those issued following remand to the Board for reconsideration by the circuit courts or reconsidered by it sua sponte in the light of Gissel. There were 61 such orders. NLRB, Study of the NLRB Cases Involving A Bargaining Order Under The Guidelines of Gissel Packing Company (June 1971). For leading Board cases interpreting Gissel, see Summer & Co., 190 NLRB No. 116, 77 LRRM 1305 (1971); United Packing Co., 187 NLRB No. 132, 76 LRRM 1156 (1971); Wilder Mfg. Co., 185 NLRB No. 76, 75 LRRM 1023 (1970); General Steel Prods., Inc., 180 NLRB No. 8, 72 LRRM 1579 (1969).

CHAPTER V

PETITIONS BEFORE LABOR BOARD

Anticipating the employer's refusal to grant recognition by a card count, the union usually files a petition for certification with the NLRB. To appreciate the procedure when a petition for an election is filed, it is helpful first to examine the Board's structure (see Facsimile No. 15, page 78).[1]

NLRB STRUCTURE

The Board is composed of five members. Its principal office is at 1717 Pennsylvania Avenue, N. W., Washington, D. C. Board members serve for five-year periods on appointment of the President, with approval of the Senate.

The duties of the Board are two-fold. One is to conduct secret ballot elections among employees in appropriate units to determine whether or not the employees desire to be represented by a labor organization. The other is to prevent and remedy unfair labor practices.[2]

The General Counsel is appointed by the President for a term of four years, with the approval of the Senate. He exercises supervision over all attorneys employed by the Board except for those attorneys on the Washington staff of Board members. He also exercises supervision over the officers and employees in the Regional offices. By statute he has final authority to investigate unfair labor practice charges and issue or refuse to issue complaints and prosecute them.[3]

The Board appoints an executive secretary and such attorneys, examiners, regional directors and other employees as it may find necessary for the proper performance of its duties.[4]   There are 31 regional offices.   They are headed by regional directors who are appointed by the Board on recommendation of the General Counsel.   Some regions have sub-regional offices or resident offices.   The regions are numbered from "1" on up.   These numbers are used in case designations.   For example, 1-RC-102 means Region 1, and refers to a representation case numbered 102.[5]

The Board publishes its "Rules and Regulations and Statements of Procedure," which as the title states, describes in detail the rules, regulations and procedures under which it operates.[6] The Board also publishes a *Field Manual* for use of its field personnel in performing their duties.   It is available to the public.[7]

FILING A PETITION

A petition is filed with the regional director for the region where the bargaining unit is located.   The Rules require an original and four copies be filed.[8]

Union or Individual as Petitioner

A petition may be filed by a union alleging that a substantial number of employees wish to be represented for purposes of collective bargaining and that it desires to be certified as their representative.   (See Facsimile No. 16, page 79, Item 1, first box, "RC — Certification of Representative.")

Item 7a of the petition form inquires as to the date on which the petitioner requested recognition from the employer.   However, it is not a condition precedent to the filing of such a petition that a demand for recognition be made.[9]

On rare occasions an individual petitions on behalf of employees. The individual need not be an employee. When this is done, the employees vote for or against the petitioning individual. If he wins, he is certified as the bargaining representative.[10]

Occasionally two or more unions petition together and are known as joint petitioners. When this occurs, the two unions appear jointly on the ballot. If they are successful in the election, they will be certified jointly, and the employer then may insist that they bargain together.[11]

The petitioner, whether it be an individual, a union, or two unions petitioning jointly, must allege and be able to submit proof that the petition is supported by thirty (30%) percent or more of the employees in the unit. (Item 6b.) This proof is presented when the petition is filed or within 48 hours thereafter.[12]

Upon the filing of the petition, the regional director commences an investigation. This may disclose that no question concerning representation (QCR) exists; for example, the employer's business is not in interstate commerce or does not affect commerce, the unit is not appropriate, a written collective bargaining agreement is in effect which bars the filing of the petition, or the showing of representation among the employees is insufficient (less than 30%).[13]

In any of these circumstances, the regional director may request the petitioner to withdraw its petition. If the petitioner refuses, the regional director may dismiss it, stating the grounds for the dismissal. The petitioner may appeal the dismissal to the Board in Washington.[14]

In the usual case, a petition is not dismissed, but processed. The regional director notifies the employer that a petition has been filed, requests a list of employees' names and job class-

FACSIMILE No. 15

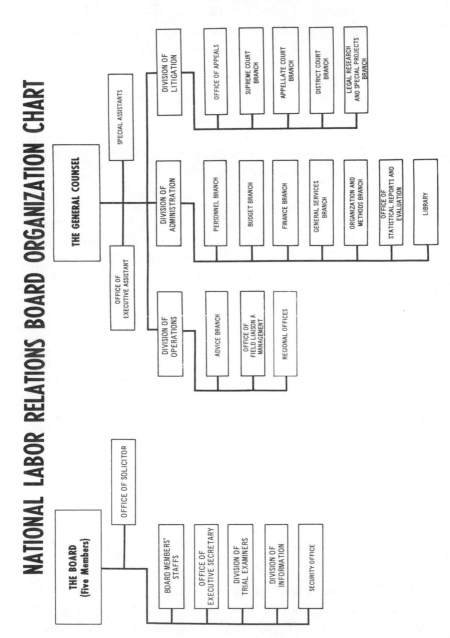

NATIONAL LABOR RELATIONS BOARD ORGANIZATION CHART

FACSIMILE No. 16

Form NLRB-502
(11-64)

UNITED STATES OF AMERICA
NATIONAL LABOR RELATIONS BOARD

Form Approved
Budget Bureau No. 64-R002.14

PETITION

DO NOT WRITE IN THIS SPACE
CASE NO
DATE FILED

INSTRUCTIONS — Submit an original and four (4) copies of this Petition to the NLRB Regional Office in the Region in which the employer concerned is located.
If more space is required for any one item, attach additional sheets, numbering item accordingly.

The Petitioner alleges that the following circumstances exist and requests that the National Labor Relations Board proceed under its proper authority pursuant to Section 9 of the National Labor Relations Act.

1. Purpose of this Petition *(If box RC, RM, or RD is checked and a charge under Section 8(b)("") of the Act has been filed involving the Employer named herein, the statement following the description of the type of petition shall not be deemed made.)*
(Check one)

☐ RC—CERTIFICATION OF REPRESENTATIVE —A substantial number of employees wish to be represented for purposes of collective bargaining by Petitioner and Petitioner desires to be certified as representative of the employees.

☐ RM—REPRESENTATION (EMPLOYER PETITION)—One or more individuals or labor organizations have presented a claim to Petitioner to be recognized as the representative of employees of Petitioner.

☐ RD—DECERTIFICATION —A substantial number of employees assert that the certified or currently recognized bargaining representative is no longer their representative.

☐ UD—WITHDRAWAL OF UNION SHOP AUTHORITY —Thirty percent (30%) or more of employees in a bargaining unit covered by an agreement between their employer and a labor organization desire that such authority be rescinded.

☐ UC—UNIT CLARIFICATION—A labor organization is currently recognized by employer, but petitioner seeks clarification of placement of certain employees *(Check one)* ☐ In unit not previously certified
☐ In unit previously certified in Case No.

☐ AC—AMENDMENT OF CERTIFICATION—Petitioner seeks amendment of certification issued in Case No.
Attach statement describing the specific amendment sought.

2. NAME OF EMPLOYER	EMPLOYER REPRESENTATIVE TO CONTACT	PHONE NO

3. ADDRESS(ES) OF ESTABLISHMENT(S) INVOLVED *(Street and number, city, State, and ZIP Code)*

4a. TYPE OF ESTABLISHMENT *(Factory, mine, wholesaler, etc.)*	4b. IDENTIFY PRINCIPAL PRODUCT OR SERVICE

5. Unit Involved *(In UC petition, describe PRESENT bargaining unit and attach description of proposed clarification.)*

Included

Excluded

6a. NUMBER OF EMPLOYEES IN UNIT
PRESENT
PROPOSED (BY UC/AC)

6b. IS THIS PETITION SUPPORTED BY 30% OR MORE OF THE EMPLOYEES IN THE UNIT?
☐ YES ☐ NO
Not applicable in RM, UC, and AC

(If you have checked box RC in 1 above, check and complete EITHER item "a" or "b", whichever is applicable)

☐ a. Request for recognition as Bargaining Representative was made on .... *(Month, day, year)* .... and Employer declined recognition on or about .... *(If no reply received, so state.)* *(Month, day, year)*

☐ b. Petitioner is currently recognized as Bargaining Representative and desires certification under the act.

8. Recognized or Certified Bargaining Agent *(If there is none, so state)*

NAME	AFFILIATION
ADDRESS	DATE OF RECOGNITION OR CERTIFICATION

9. DATE OF EXPIRATION OF CURRENT CONTRACT, IF ANY *(Show month, day, and year)*	10. IF YOU HAVE CHECKED BOX UD IN 1 ABOVE, SHOW HERE THE DATE OF EXECUTION OF AGREEMENT GRANTING UNION SHOP *(Month, day and year)*

11a. IS THERE NOW A STRIKE OR PICKETING AT THE EMPLOYER'S ESTABLISHMENT(S) INVOLVED? YES NO	11b. IF SO, APPROXIMATELY HOW MANY EMPLOYEES ARE PARTICIPATING?

11c. THE EMPLOYER HAS BEEN PICKETED BY OR ON BEHALF OF .... *(Insert name)* .... A LABOR ORGANIZATION OF .... *(Insert address)* .... SINCE .... *(Month, day, year)*

12. ORGANIZATIONS OR INDIVIDUALS OTHER THAN PETITIONER (AND OTHER THAN THOSE NAMED IN ITEMS 8 AND 11c), WHICH HAVE CLAIMED RECOGNITION AS REPRESENTATIVES AND OTHER ORGANIZATIONS AND INDIVIDUALS KNOWN TO HAVE A REPRESENTATIVE INTEREST IN ANY EMPLOYEES IN THE UNIT DESCRIBED IN ITEM 5 ABOVE. (IF NONE, SO STATE.)

NAME	AFFILIATION	ADDRESS	DATE OF CLAIM *(Required only if Petition is filed by Employer)*

I declare that I have read the above petition and that the statements therein are true to the best of my knowledge and belief.

.... *(Petitioner and affiliation, if any)*

By .... *(Signature of representative or person filing petition)* .... *(Title, if any)*

Address .... *(Street and number, city, State, and ZIP Code)* .... *(Telephone number)*

WILLFULLY FALSE STATEMENT ON THIS PETITION CAN BE PUNISHED BY FINE AND IMPRISONMENT (U.S. CODE, TITLE 18, SECTION 1001)

ifications, and schedules a conference. (See Facsimile No. 17, page 81.) At this point, counsel will enter his appearance. All further documents and written communications will then be served upon counsel as well as his client. However, where counsel prefers to receive exclusive service he should have his client execute and file NLRB Form 4814. (Appendix K is a reproduction of this form.)

Should an employer submit a list of employees? It depends upon the circumstances. Some employers are reluctant to do so because the list may somehow become accessible to the union. It also is preferable not to submit a list because by including or excluding names the employer may thereby unwittingly have committed himself to a unit position which he may later feel was unwise.

Where, however, the union has grossly understated the number of employees in the unit (Facsimile No. 16, page 79, Item 6a) and the employer believes that the union does not have 30% of the accurate number, it may be advisable to submit the list and request dismissal of the petition.

When the employer is first notified of the filing of the petition, he also will receive a "Notice to Employees" for posting. (See Facsimile No. 18, pages 82-83.) There is no obligation to post this notice. An employer may refuse to do so because of the emphasis upon examples of employer misconduct.

Employer as Petitioner

A petition filed by an employer is commonly known as an RM petition, from the word "representation-management." It may be filed under various circumstances:[15]

(a) where a union requests recognition

In the preceding chapter we discussed the union's request for recognition and the employer's response. When an employer

FACSIMILE No. 17

UNITED STATES OF AMERICA
BEFORE THE NATIONAL LABOR RELATIONS BOARD
REGION 29

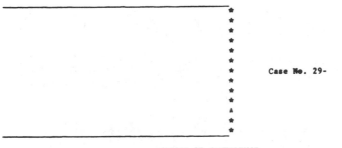

Case No. 29-

NOTICE OF CONFERENCE

PLEASE TAKE NOTICE that a petition has been filed in the above proceeding alleging that a question concerning representation exists in a unit of employees alleged to be appropriate for the purposes of collective bargaining, as set forth in the petition. The unit described is as follows:

PLEASE TAKE FURTHER NOTICE that a conference will be held in this matter at the Regional office, on

at o'clock, before

ALL PARTIES are requested to bring any contract or correspondence between any individuals or labor organizations and the employer pertaining to the representation of any of the employees in the unit or to a contract.

The Employer is requested to produce the completed commerce questionnaire and an alphabetized current list of employees in the unit together with their job classifications including employees who are ill, on vacation, in military service, or temporarily laid off.

Individuals or labor organizations claiming to represent employees in the unit, which have not already furnished the Board with proof of representation in the form of membership or application cards, dues records, contract, etc., must produce such evidence at the conference.

Labor organizations involved may, in certain situations, be deemed not to be a party in the proceeding if they do not present proof of interest at this conference.

PLEASE TAKE FURTHER NOTICE that if this conference does not result in a disposition of this matter a formal hearing will take place on at o'clock at the Regional office.

Dated: Brooklyn, New York

TO:

Regional Director

FACSIMILE No. 18

★ NOTICE TO EMPLOYEES
FROM THE
National Labor Relations Board

A PETITION has been filed with this Federal agency seeking an election to determine whether certain employees want to be represented by a union.

The case is being investigated and NO DETERMINATION HAS BEEN MADE AT THIS TIME by the National Labor Relations Board.   IF an election is held Notices of Election will be posted giving complete details for voting.

It was suggested that your employer post this notice so the National Labor Relations Board could inform you of your basic rights under the National Labor Relations Act.

YOU HAVE THE RIGHT under Federal Law

- To self-organization
- To form, join, or assist labor organizations
- To bargain collectively through representatives of your own choosing
- To act together for the purposes of collective bargaining or other mutual aid or protection
- To refrain from any or all such activities

It is possible that some of you will be voting in an employee representation election as a result of the request for an election having been filed.   While NO DETERMINATION HAS BEEN MADE AT THIS TIME, in the event an election is held, the NATIONAL LABOR RELATIONS BOARD wants all eligible voters to be familiar with their rights under the law IF it holds an election.

Board applies rules which are intended to keep its elections fair and honest and which result in a free choice. If agents of either Unions or Employers act in such a way as to interfere with your right to a free election, the election can be set aside by the Board.   Where appropriate the Board provides other remedies, such as reinstatement for employees fired for exercising their rights, including backpay from the party responsible for their discharge.

FACSIMILE No. 18

NOTE:

The following are examples of conduct which interfere with the rights of employees and may result in the setting aside of the election

- Threatening loss of jobs or benefits by an Employer or a Union
- Misstating important facts by a Union or an Employer where the other party does not have a fair chance to reply
- Promising or granting promotions, pay raises, or other benefits, to influence an employee's vote by a party capable of carrying out such promises
- An Employer firing employees to discourage or encourage union activity or a Union causing them to be fired to encourage union activity
- Making campaign speeches to assembled groups of employees on company time within the 24-hour period before the election
- Incitement by either an Employer or a Union of racial or religious prejudice by inflammatory appeals
- Threatening physical force or violence to employees by a Union or an Employer to influence their votes

Please be assured that IF AN ELECTION IS HELD every effort will be made to protect your right to a free choice under the law.   Improper conduct will not be permitted.   All parties are expected to cooperate fully with this agency in maintaining basic principles of a fair election as required by law.   The National Labor Relations Board as an agency of the United States Government does not endorse any choice in the election.

NATIONAL LABOR RELATIONS BOARD
an agency of the
UNITED STATES GOVERNMENT

THIS IS AN OFFICIAL GOVERNMENT NOTICE AND MUST NOT BE DEFACED BY ANYONE

declines recognition, he also has the option of filing a petition for an election. The same form used by unions or individuals is filed. (See Facsimile No. 16, page 79.) The employer checks the second box in Item 1, alleging that "one or more individuals or labor organizations have presented a claim (to the employer) to be recognized." In completing the petition form counsel should observe that in reciting a unit in Item 5 he is not acknowledging its appropriateness. However, the careful practitioner will state that it is the unit "alleged by the union" as appropriate which he is reciting.

The petition should be accompanied with proof of the union's request for recognition. This proof may be in affidavit form, reciting the request, if oral, or attaching the letter, if made in writing. If this proof is not submitted within 48 hours after the petition has been filed, the petition may be dismissed.[16]

(b) where the employer doubts incumbent union's majority

An employer also may file a petition when he has been unable to reach an initial agreement with a union and doubts that the union represents a majority of his employees.[17] The petition is not timely, however, until after the expiration of the union's certification year.[18]

Another circumstance in which an employer may file a petition is when he doubts that the union with which he has a contract currently represents a majority of his employees.[19] In such event, he may file a petition for an election either between the 90th and 60th day prior to the expiration of the contract, or after the contract has expired where no new agreement has been executed.[20]

In order to file a petition where there is an incumbent union, the employer must submit objective proof of the basis for his doubt of the union's majority status.[21] Examples of "objective proof" which may satisfy this requirement are personnel reductions due to administrative reorganization,[22] high turnover of employees,[23] changes in personnel and composition of the bargaining unit during a strike,[24] request by a majority of the employees that the employer discontinue bargaining,[25] and an admission by the union that it no longer represents a majority.[26] Employee revocation of dues deduction authorizations also may evidence employee disaffection.[27] However, the fact that only a minority of employes are on check-off is not by itself sufficient, since the Board presumes that employees are paying dues in some other way or that they continue to support the union, although not financially.[28]

The employer who doubts an incumbent union's majority need not file a petition. He need only withdraw recognition. The Board has stated:

> After the certification year has run, an Employer may lawfully withdraw recognition from an incumbent union because of an asserted doubt of the union's continued majority if its assertion of doubt is raised in a context free of unfair labor practices and is supported by a showing of objective considerations providing reasonable grounds for a belief that a majority of the employees no longer desire union representation.[29]

However, in practical terms, a withdrawal of recognition, unaccompanied by a petition, usually will cause the union to file an unfair labor practice charge alleging a refusal to bargain. The employer must then show its objective considerations for doubting the union's majority status. These are the same as the objective proof which an employer must submit when he has filed a petition.

A union also may file an unfair labor practice charge where an employer has filed a petition. In commo parlance, this is called a "blocking" charge.[30] If such a charge is filed, the petition is held in abeyance while the Board investigates the charge.[31] The union may use this stratagem when it doubts its chances of winning an election.

If the union desires the regional director to continue to process the representation case, notwithstanding the charge, it will execute a "Request to Proceed" form.[32]   (See Facsimile No. 19, page 87.)   The representation case and the investigation of the unfair labor practice charge will then proceed simultaneously. However, where the charge alleges company domination of a labor organization (§ 8(a)(2)), or refusal to bargain (§ 8(a) (5)), the representation proceedings normally will be stayed until the charge is decided.[33]

(c) where a union pickets for recognition

An employer may also file a petition when he is confronted with picketing for recognition.[34]   The considerations and procedure involved in filing a petition under these circumstances are discussed in Appendix I.

Decertification Petitions

Another form of petition leading to an election is a decertification petition. The third box in Item 1 of the petition form (Facsimile No. 16, page 79), is entitled "RD-Decertification."   It recites that "a substantial number of employees assert that the certified or currently recognized bargaining representative is no longer their representative." The RD petition must be supported by a 30% showing of interest.[35]

A petition for decertification may not be filed by an employer, nor may he sponsor or assist in the preparation of such a petition by his employees.[36]   Such conduct will invalidate the petition.[37] It may only be filed between the 90th and 60th day prior to the expiration of a contract or, if the contract has not been renewed, after it has expired.[38]   The NLRB proceedings continue in the same manner as with an RC or RM petition.

Deauthorization Petitions

Another, but less used petition, is a deauthorization petition. (See fourth box of Item 1 of Facsimile No. 16, page 79, "UD—

FACSIMILE No. 19

UNITED STATES OF AMERICA
NATIONAL LABOR RELATIONS BOARD

REQUEST TO PROCEED

In the matter of _____ _____
(Name of Case)   (Number of Case)

The undersigned hereby requests the Regional Director to proceed with the above-captioned representation case, notwithstanding the charges of unfair labor practices filed in Case No. _____.
It is understood that the Board will not entertain objections to any election in this matter based upon conduct occurring prior to the filing of the petition.

Date _____   _____

By _____

_____
(Title)

Withdrawal of Union Shop Authority.") It is authorized by Section 9(e)(1) of the Act.

A deauthorization petition may be filed by employees when their employer has a collective bargaining agreement containing a union shop clause which requires union membership as a condition of employment.[39] If thirty percent or more of the employees decide that they do not want such a condition of compulsory membership to continue, they may file a petition stating their desire to rescind the union's authority to compel membership under the union shop clause.[40]

The employer, as with a decertification petition, may not sponsor or assist in this petition. Unlike a decertification petition, a deauthorization petition may be filed at any time during the term of an existing contract,[41] and within twelve months of an earlier certification election.[42]

A vote of a majority of bargaining unit employees (not of those voting, as is the case with other elections) in favor of rescinding the union's authority, leaves the union as the bargaining agent, but bereft of its union security clause. The employees thereafter may not be compelled to join the union. The contract continues in all other respects for the balance of its term.[43]

Unit Clarification (UC)

An employer or a union may file a petition for a unit clarification. It is useful when there is a dispute as to the unit placement of individual employees. As the form indicates (Facsimile No. 16, page 79, Item 1, box 5), the petition may be filed in the case of either a recognized or a certified union.[44] No vote is held. The Board decides whether the employees should be part of the unit.

Amendment of Certification (AC)

In 1964, the NLRB amended its rules to provide for a petition to amend an existing certification. It may be filed by an employer or a union to reflect changed circumstances, such as changes in the name or affiliation of the union, or in the name or location of the employer.[45]

Affiliated unions who seek to substitute themselves for certified independents often avail themselves of this procedure. A more detailed description may be found in Appendix I.

COMMERCE FINDING

Whenever one of the petitions previously discussed is filed, the Board must, as part of its investigation, find that the employer is engaged in interstate commerce within the meaning of the Act.

The Board generally will attempt to make this determination in advance of hearing by asking the employer to complete its "Commerce Questionnaire." Some of the questions asked are as follows:

a. Gross annual *revenue* from sales: $500,000 or more   ☐

Less than $500,000   ☐

b. Annual *purchases* of goods, supplies, commodities or services purchased directly from other firms located *outside* the State:

$50,000 or more   ☐

Less than $50,000   ☐

c. Annual *purchases* of goods, supplies, commodities, or services purchased from firms located *inside* the State, but which *originated outside* the State:

$50,000 or more   ☐

Less than $50,000   ☐

d. Annual *revenue* from sales of goods, products, or commodities delivered directly to points *outside* the

State, or from services to firms located outside the
State:

$50,000 or more ☐

Less than $50,000 ☐

e. Annual *revenue* from sales of goods, products, or
commodities delivered to, or from services performed
for, firms located *within* the State, which firms, in
turn, made sales to customers located *outside* the
State:

$50,000 or more ☐

Less than $50,000 ☐

The commerce questionnaire is sent to the employer by the
Board in its first communication. There is no penalty for failing to submit the completed questionaire, except that in such
a case the Board will exercise its wide statutory authority in
deciding whether to take jurisdiction.

The Board has developed industry standards based upon dol-
lar volume minimums for its assertion of jurisdiction.[46] Familiarity with these standards is desirable when completing the questionnaire. These standards appear in Appendix J.

Any labor dispute occurring in interstate commerce is subject to the Act [47] and the jurisdiction of the Board.[48] Even when
a business is not engaged in interstate commerce, it may be subject to NLRB jurisdiction, if its operations "affect commerce." [49]
Thus the Board may assert jurisdiction over even a purely local
business, if its operations, interrupted by a labor dispute, could
have a substantial impact on the flow of commerce. Companies
performing construction work, engaging in janitorial services or
in local retailing are covered by the Act as a result.[50] In recent
years, the Board has expanded its jurisdiction to include universities, profit-making hospitals, and nursing homes.[51]

Whether the Board will assert jurisdiction over a particular company may be ascertained, under certain circumstances, by means of a Petition for an Advisory Opinion.[52] This is permissible only when the person seeking the opinion is a party to a proceeding before a state agency or court. Unlike other petitions, this type of petition must be filed directly with the Board in Washington.

CONSENT AGREEMENT ELECTION

We noted previously that the regional director schedules a conference soon after the filing of a petition. At the conference the NLRB representative will explore the parties' positions concerning the appropriate unit, and the eligibility of individuals to vote. In the interest of monetary and manpower economy, the Board seeks to effect an agreement between the parties concerning these matters. The *Field Manual* states:

> In advance of the date of hearing, every effort should have been made to procure an agreement for a consent election.[53]

There are two types of consent agreements. It is advisable to be aware of their points of difference prior to attending the conference. One is referred to as an "Agreement for Consent Election." (See Facsimile No. 20, pages 92-93). This form of agreement provides that the rulings of the regional director are final and binding on all questions relating to the election (such as voter eligibility, challenges to ballots, and objections to the conduct of the election or conduct affecting the results of the election).[54]

The other type of consent election agreement is called a "Stipulation for Certification Upon Consent Election." (See Facsimile No. 21, page 94. Only the first half of the form is reproduced. The second half is identical to the second half of the agreement for consent election shown at page 93.) The

FACSIMILE No. 20

UNITED STATES OF AMERICA
NATIONAL LABOR RELATIONS BOARD

AGREEMENT FOR CONSENT ELECTION

Pursuant to a Petition duly filed under Section 9 of the National Labor Relations Act as amended, and subject to the approval of the Regional Director for the National Labor Relations Board (herein called the Regional Director), the undersigned parties hereby waive a hearing and AGREE AS FOLLOWS:

1. SECRET BALLOT.—An election by secret ballot shall be held under the supervision of the said Regional Director, among the employees of the undersigned Employer in the unit defined below, at the indicated time and place, to determine whether or not such employees desire to be represented for the purpose of collective bargaining by (one of) the undersigned labor organization(s). Said election shall be held in accordance with the National Labor Relations Act, the Board's Rules and Regulations, and the applicable procedures and policies of the Board, provided that the determination of the Regional Director shall be final and binding upon any question, including questions as to the eligibility of voters, raised by any party hereto relating in any manner to the election, and provided further that rulings or determinations by the Regional Director in respect of any amendment of any certification resulting therefrom shall also be final.

2. ELIGIBLE VOTERS.—The eligible voters shall be those employees included within the Unit described below, who were employed during the payroll period indicated below, including employees who did not work during said payroll period because they were ill or on vacation or temporarily laid off, employees in the military services of the United States who appear in person at the polls, employees engaged in an economic strike which commenced less than twelve (12) months before the election date and who retained their status as such during the eligibility period and their replacements, but excluding any employees who have since quit or been discharged for cause and employees engaged in a strike who have been discharged for cause since the commencement thereof, and who have not been rehired or reinstated prior to the date of the election, and employees engaged in an economic strike which commenced more than 12 months prior to the date of the election and who have been permanently replaced. At a date fixed by the Regional Director, the parties, as requested, will furnish to the Regional Director, an accurate list of all the eligible voters, together with a list of the employees, if any, specifically excluded from eligibility.

3. NOTICES OF ELECTION.—The Regional Director shall prepare a Notice of Election and supply copies to the parties describing the manner and conduct of the election to be held and incorporating therein a sample ballot. The parties, upon the request of and at a time designated by the Regional Director, will post such Notice of Election at conspicuous and usual posting places easily accessible to the eligible voters.

4. OBSERVERS.—Each party hereto will be allowed to station an equal number of authorized observers, selected from among the nonsupervisory employees of the Employer, at the polling places during the election to assist in its conduct, to challenge the eligibility of voters, and to verify the tally.

5. TALLY OF BALLOTS.—As soon after the election as feasible, the votes shall be counted and tabulated by the Regional Director, or his agent or agents. Upon the conclusion of the counting, the Regional Director shall furnish a Tally of Ballots to each of the parties. When appropriate, the Regional Director shall issue to the parties a certification of representatives or of results of election, as may be indicated.

6. OBJECTIONS, CHALLENGES, REPORTS THEREON.—Objections to the conduct of the election or conduct affecting the results of the election, or to a determination of representatives based on the results thereof, may be filed with the Regional Director within 5 days after issuance of the Tally of Ballots. Copies of such objections must be served upon the other parties at the time of filing with the Regional Director. The Regional Director shall investigate the matters contained in the objections and issue a report thereon. If objections are sustained, the Regional Director may in his report include an order voiding the results of the election and, in that event, shall be empowered to conduct a new election under the terms and provisions of this agreement at a date, time, and place to be determined by him. If the challenges are determinative of the results of the election, the Regional Director shall investigate the challenges and issue a report thereon. The method of investigation of objections and challenges, including the question whether a hearing should be held in connection therewith, shall be determined by the Regional Director, whose decision shall be final and binding.

7. RUN-OFF PROCEDURE.—In the event more than one labor organization is signatory to this agreement, and in the event that no choice on the ballot in the election receives a majority of the valid ballots cast, the Regional Director shall proceed in accordance with the Board's Rules and Regulations.

8. COMMERCE.—The Employer is engaged in commerce within the meaning of Section 2 (6) (7) of the National Labor Relations Act.

FACSIMILE No. 20

9. WORDING ON THE BALLOT.—Where only one labor organization is signatory to this agreement, the name of the organization shall appear on the ballot and the choice shall be "Yes" or "No." In the event more than one labor organization is signatory to this agreement, the choices on the ballot will appear in the wording indicated below and in the order enumerated below, reading from left to right on the ballot, or if the occasion demands, from top to bottom. (If more than one union is to appear on the ballot, any union may have its name removed from the ballot by the approval of the Regional Director of a timely request, in writing, to that effect.)

First.

Second.

Third.

10. PAYROLL PERIOD FOR ELIGIBILITY.—

11. DATE, HOURS, AND PLACE OF ELECTION.—

12. THE APPROPRIATE COLLECTIVE BARGAINING UNIT.—

If Notice of Representation Hearing has been issued in this case, the approval of this agreement by the Regional Director shall constitute withdrawal of the Notice of Representation Hearing heretofore issued.

....
(Employer)

By ....
(Name and title)   (Date)

Recommended:

....
(Board Agent)   (Date)

Date approved ....

....
Regional Director,
National Labor Relations Board.

....
(Name of Organization)

By ....
(Name and title)   (Date)

....
(Name of other Organization)

By ....
(Name and title)   (Date)

Case No. ....

FACSIMILE No. 21

UNITED STATES OF AMERICA
NATIONAL LABOR RELATIONS BOARD

STIPULATION FOR CERTIFICATION UPON CONSENT ELECTION

Pursuant to a Petition duly filed under Section 9 of the National Labor Relations Act, as amended, and subject to the approval of the Regional 'Director for the National Labor Relations Board (herein called the Regional Director), the undersigned parties hereby AGREE AS FOLLOWS:

1. SECRET BALLOT.—An election by secret ballot shall be held under the supervision of the said Regional Director, among the employees of the undersigned Employer in the unit defined below, at the indicated time and place, to determine whether or not such employees desire to be represented for the purpose of collective bargaining by (one of) the undersigned labor organization(s). Said election shall be held in accordance with the National Labor Relations Act, the Board's Rules and Regulations, and the applicable procedures and policies of the Board.

2. ELIGIBLE VOTERS.—The eligible voters shall be those employees included within the Unit described below, who were employed during the payroll period indicated below, including employees who did not work during said payroll period because they were ill or on vacation or temporarily laid off, and employees in the military services of the United States who appear in person at the polls, also eligible are employees engaged in an economic strike which commenced less than twelve (12) months before the election date and who retained their status as such during the eligibility period and their replacements, but *excluding* any employees who have since quit or been discharged for cause and employees engaged in a strike who have been discharged for cause since the commencement thereof, and who have not been rehired or reinstated prior to the date of the election, and employees engaged in an economic strike which commenced more than twelve (12) months prior to the date of the election and who have been permanently replaced. At a date fixed by the Regional Director, the parties, as requested, will furnish to the Regional Director, an accurate list of all the eligible voters, together with a list of the employees, if any, specifically excluded from eligibility.

3. NOTICES OF ELECTION.—The Regional Director shall prepare a Notice of Election and supply copies to the parties describing the manner and conduct of the election to be held and incorporating therein a sample ballot. The parties, upon the request of and at a time designated by the Regional Director, will post such Notice of Election at conspicuous and usual posting places easily accessible to the eligible voters.

4. OBSERVERS.—Each party hereto will be allowed to station an equal number of authorized observers, selected from among the nonsupervisory employees of the Employer, at the polling places during the election to assist in its conduct, to challenge the eligibility of voters, and to verify the tally.

5. TALLY OF BALLOTS.—As soon after the election as feasible, the votes shall be counted and tabulated by the Regional Director, or his agent or agents. Upon the conclusion of the counting, the Regional Director shall furnish a Tally of Ballots to each of the parties.

6. POST-ELECTION AND RUN-OFF PROCEDURE.—All procedure subsequent to the conclusion of counting ballots shall be in conformity with the Board's Rules and Regulations.

7. RECORD.—The record in this case shall be governed by the appropriate provisions of the Board's Rules and Regulations and shall include this stipulation. Hearing and notice thereof, Direction of Election, and the making of Findings of Fact and Conclusions of Law by the Board prior to the election are hereby expressly waived.

8. COMMERCE.—The Employer is engaged in commerce within the meaning of Section 2(6) of the National Labor Relations Act, and a question affecting commerce has arisen concerning the representation of employees within the meaning of Section 9(c). *(Insert commerce facts.)*

difference between the two consent election forms is that with the stipulated agreement appeal is permitted to the Board in Washington for the final determination of any disputed matters following the election. A comparison of paragraph 6 of both forms will readily reveal this difference.

Counsel should weigh the choice between the two types very carefully. The stipulated consent agreement can afford the employer an added opportunity to argue his position. Some practitioners prefer a final ruling by the Board to that of a particular regional office. Others are content to rely upon the regional director's determination as final.

It is sometimes advisable in a consent agreement (this term is hereafter used generically to apply to both types) to name all employees who will be included in or excluded from the voting unit, rather than simply define the unit in general terms. This is permitted under the Board's decision in *Norris-Thermador Corp.*[55] Such an agreement normally will obviate litigation concerning ballot challenges.

However, the parties cannot, by their agreement, resolve an issue that would be in contravention of either the Act or established Board policy. A union therefore is not precluded from challenging the ballots of employees whom it alleges are supervisors, notwithstanding a prior "Norris-Thermador agreement," because it would contravene the policies of the Act to permit supervisors to vote.[56]

Execution of a consent election agreement presupposes agreement on the unit. When eligibility questions cannot be resolved at the conference, a hearing will be required, irrespective of other considerations.

Since parties are not required to execute either type of consent agreement, under what circumstances should an employer sign one? The answer is only when he is satisfied with the unit, the specific employees eligible to vote, and the election date.

SELECTING THE DATE OF ELECTION

The optimum election date is often the most difficult decision to make. There are two prime considerations: (1) the employer's degree of confidence that the union will be rejected, and (2) the amount of time needed to provide employees with information to make an informed decision. These questions are complex, the answers to which involve speculative and subjective reasoning.

Should an employer seek an early election date on the theory that the union will then not have time to "sell" his employees? Should he agree to an election in 10 days [57] because he has a "gut feeling" that "his people" will not let him down?

More often than not, an employer's decision to expedite the election is unwise. The union will have done its homework. The employer will have done little or nothing. He is overconfident.

It is only when an employer is convinced that the union will be rejected that he should agree on an early date. Since few employers can have that degree of confidence with any certainty, counsel should seek the maximum time interval.

This can be accomplished by conditioning the execution of a consent agreement on the holding of the election no earlier than 30 days hence. No subtlety in doing so is involved. The employer simply feels that he wants an informed electorate. He requires sufficient time. Absent an agreement on a satisfactory date, the employer may insist on a formal hearing.

When an election date has been scheduled, it is advisable to inform the employees as quickly as possible. A brief notice is all that is required. (See Facsimile No. 22, page 97.) In this way, the employees will hopefully begin looking to the employer, rather than the union, as their source for prompt, and factual data.

FACSIMILE No. 22

BULLETIN BOARD NOTICE

TO ALL EMPLOYEES:

This morning agreement was reached to hold an election on Friday, January 29th, to determine if the union will represent our employees.

The election will be held at our plant facilities under the supervision of the National Labor Relations Board.

The vote will be by secret ballot. The fact that you may have signed a union "authorization card" does not mean you have to vote for the union in the election. We will provide additional details concerning the election and the issues involved in the near future.

General Manager

NOTES TO CHAPTER V

1. The organization chart is reproduced from the NLRB Rules & Regulations and Statements of Procedure, Series 8, as amended, p. 183.

2. NLRB Organization & Functions § 201, 32 Fed. Reg. 9588 (1967).

3. LMRA § 101.3(d), 29 U.S.C. § 153(d) (1964).

4. LMRA § 101.4(a), 29 U.S.C. § 154(a) (1964).

5. NLRB Organization & Functions at Appendix, 32 Fed. Reg. 9590-592 (1967).

6. The Board's Rules & Regulations are available for purchase in looseleaf form from the Superintendent of Documents, U.S. Government Printing Office, Washington, D.C. 20402.

7. The *Field Manual* first became available to the public upon the passage of the Freedom of Information Act. [Act of Sept. 6, 1966, Pub. L. No. 89-554, § 1(552), 80 Stat. 383, *amending* Administrative Procedure Act § 3, 5 U.S.C. § 552 (codified at 23 U.S.C. § 552) (1964)]. *See,* 1965 ABA Lab. Rel. Section, Ann. Comm. Rep. 388, for a discussion of efforts to obtain public disclosure prior to passage of this law.

The manual may be purchased from the U.S. Government Printing Office, Public Documents Department, Washington, D.C. Although the preface to the manual states that the instructions are not Board rulings or binding directives, the Board has cited it. Allied Foods, Inc., 189 NLRB No. 79, 77 LRRM 1153, 1155 n. 5 (1971).

8. NLRB Rules & Regulations § 102.60(a), 29 C.F.R. § 102.60(a) (1971).

9. Advance Pattern, 80 NLRB 29, 23 LRRM 1022 (1948), *rev'g* 79 NLRB 209, 22 LRRM 1366 (1948).

10. Penn-Keystone Realty Corp., 191 NLRB No. 105, 77 LRRM 1600, 1602 (1971).

11. NLRB v. Winchell Processing Corp., __ F.2d __, 78 LRRM 2929, 2931 (9th Cir., No. 71-1206, decided Nov. 18, 1971), *denying enforcement to* 183 NLRB No. 135, 74 LRRM 1656 (1970); Mid-South Packers, Inc., 120 NLRB 495 n. 1, 41 LRRM 1526 (1958); Stickless Corp., 115 NLRB 979, 37 LRRM 1466 (1956).

12. NLRB Statements of Procedure § 101.17, 29 C.F.R. § 101.17 (1971).

13. *Id.* at § 101.18(b), 29 C.F.R. § 101.18(b) (1971). Cards solicited by supervisors are deducted in determining whether the union has an

adequate showing of interest. *See*, WKRG-TV, Inc., 190 NLRB No. 34, 77 LRRM 1078 (1971); Juniata Packing Co., 182 NLRB No. 140, 74 LRRM 1241 (1970).

14. NLRB Statements of Procedure § 101.18(c), 29 C.F.R. § 101.18(c) (1971).

15. *See*, Lewis, *Employer Petitions—New York and Federal—A Comparison*, 5 NYU Conf. on Labor 249 (1952), for a review of employer petitions under the National Labor Relations Act and a discussion of the Congressional debates and hearings which led to the statutory changes incorporated in the Labor Management Relations Act.

16. NLRB Statements of Procedure § 101.17, 29 C.F.R. § 101.17 (1964).

17. Southern Mfg. Co., 144 NLRB 784, 54 LRRM 1118 (1963).

18. Kimberly-Clark Co., 61 NLRB 90, 16 LRRM 77 (1945).

19. United States Gypsum Co., 157 NLRB 652, 61 LRRM 1384 (1966).

20. Leonard Wholesale Meats, 136 NLRB 1000, 49 LRRM 1901 (1962), *modifying* Deluxe Metal Furniture Co., 121 NLRB 995, 42 LRRM 1470 (1958).

21. NLRB Statements of Procedure § 101.17, 29 C.F.R. § 101.17 (1964).

22. Convair Div. of General Dynamics Corp., 169 NLRB 131, 67 LRRM 1091 (1968).

23. Southern Wipers, Inc., 192 NLRB No. 135, 78 LRRM 1070 (1971) (turnover of 398 in a work force of 100). *Cf.* Massey-Ferguson, Inc. v. NLRB, __ F.2d __, 78 LRRM 2289 (5th Cir., No. 18767, decided Sept. 20, 1971), *enforcing* 184 NLRB No. 69, 74 LRRM 1565 (1970).

24. Mid-Western Instruments, Inc., 133 NLRB 1132, 1136-37, 48 LRRM 1793 (1961); Celanese Corp. of America, 95 NLRB 664, 28 LRRM 1362 (1951). However, a strike supported by only a minority of employees does not necessarily evidence rejection of union representation. Dayton Motels, Inc., 192 NLRB No. 112, 78 LRRM 1067 (1971).

25. Frito-Lay, Inc., 151 NLRB 28, 58 LRRM 1328 (1965).

26. Convair, *supra* note 22.

27. *Id.*

28. Gulfmont Hotel Co., 147 NLRB 997, 56 LRRM 1379 (1964), *enf'd*, 362 F.2d 588 (5th Cir. 1966). *Cf.* Ingress-Plastene, Inc. v.

NLRB, 430 F.2d 542 (7th Cir. 1970), *denying enforcement to* 177 NLRB No. 70, 71 LRRM 1398 (1969), *modified,* ___ F.2d ___, 75 LRRM 2048 (7th Cir., No. 17739, decided July 7, 1970).

29. Southern Wipers, *supra* note 23, at 78 LRRM 1071, reversing trial examiner's finding that employer's failure to file petition was evidence of bad faith. *Cf.* Bally Case & Cooler, Inc., 172 NLRB No. 106, 68 LRRM 1387 (1968), *enf'd,* 416 F.2d 902 (6th Cir. 1969). *See also,* Brooks v. NLRB, 348 U.S. 96, 104 n. 18 (1954); NLRB v. Keystone Valve Corp., ___ F.2d ___, 78 LRRM 2620 (5th Cir., No. 71-1445, decided Oct. 27, 1971), *enforcing* 186 NLRB No. 9, 75 LRRM 1386 (1970); Wigwam Stores, Inc., 193 NLRB No. 75, 78 LRRM 1263 (1971).

30. Suprenant Mfg. Co. v. Alpert, 318 F.2d 396 (1st Cir. 1963).

31. *Compare* NLRB Field Manual § 11730 *and* Dufresne v. McCann Steel Co., ___ F.Supp. ___, 78 LRRM 2331 (M.D. Tenn., No. 6171, decided Sept. 10, 1971) *with* Templeton v. Dixie Color Printing Co., 444 F.2d 1064, 77 LRRM 2392 (5th Cir. 1971), *vacating and remanding* 313 F.Supp. 105, 74 LRRM 2206 and 74 LRRM 2319 (N.D. Ala. 1970), *rehearing denied,* ___ F.2d ___, 77 LRRM 3156 (5th Cir., No. 299921, decided July 28, 1971) *and* Surratt v. NLRB, ___ F.Supp. ___, 78 LRRM 2115 (N.D. Ala., No. 71-476, decided July 27, 1971). *See also,* Commarto v. McLeod, ___ F.Supp. ___, 78 LRRM 2741 (S.D. N.Y., No. 71 Civ. 2594, decided Nov. 3, 1971).

32. NLRB Field Manual §§ 11730, 11730.1.

33. Panda Terminals, Inc., 161 NLRB 1215, 1223-224, 63 LRRM 1419, 1424 (1966).

34. LMRA § 101.8(b)(7), 29 U.S.C. § 158(b)(7) (1959).

35. NLRB Statements of Procedure § 101.18(a), 29 C.F.R. § 101.18 (a) (1971).

36. LMRA §§ 101.9(c)(1)(A), 101.9(c)(1)(B), 29 U.S.C. §§ 159(c) (1)(A), 159c)(1)(B) (1964). NLRB Rules & Regulations § 102.60(a), 29 C.F.R. § 102.60(a) (1971). NLRB Statements of Procedure § 101.17, 29 C.F.R. § 101.17 (1971). Clyde J. Merris and W. S. Monroe, 77 NLRB 1375, 22 LRRM 1142 (1948). *See also,* Star Brush Mfg. Co., 100 NLRB 679, 30 LRRM 1335 (1952), holding that confidential employees may not file decertification petitions.

37. Irv's Mkt., 188 NLRB No. 35, 76 LRRM 1319 (1971).

38. *Id.* However, if the contract is for a term longer than three years, a RD petition may be filed between 90 and 60 days prior to the end of the third year. Duke Power, 173 NLRB No. 41, 69 LRRM 1319 (1968). *Cf.* Montgomery Ward, 137 NLRB 346, 50 LRRM 1137 (1962) (RM petition barred until expiration of five-year contract).

39. LMRA § 101.8(a)(3), 29 U.S.C. § 158(a)(3) (1964).

40. LMRA § 101.9(e)(1), 29 U.S.C. § 159(e)(1) (1959).

41. Great Atlantic & Pacific Tea Co., 100 NLRB 1494, 30 LRRM 1472 (1952).

42. Monsanto Chem. Co., 147 NLRB 49, 56 LRRM 1136 (1964).

43. Great Atlantic & Pacific Tea Co., *supra* note 41.

44. Manitowoc Co., 191 NLRB No. 137, 77 LRRM 1534 (1971); A.D.T. Co., 177 NLRB No. 112, 71 LRRM 1513 (1969); Bhd. of Locomotive Firemen, 145 NLRB 1521, 55 LRRM 1177 (1964).

45. NLRB Rules & Regulations § 102.61(e), 29 C.F.R. § 102.61(e) (1971). *See also,* NLRB Statements of Procedure § 101.17, 29 C.F.R. § 101.17 (1971).

46. The Act was amended in 1959 to permit the adoption of jurisdictional standards. LMRA § 101.14(c)(1), 29 U.S.C. § 164(c)(1) (1964). The Board previously had established a revised set of standards on October 2, 1958. See 23 NLRB Ann. Rep. 8 (1958).

47. LMRA § 101.2(6), 29 U.S.C. § 152(6) (1964).

48. The NLRB considers the total operation of the employer even though the particular labor dispute involves only a portion of those operations. Man Prods., Inc., 128 NLRB 546, 46 LRRM 1353 (1960); Siemons Mailing Serv., 122 NLRB 81, 43 LRRM 1056 (1958); Potato Growers Cooperative Co., 115 NLRB 1281, 38 LRRM 1045 (1956).

49. LMRA § 101.2(7), 29 U.S.C. § 152(7) (1964).

50. *Construction work:* NLRB v. Denver Bldg. Trades Council, 341 U.S. 675 (1951), IBEW, Local 501 v. NLRB, 341 U.S. 694 (1951). *Janitorial service:* Mistletoe Operating Co., 122 NLRB 1534, 43 LRRM 1333 (1959). *Retailing:* Howell Chevrolet Co. v. NLRB, 346 U.S. 482 (1953), *affirming* 204 F.2d 79 (9th Cir. 1953), *enforcing* 95 NLRB 410, 28 LRRM 1340 (1951).

51. *Universities & Schools:* Children's Village, 186 NLRB No. 137, 76 LRRM 1383 (1970); New York Univ., 186 NLRB No. 135, 75 LRRM 1440 (1970); Cornell Univ., 183 NLRB No. 41, 74 LRRM 1269 (1970). *Profit-making hospitals:* Butte Medical Properties, d/b/a Medical Center Hosp., 168 NLRB 266, 66 LRRM 1259 (1967). *Nursing homes:* Univ. Nursing Home, Inc., 168 NLRB 263, 66 LRRM 1263 (1967). *See also,* 33 NLRB Ann. Rep. 28 (1968).

52. The contents of the petition and the procedures to be followed are set forth in NLRB Rules & Regulations §§ 102.98, 102.99, and the Board's Statements of Procedure § 101.39.

53. NLRB Field Manual § 11188.

54. NLRB Statements of Procedure § 101.19(a)(5), 29 C.F.R. § 101.19(a)(5) (1971).

55. 119 NLRB 1301, 41 LRRM 1283 (1958).

56. Fisher-New Center Co., 184 NLRB No. 92, 74 LRRM 1609 (1970).

57. In *Excelsior Underwear Inc.*, 156 NLRB 1236, 61 LRRM 1217 (1966), the Board ruled that an employer must furnish the names and addresses of employees to a union prior to an election. *See* pp. 116-117, *infra.* Since a union must have the Excelsior list within its possession for ten days, this is the minimum time permitted for scheduling a consent election. The union may not waive this rule.

CHAPTER VI

HEARING AND DIRECTION OF ELECTION

When the parties are unwilling to agree to a consent election, the regional director issues a Notice of Representation Hearing.[1] (See Facsimile No. 23, page 104.) On the date of the hearing, another effort is made to consummate a consent agreement. The *Field Manual* states:

> Before opening the hearing, the hearing officer should again explore the possibility of a consent election, and, if the parties indicate a willingness to execute a consent-election agreement, the opening of the hearing should be delayed until after the possibility has been completely explored. . . .[2]

Where this further effort is unproductive, the hearing officer will formally open the hearing. The following discussion is based on the premise that the petition has been filed by a union, although the procedure is the same in the case of other petitioners.

Since a representation hearing is non-adversary in nature, technical rules of evidence are not followed.[3] The hearing officer, who conducts it, is responsible for developing a full statement of all pertinent facts.

He asks counsel to note their appearances and inquires whether there is any other labor organization in the hearing

FACSIMILE No. 23

UNITED STATES OF AMERICA

BEFORE THE NATIONAL LABOR RELATIONS BOARD

Case No.

NOTICE OF REPRESENTATION HEARING

The Petitioner, above named, having heretofore filed a Petition pursuant to Section 9(c) of the National Labor Relations Act, as amended, 29 U.S.C. Sec. 151 et seq., copy of which Petition is hereto attached, and it appearing that a question affecting commerce has arisen concerning the representation of employees described by such Petition,

YOU ARE HEREBY NOTIFIED that, pursuant to Sections 3(b) and 9(c) of the Act, on the day of   , 19   , at

a hearing will be conducted before a hearing officer of the National Labor Relations Board upon the question of representation affecting commerce which has arisen, at which time and place the parties will have the right to appear in person or otherwise, and give testimony.

 Signed at   on the   day of   , 19

Regional Director, Region
National Labor Relations Board

room which claims an interest in the proceeding or wishes to intervene. When another labor organization is present, it will normally make a formal motion to intervene. The proposed intervenor must state the basis for its assertion that it has an interest in the proceeding. Its claim may be based upon a contract covering all or part of the employees in the proposed unit, or upon its possession of signed authorization cards.[4]

Where a union seeks to intervene based upon authorization cards, the extent to which it will be permitted to participate in the hearing is premised upon the number of cards it has.

1. It needs only one authorization card to appear on the ballot in the unit requested by the petitioning union.[5]

2. If it has a ten percent showing of interest, it may block an agreement between the other parties for a consent election and force the matter to a hearing.[6]

3. If it has a thirty percent showing of interest, it may oppose the unit sought by the petitioning union and seek its own unit.[7]

STIPULATIONS

The parties are asked to stipulate that the employer is engaged in interstate commerce. If the employer refuses to stipulate, it becomes a contested issue on which testimony will be taken. (The Board's jurisdictional standards set forth in Appendix J may be consulted.)

In most cases, the commerce question is not an issue. However, in order to assert jurisdiction a finding of "commerce" must be made by the regional director in his decision. Employer's counsel may therefore state for the record, for example, that the employer purchases more than $50,000 in goods directly or indirectly from without the state or has sales directly or indirectly out of state of more than $50,000. The employer's actual business volume need not be stated.

The parties also are asked to stipulate that the petitioner is a labor organization. On occasion, counsel will refuse to do so because he is unfamiliar with the particular local union or because of a serious question as to its *bona fides*. The petitioner then must prove that it satisfies the elements of a labor organization as defined in the Act.[8] It must demonstrate that it "exists for the purpose, in whole or in part, of dealing with employers concerning grievances, labor disputes, wages, rates of pay, hours of employment, or conditions of work."[9] The hearing officer often assists in eliciting the requisite information from the union's witness. The employer also may examine the union representative. Such examination may be helpful in learning more about the union, such as the names of other companies with whom it has contracts.

The hearing officer will not receive testimony to show that an independent union is company dominated. This is an allegation of an unfair labor practice, which is not permitted in a representation proceeding.[10]

The hearing officer will inquire into the circumstances of the filing of the representation petition. He is instructed to ask the question: "Does the company decline at this time to recognize the petitioner as exclusive bargaining agent for the employees in the unit petitioned for until such time as it is certified as such in the appropriate unit determined by the Board?" If the company responds affirmatively, the hearing officer may incorporate the question and answer into a stipulation.[11] The Board has sometimes used such answers in representation hearings as evidence of a refusal to bargain in a subsequent unfair labor practice proceeding.[12] Counsel, therefore, should be careful in his response.

DETERMINING THE UNIT—A KEY QUESTION

A management official normally will be the first witness since the employer has possession and access to the facts relevant to the unit issues.

The major task of a hearing officer in a representation hearing is to make a complete record concerning the appropriate unit. The *Field Manual* states his responsibilities:

> The hearing officer should conduct whatever necessary cross-examination has been omitted by the parties. He may call witnesses himself to fill the gaps in the situation.[18]

Early in the hearing the hearing officer will request the parties to state their positions concerning the appropriateness of the unit. Counsel may do so, or he may prefer to wait until all the evidence is introduced and state his position at the conclusion of the hearing. Or, counsel may prefer to initially state his position in his brief, after he has had an opportunity to review the transcript of the hearing. Alternatively, counsel may decide not to state a position at all.

The position that the employer takes may have an important bearing on the results of the election and the future course of his labor relations. Shall he seek to limit the unit to the employees sought in the union's petition? In this way, if the union prevails in the election, its influence will not, immediately at least, spread too far into the establishment. Or shall he try to enlarge the unit beyond that requested by the union, in order to garner favorable votes from employees the union did not attempt to organize or had no success in organizing?

The decision is a difficult one. Assume that the union has not petitioned for the employer's plant clericals. The employer may not wish to risk introducing the union into this area, even though these employees may be more likely to vote against representation. He, therefore, would prefer to have the contest in the narrower group sought by the petitioning union and not incur the risks inherent in enlarging the unit.

On the other hand, the employer may wish to take this calculated risk. If counsel presents a good case the Board may include them in the eligible voting unit. At times, such votes make the difference between winning and losing.

What then are the indicia for including or excluding employees from a voting unit? What is an "appropriate unit"? The Act does not say. Counsel must look to decisions of the Board for guidelines.

The following are examples of indicia which the Board considers in determining whether employees have a community or similarity of interests and therefore should be included in the same unit:

> Same hours of work
> Same job duties
> Same compensation
> Same rest periods and lunch hours
> Same holidays, vacations, pensions, and insurance
> Same employee facilities
> Similar production methods
> Transfers between departments and plants
> Similarity of tools, equipment, and skills
> Same overall supervision
> Integration of work flow

Of course, when the exclusion of an employee or group of employees is sought, the proof must be directed toward dissimilarity of working conditions to show an absence of a community of interest.

It is quite evident that there must be careful preparation to collect the data to support a claimed appropriate unit. The checklist set forth in Chapter I should prove helpful.

There always are certain exclusions from the bargaining unit, some by statute and some by Board rulings. Section 2(3) of the Act mandates the exclusion of agricultural laborers, domestic servants, individuals employed by a parent or spouse, independent contractors, supervisors and any one employed by an employer subject to the Railway Labor Act or by an employer who does not fall within the coverage of the Act. Similarly, the Board is forbidden to find that a unit is appropriate which groups guards and other employees together,[14] or which includes professional with non-professional employees, unless a majority of the professional employees vote expressly for such inclusion.[15]

Employee inclusion and exclusion is the subject of thousands of cases. Typical disputed classifications are: part-time employees,[16] students,[17] casual employees,[18] seasonal employees,[19] trainees,[20] confidential employees,[21] and office and plant clerical employees.[22]

The most frequently litigated job classification issue is whether a particular employee is a supervisor as defined by the Act.[23] The Act defines a supervisor as:

> [A]ny individual having authority, in the interest of the employer, to hire, transfer, suspend, lay off, recall, promote, discharge, assign, reward, or discipline other employees, or responsibly to direct them, or to adjust their grievances, or effectively to recommend such action, if in connection with the foregoing the exercise of such authority is not of a merely routine or clerical nature, but requires the use of independent judgment.[24]

The statute is to be read in the disjunctive.[25] The authority to do or effectively recommend any of the actions mentioned establishes supervisory status.[26]

The following checklist and citations will assist counsel in initiating his investigation as to the supervisory status of an employee. Inquiry should be made as to whether the employee:

Assigns work [27]
Directs employees [28]
Grants time off [29]

Evaluates work [30]
Schedules work hours [31]
Recommends or executes discipline [32]
Hires and fires employees [33]
Receives a salary [34]
Receives higher pay than other employees [35]
Interviews job applicants [36]
Keeps workers' time records [37]
Consults with management on production problems [38]
Exercises independent judgment [39]
Selects employees for overtime [40]
Has authority to adjust grievances [41]
Participates in a profit sharing plan [42]
Attends supervisory meetings [43]

There are certain supervisors in every company who are clearly a part of management. There is no question as to their status. However, there may be other employees whose eligibility or ineligibility is borderline. An employer must seriously ponder the inclusion or exclusion of these employees. If the employees are included in the unit and the union wins the election, they will be covered by the contract. Conversely, some elections are lost by one or two votes. With the benefit of hindsight, the employer rues the day his caution influenced him to exclude these employees from the voting unit.

Closing the Hearing

After the testimony is presented, the parties are given an opportunity for oral argument. The hearing officer then will inquire as to whether any party wishes to file a brief. The rules provide that briefs are due within seven days.[44] The court reporter usually does not transcribe the testimony immediately. Where counsel requests expedited handling, he may receive the transcript a few days after the close of the hearing. It is therefore always necessary to request an extension of time for the filing of briefs. The hearing officer may grant such an extension, not to exceed an additional 14 days. The hearing is then closed.[45]

It is well to keep employees informed of the progress of the proceedings before the NLRB. (See Facsimile No. 24, page 112.)

Reviewing the Record

After the hearing is closed and briefs filed, the entire record is reviewed by the regional director or his designee. To assist in this review, the hearing officer makes an analysis of the evidence. At this stage, his role is limited. He makes no recommendations to the regional director concerning resolution of the issues.[46]

Section 9(b) of the Act sets forth alternative units for the regional director to choose from.[47] It may be the employer's entire establishment,[48] a craft unit,[49] a single plant unit,[50] or a subdivision of a plant.[51] He will not, however, certify a one-man unit.[52]

Section 9(c)(5) of the Act prohibits the regional director, in determining whether a particular unit is appropriate, from giving controlling weight to the extent to which the employees have been organized.[53] For example, the employer may have demonstrated at the hearing that the union sought to represent only assembly line employees in a factory and excluded all other production workers. In the case of a retail chain, the union may have confined its organizing to only one of several stores. In any event, the extent of the union's organizing efforts may not, of itself, define the unit. It may be considered by the regional director as one of many factors in his unit determination, providing it is not given "controlling weight." [54]

The regional director may find that more than one grouping of employees is appropriate, and then choose between them.[55] He need not find the most appropriate unit, but only "an" appropriate unit, and may rely on the unit requested by the union in making the choice.[56] The regional director will set forth his unit determination in his Decision and Direction of Election.

FACSIMILE No. 24

BULLETIN BOARD NOTICE

TO ALL EMPLOYEES:

I have just returned from a National Labor Relations Board hearing.   We described the work we do here and the classifications of employees who perform it.

The Board will now study the case.   If it decides to hold an election, you will be advised as to who will be eligible to vote.

If there is an election, there will be two choices: the union or no union.   If 50% or more of the employees voting cast their vote against having a union, that will be the end of the matter.   The company has faith in your good judgment.

General Manager

Election Arrangements

When the parties are waiting for the regional director's decision and direction of election,[57] the campaign is at a low key, with little literature, few letters and muted polemics.

When the election is directed, the final stage of the contest begins. Soon thereafter one can expect to receive a phone call from the Board's field examiner. His purpose is to convene the parties to discuss the arrangements for the election. If the parties are geographically widespread, the arrangements may be made by phone.

The primary purpose of the conference is to discuss the date on which the election will be held. Once this is agreed upon, the hours of the election are scheduled.

The location of the balloting is then discussed. Elections usually are held on the employer's premises. It saves the Board rental charges and is convenient for the electorate. On occasion, unions object to this. The regional director, exercising his discretion, may then make arrangements for the balloting elsewhere. The balloting place, if on the employer's premises, must not be in or near the executive offices. Some area familiar to the employees and away from general supervisory view will be approved.

About ten days before the election, but no less than five, the regional director will mail a number of copies of a Notice of Election to the parties.[58] (See Facsimile No. 25, pages 114-115.) The employer is required to post them. The usual posting places are at the time clock and employee bulletin boards. The object is to be certain that every employee has the opportunity to read them.

The notices are not to be defaced in any way. Marking an "X" in any box of a posted notice is a defacement which may operate to void an election.[59] The employer must police this and, if need be, replace the notice. The problem may be avoided by placing the notices under a glass or plastic cover.

FACSIMILE No. 25

NATIONAL LABOR RELATIONS BOARD
NOTICE OF ELECTION

EMPLOYEES OF:

VOTING UNIT

INCLUDED: All production and maintenance employees, shipping and receiving
employees, and drivers employed by the Employer at its premises
during
the payroll period as of the week ending
EXCLUDED: All office clerical employees, professional employees, guards and
supervisors as defined in the Act.

TIME & PLACE OF ELECTION

DATE: FRIDAY, JANUARY 2,   TIME:

PLACE: EMPLOYER'S PREMISES

UNITED STATES OF AMERICA

National Labor Relations Board

OFFICIAL SECRET BALLOT

SAMPLE

FOR CERTAIN EMPLOYEES OF

Do you wish to be represented for purposes of collective bargaining by -

MARK AN "X" IN THE SQUARE OF YOUR CHOICE

YES	NO
☐	☐

DO NOT SIGN THIS BALLOT. Fold and drop in ballot box.
If you spoil this ballot return it to the Board Agent for a new one.

PURPOSE OF THIS ELECTION

This election is to determine the representative, if any, desired by the eligible employees for purposes of collective bargaining with their employer. (See VOTING UNIT in this Notice of Election, for description of eligible employees.) A majority of the valid ballots cast will determine the results of the election.

SECRET BALLOT

The election will be by SECRET ballot under the supervision of the Regional Director of the National Labor Relations Board. Voters will be allowed to vote without interference, restraint, or coercion. Electioneering will not be permitted at or near the polling place. Violations of these rules should be reported immediately to the Regional Director or his agent in charge of the election. Your attention is called to Section 12 of the National Labor Relations Act:

ANY PERSON WHO SHALL WILLFULLY RESIST, PREVENT, IMPEDE, OR INTERFERE WITH ANY MEMBER OF THE BOARD OR ANY OF ITS AGENTS OR AGENCIES IN THE PERFORMANCE OF DUTIES PURSUANT TO THIS ACT SHALL BE PUNISHED BY A FINE OF NOT MORE THAN $5,000 OR BY IMPRISONMENT FOR NOT MORE THAN ONE YEAR, OR BOTH.

An agent of the Board will hand a ballot to each eligible voter at the voting place. Mark your ballot in secret in the voting booth provided. DO NOT SIGN YOUR BALLOT. Fold the ballot before leaving the voting booth, then personally deposit it in a ballot box under the supervision of an agent of the Board.

A sample of the official ballot is shown at the center of this Notice.

ELIGIBILITY RULES

Employees eligible to vote are those described under VOTING UNIT in this Notice of Election, including employees who did not work during the designated payroll period because they were ill or on vacation or temporarily laid off, and also including employees in the military service of the United States who appear in person at the polls. Employees who have quit or been discharged for cause since the designated payroll period and who have not been rehired or reinstated prior to the date of this election are not eligible to vote.

CHALLENGE OF VOTERS

An agent of the Board or an authorized observer may question the eligibility of a voter. Such challenge MUST be made before the voter has deposited his ballot in the ballot box.

AUTHORIZED OBSERVERS

Each of the interested parties may designate an equal number of observers, this number to be determined by the Regional Director or his agent in charge of the election. These observers (a) act as checkers at the voting place and at the counting of ballots, (b) assist in the identification of voters, (c) challenge voters and ballots, and (d) otherwise assist the Regional Director or his agent.

INFORMATION CONCERNING ELECTION

The Act provides that only one valid representation election may be held in a 12 month period. Any employee who desires to obtain additional information concerning the terms and conditions under which this election is to be held or who desires to raise any question concerning the holding of an election, the voting unit, or eligibility rules may do so by communicating with the Regional Director or his agent in charge of the election.

RIGHTS OF EMPLOYEES

Under the National Labor Relations Act, employees have the right:

- To self-organization
- To form, join, or assist labor organizations
- To bargain collectively through representatives of their own choosing
- To act together for the purposes of collective bargaining or other mutual aid or protection
- To refrain from any or all such activities

It is the responsibility of the National Labor Relations Board to protect employees in the exercise of these rights.

The Board wants all eligible voters to be fully informed about their rights under Federal law and wants both Employers and Unions to know what is expected of them when it holds an election.

If agents of either Unions or Employers interfere with your right to a free, fair, and honest election, the election can be set aside by the Board. Where appropriate the Board provides other remedies, such as reinstatement for employees fired for exercising their rights, including backpay from the party responsible for their discharge.

The following are examples of conduct which interfere with the rights of employees and may result in the setting aside of the election:

- Threatening loss of jobs or benefits by an Employer or a Union
- Misstating important facts by a Union or an Employer where the other party does not have a fair chance to reply
- Promising or granting promotions, pay raises, or other benefits, to influence an employee's vote by a party capable of carrying out such promises
- An Employer firing employees to discourage or encourage union activity or a Union causing them to be fired to encourage union activity
- Making campaign speeches to assembled groups of employees on company time within the 24-hour period before the election
- Incitement by either an Employer or a Union of racial or religious prejudice by inflammatory appeals
- Threatening physical force or violence to employees by a Union or an Employer to influence their votes

The National Labor Relations Board protects your right to a free choice

Improper conduct will not be permitted. All parties are expected to cooperate fully with this agency in maintaining basic principles of a fair election as required by law. The National Labor Relations Board as an agency of the United States Government does not endorse any choice in the election.

NATIONAL LABOR RELATIONS BOARD
an agency of the
UNITED STATES GOVERNMENT

Employees' Names and Addresses

In 1966, the Board decided in *Excelsior Underwear Inc.*,[60] that it would require employers to furnish unions with a list of employees' names and home addresses. Accordingly, an employer must, within seven days after the regional director's decision (or within seven days after a consent agreement is approved), send a list of the names and addresses of all employees in the bargaining unit to the regional director. The regional director then sends a copy of this list to the union. How the unions make use of the list is graphically shown in *Organizing and the Law*, a book written for union organizers. It states:

Suggestions to Organizers Based on Excelsior

1. Organizing campaigns will now need a different type of planning geared to the availability of employee address lists after direction of election or employer consent. This planning should consider extensive house calls, phone contacts, and home mailing campaigns in addition to other organizing methods. This should not be a 'one-man show' but should be a cooperative effort mobilizing as many key in-plant people as possible.

2. All mailing should contain materials designed on a *positive basis*. Unions must realize that they are approaching the worker and his family in their home and community environment rather than in that of the factory. They should talk about what the union can accomplish in terms of security for the family breadwinner and economic benefits and protections for the family group. Name-calling or attacks upon the employer should be carefully avoided. Mailings should be cleared with organizing directors prior to mailing.

3. These lists must be kept locked in a safe place at all times and never shown or given to any outsiders. Misuse of such lists could jeopardize the communications gain made in the *Excelsior* decision.

4. When an election is won, preserve the list. It can come in handy later.

5. If an election is lost, again *preserve* the mailing list. It may be invaluable for a later campaign.

Remember, the techniques made possible by the availability of the mailing lists are not a substitute for a regular campaign or traditional methods but, rather, an aid and adjunct to them.

Organizers should not rely on the NLRB's automatically making the list available, even though it will do so. Tell the NLRB regional director or his agent that you want the list *as soon as it is received* from the employer. If you are located near the NLRB office, it would be wise to pick up the list. The sooner you have it, the better you can use it to inform those in the unit.[61]

The union is given a minimum of 10 days to make use of the list. Therefore, the regional director will not set the election date earlier than 10 days after the union receives the list.[62] Since the employer has 7 days to furnish the list, and the union has 10 days to use it, the election date normally will be no earlier than 17 days from the date of the regional director's direction of election or the execution of a consent agreement.[63]

When *Excelsior* was first decided, employers railed at the manifest injustice whereby they are prohibited by the Board from visiting the homes of employees, but the union representative, in effect, is shown the way by the employer.[64] Employers' protests, however, fell on deaf ears and a few years later the Supreme Court upheld the rule.[65]

At this point, the employer may desire to write his employees stating, for example:

We did not want to turn over this information, which we have always regarded as confidential. We did so only in response to a written instruction from the NLRB. We regret this invasion of your privacy and any annoyance the union may cause you as a result.[66]

REQUEST FOR REVIEW

If a party disagrees with the regional director's decision, he may request review by the Board in Washington within 10 days after service of the decision.[67] The other party may file a statement in opposition to the request for review.[68] The Board will grant review only upon one or more of the following grounds:

(1) That a substantial question of law or policy is raised because of (i) the absence of, or (ii) a departure from, officially reported Board precedent.

(2) That the regional director's decision on a substantial factual issue is clearly erroneous on the record and such error prejudicially affects the rights of a party.

(3) That the conduct of the hearing or any ruling made in connection with the proceeding has resulted in prejudicial error.

(4) That there are compelling reasons for reconsideration of an important Board rule or policy.[69]

A request for review should always be filed where there is disagreement with the regional director's decision. The Board's rule is that:

Failure to request review shall preclude . . . relitigating, in any related subsequent unfair labor practice proceeding, any issue which was, or could have been, raised in the representation proceeding.[70]

This rule would apply should the union later win the election and the employer refuses to bargain, claiming that the regional director's decision was erroneous. The union will then file an unfair labor practice charge, alleging the refusal to bargain. An employer who did not previously request review in the representation case may not then litigate the claimed error in the unfair labor practice case,[71] or before a court of appeals.[72]

When a request for review is filed, the regional director need not wait for the Board's decision but may make the election arrangements. However, he will not schedule the election until a date between the 20th and 30th day after the date of his decision in order to allow the Board time to pass on the request.[73] A date closer to the 30th day is customary. Under present practice, the Board issues its ruling shortly before the scheduled election date. Should it grant the request, it may stay the election, or direct that the election be held and the ballots impounded.

If the Board should grant the request for review, it will affirm or reverse the decision of the regional director in whole or in part.[74] In practice, however, very few requests for review are granted by the Board.[75] Infrequently a regional director will transfer the representation case to Washington, without deciding it.[76] In such circumstances, the Board will make the decision.

EMPLOYER CAMPAIGN TECHNIQUES

Agreement on the date of the election will herald an escalation of efforts by both parties. The union will step up its home visits, intensify its handbilling, and call mass meetings. The employer will make the same intense effort, using different media to communicate. Generally, at this point, neither side will have a truly firm majority. There will be a group of workers, usually about 25%, who have not yet firmly made up their minds. It is this group to whom the final effort is mainly directed.

What is the most effective technique that an employer can use? Experience has shown that it is oral communication. A survey of employees, participants in NLRB elections in Los Angeles and Orange Counties, California, substantiated this conclusion.[77] They were asked: "What do you think influenced you or your co-workers most in the union campaign?" The overwhelming consensus was that the most influential employer technique was the group meeting at which employees were addressed by top company executives. The second most effective technique was the individual talk by supervisors. Rated third was home mailing.

The best results will be produced by combining, in appropriate measure, all three techniques. In implementing this program of communication, the employer will not concentrate on asking the employees to vote for the company. The better approach is to seek to persuade them to vote against the union. It has been noted that in political elections, people do not vote *for* a candidate, but *against* one. Roosevelt was elected in 1932, not because people voted for him, but because they voted against Hoover.[78] In the Johnson-Goldwater election, it was stated that Johnson was elected because people feared Goldwater's candidacy and voted *against* him.[79]

EMPLOYER'S RIGHT TO FREE SPEECH

It is now appropriate to review the rules of the contest. Neither side may threaten or coerce. Neither side may engage in gross misrepresentations about material issues at a time when the other party cannot reply.[80] The union may promise. The employer may not.[81]

Counsel is often asked whether the Board would construe a proposed statement as a promise of a benefit and therefore unprotected as "free speech." For example, an employer may inquire whether it is unlawful to compare his existing profit-sharing plan with the union's pension plan. Is he promising a benefit when he states that the employees will receive more from his plan than from the union's?

In *Pure Chem Corporation*,[82] the Board approved the following statement contained in a letter mailed to employees four days before the election:

> You have a right to ask what kind of financial future you are going to have if you stay non-union.
>
> We are restricted by law as to what we can tell you during a union organizing campaign. We can lawfully tell you the things that are in existence.
>
> You may choose to share in our Profit Sharing Plan which is known as one of the finest programs for working people. If you stay with the company and develop, as we are sure that you will, you should have much more money in this plan compared with any Teamster plan.
>
> You get to take all or part of this money with you after the very first year that you are in the plan. Under Teamster plans you would, in most cases, forefeit all that had been put into it for you if you leave while you are young.[83]

In other words, a comparison of plans is lawful and not a promise of benefit.

Counsel frequently is asked by his client how far he can go in stating his opinion concerning the adverse consequences of unionization. For example, may he tell his employees that resistance to union demands may cause a strike, resulting in employee hardship?

The answer to this and similar questions is to be found in Board decisions. In general, the Board has stated:

> . . . In outlining the advantages and disadvantages of unionization, an employer is not prohibited from pointing out that the strike is a union's chief economic lever,

and that strike action might entail certain consequences. But the more the employer persists in referring to strikes and what they might entail—replacement, violence, unemployment, walking picket lines, unpaid bills—the more the employee is likely to believe that the employer has already determined to adopt an intransigent bargaining stance which will force employees to strike in order to gain any benefits. An employer who campaigns on the theory that a strike is an inevitable result of unionization leaves himself open to the construction that he does not intend to bargain in any meaningful sense.[84]

Thus, an employer may state, as in *Babcock & Wilcox Co.*:[85] "We know, and you know, that in trying to use force, unions have shut plants down. We don't want to see that happen here, because of some men who don't even work here and who would not lose anything while you were out on strike." (The context in which this statement was made may be examined by reference to Appendix H which contains the full text of the statement as reported in the official volumes of NLRB decisions.)

May an employer tell his employees that the granting of union demands for increased wages and benefits will result in higher prices and less demand for products with adverse effects on the employees?

When asked for advice in this and related areas of the law, counsel's safest course is to advise the use of the actual language approved by the Board. In *Lord Baltimore Press*,[86] for example, the following statement in a pre-election speech was approved: "If a union imposes uncompetitive conditions on an employer, it can make it almost impossible for the Company to secure enough sales to provide full and regular employment." (See Appendix H.)

Of course, counsel will check whether a particular Board decision was reviewed by the appellate courts. In general, a Board approved employer statement will receive court approval.

Conversely, Board disapproval will not necessarily beget court concurrence, for the courts of appeals generally take a broader view of free speech.[87] For example, in one case, the Board held that an employer's letter discussing the adverse consequences of unionization was coercive. When the Board sought to enforce its order in the Seventh Circuit, it was confronted by the court with its *Excelsior* decision. The Board, in *Excelsior*, stated that one of the reasons an employer should furnish a union with a list of employee names and home addresses was that: "[A]n employee who has had an effective opportunity to hear the arguments concerning representation is in a better position to make a more fully informed and reasonable choice."[88]

The court, noting this rationale, stated:

> If . . . 'employees are . . . to exercise an informed and reasoned choice after hearing all sides of the question concerning the desirability of union representation,' then we must guard against the Board adopting an overly restrictive attitude toward permissible employer communications.[89]

NOTES TO CHAPTER VI

1. NLRB Rules & Regulations § 102.63(a), 29 C.F.R. § 102.63(a) (1971). A copy of the petition is sent with the notice.

2. NLRB Field Manual § 11188.

3. Avondale Shipyards, Inc., 174 NLRB No. 14, 70 LRRM 1103, 1105 n. 5 (1969).

4. NLRB Rules & Regulations § 102.65(b), 29 C.F.R. § 102.65(b) (1971). The tests for intervention are found in NLRB *Field Manual* § 11022 *et seq.*

5. Beneke Corp., 109 NLRB 1191, 34 LRRM 1537 (1954).

6. 17 NLRB Ann. Rep. 31 n. 19 (1952).

7. Boeing Airplane Co., 86 NLRB 368, 24 LRRM 1624 (1949).

8. LMRA § 101.2(5), 29 U.S.C. § 152(5) (1964).

9. *Id.*

10. Foothill Elec. Corp., 120 NLRB 1350, 42 LRRM 1184 (1958).

11. NLRB Field Manual § 11200(g).

12. Aero Corp., 149 NLRB 1283, 1285 n. 3, 57 LRRM 1483 (1964), *enf'd*, 363 F.2d 702 (D.C. Cir. 1966), *cert. denied*, 385 U.S. 973 (1966).

13. NLRB Field Manual § 11200(m).

14. LMRA § 101.9(b)(3), 29 U.S.C. § 159(b)(3) (1964).

15. LMRA § 101.9(b)(1), 29 U.S.C. § 159(b)(1) (1964).

16. Display Sign Serv., Inc., 180 NLRB No. 6, 72 LRRM 1577 (1969); Bowman Transp., Inc., 166 NLRB 982, 65 LRRM 1716 (1967).

17. Cromwell Printery Inc., 172 NLRB No. 212, 69 LRRM 1182 (1968); Crest Wine & Spirits Ltd., 168 NLRB 754, 66 LRRM 1364 (1967).

18. Blade-Tribune Publishing Co., 161 NLRB 1512, 1520, 63 LRRM 1484 (1966), *remanded*, __ F.2d __, 71 LRRM 3104 (9th Cir., No. 21860, decided July 14, 1969), *rev'd on other grounds*, 180 NLRB No. 56, 73 LRRM 1041 (1969).

19. R. H. Macy & Co., 185 NLRB No. 5, 74 LRRM 1730 (1970); Aspen Skiing Corp., 143 NLRB 707, 53 LRRM 1397 (1963).

20. M & M Charter Lines, Inc., 173 NLRB 605, 610, 70 LRRM 1174 (1968); Haag Drug Co., 146 NLRB 798, 55 LRRM 1417 (1964).

21. San Diego Transit Corp., 182 NLRB No. 66, 74 LRRM 1145 (1970); R. H. Macy & Co., *supra* note 19.

22. General Elec. Co. (River Works), 107 NLRB 70, 33 LRRM 1058 (1953).

23. LMRA § 101.2(11), 29 U.S.C. § 152 (11) (1964).

24. *Id.*

25. Ohio Power Co. v. NLRB, 176 F.2d 385 (6th Cir. 1949), *denying enforcement to* 78 NLRB 1134, 22 LRRM 1315 (1948) and 80 NLRB 1334, 23 LRRM 1242 (1948), *cert. denied*, 338 U.S. 899 (1949); Clark O'Neill, Inc., 147 NLRB 370, 56 LRRM 1204 (1964).

26. Jas. H. Matthews & Co. v. NLRB, 354 F.2d 432 (8th Cir. 1965), *enforcing* 149 NLRB 161, 57 LRRM 1253 (1965), *cert. denied*, 384 U.S. 1002 (1966); Sturgeon Elec. Co., 166 NLRB 210, 65 LRRM 1530 (1967), *enf'd in part and remanded in part*, 419 F.2d 51 (10th Cir. 1969), *reaff'd*, 181 NLRB No. 30, 73 LRRM 1320 (1970).

27. A.D.T. Co., 177 NLRB No. 112, 71 LRRM 1513 (1969).

28. Autotronics, Inc., 176 NLRB No. 96, 71 LRRM 1322 (1969), *enf'd,* 434 F.2d 651 (8th Cir. 1970).

29. Grand Union Co., 176 NLRB No. 28, 71 LRRM 1216 (1969).

30. Finnical Tire Co., 171 NLRB No. 41, 68 LRRM 1094 (1968).

31. Sea Life, Inc., 175 NLRB No. 168, 71 LRRM 1134 (1969).

32. Sav-on Drugs, Inc., 138 NLRB 1032, 51 LRRM 1152 (1962).

33. Paramount Press, Inc., 187 NLRB No. 65, 76 LRRM 1069 (1970).

34. Brown Specialty Co., 174 NLRB No. 177, 70 LRRM 1242 (1969), *reaff'd,* 180 NLRB No. 149, 73 LRRM 1201, *enf'd,* 436 F.2d 372 (7th Cir. 1971).

35. Eastman Broadcasting Co., 188 NLRB No. 13, 76 LRRM 1398 (1971).

36. *Id.*

37. *Id.*

38. Spotlight Co., 188 NLRB No. 128, 76 LRRM 1443 (1971).

39. Cromwell Printery Inc., *supra* note 17.

40. Shattuck School, 189 NLRB No. 118, 77 LRRM 1164 (1971).

41. Carpenters Local 101, 191 NLRB No. 108, 77 LRRM 1637 (1971).

42. Hook Drugs, Inc., 191 NLRB No. 45, 77 LRRM 1445 (1971).

43. *Cf.* Edinburg Mfg. Co., 164 NLRB 121, 123, 65 LRRM 1084 (1967), *enf'd,* 394 F.2d 1 (4th Cir. 1968).

44. NLRB Rules & Regulations § 102.67(a), 29 C.F.R. § 102.67(a) (1971). If the hearing officer denies an extension of time, an appeal may be made to the regional director.

45. NLRB Field Manual § 11246.1.

46. NLRB Statements of Procedure § 101.21(b), 29 C.F.R. § 101.21(b) (1971).

47. LMRA § 101.9(b), 29 U.S.C. § 159(b) (1964). *See also,* LMRA § 101.3(b), 29 U.S.C. § 153(b) (1964); NLRB Organization & Functions § 203.1, 32 F.R. § 9589 (1967).

48. Buckeye Village Mkts., 175 NLRB No. 46, 70 LRRM 1529 (1969); United Mercantile, Inc., 171 NLRB No. 103, 68 LRRM 1173 (1968).

49. Dundee Cement Co., 170 NLRB No. 66, 67 LRRM 1409 (1968); Buddy L Corp., 167 NLRB 808, 66 LRRM 1150 (1966); Mallinckrodt Chem. Works, 162 NLRB 387, 64 LRRM 1011 (1966).

50. Haag Drug Co., 169 NLRB 877, 67 LRRM 1289 (1968); Sav-on Drugs, Inc., *supra* note 32. *Cf.* Disco Fair Stores, Inc., 189 NLRB No. 61, 76 LRRM 1609 (1971); Star Mkt. Co., 172 NLRB No. 130, 68 LRRM 1497 (1968).

51. Weyerhaeuser Co., 173 NLRB 1170, 69 LRRM 1553 (1968); American Cyanamid Co., 172 NLRB No. 241, 69 LRRM 1161 (1968).

52. Foreign Car Center, Inc., 129 NLRB 319, 320, 46 LRRM 1538 (1960).

53. LMRA § 101.9(c)(5), 29 U.S.C. § 159(c)(5) (1964).

54. *Id.* *See also*, NLRB v. Metropolitan Life Ins. Co., 380 U.S. 438 (1965).

55. Motts Supermarkets, 182 NLRB No. 19, 74 LRRM 1023 n.3 (1970) and cases cited therein.

56. *Id.*

57. It is difficult to predict the exact date when the regional director will issue his decision. The average time is twenty days. 35 NLRB Ann. Rep. 12 (1970). But circumstances and caseloads vary from region to region. The complexity of the issues in the particular case has a bearing on the time it takes to decide it. Sometimes counsel's experience in a particular region may provide him with a basis for prediction.

58. NLRB Statements of Procedure § 101.19(a)(1), 29 C.F.R. § 101.19 (a)(1) (1971).

59. Murray Chair Co., 117 NLRB 1385, 40 LRRM 1009 (1957).

60. 156 NLRB 1236, 61 LRRM 1217.

61. S. I. Schlossberg & F. E. Sherman, *Organizing and The Law* 124-25 (1971). Reprinted with permission of Bureau of National Affairs.

62. NLRB Field Manual § 11302.1.

63. The employer may shorten this time, if he desires an earlier election, by furnishing the list in less than 7 days.

64. For a critical analysis of this decision, see Lewis, *NLRB Intrudes on the Right of Privacy*, 17 Lab. L.J. 280 (May 1966).

65. NLRB v. Wyman-Gordon Co., 394 U.S. 759 (1969).

66. *But see*, Tunica Mfg. Co., 182 NLRB No. 111, 76 LRRM 1535, 1536 (1970), where Board held that employer interfered with election by stating that such visits could result in violence.

67. NLRB Rules & Regulations § 102.67(b), 29 C.F.R. § 102.67(b) (1971).

68. *Id.* at § 102.67(e), 29 C.F.R. § 102.67(e) (1971).

69. *Id.* at § 102.67(c), 29 C.F.R. § 102.67(c) (1971).

70. *Id.* at § 102.67(f), 29 C.F.R. § 102.67(f) (1971).

71. This does not mean that when the request for review is made, but denied by the Board, an employer necessarily will be entitled to litigate the issue in a subsequent unfair labor practice proceeding. In most instances, the Board will grant General Counsel's motion for summary judgment on the refusal to bargain charge. But the necessary basis will have been laid for court review. L. F. Strassheim Co., 171 NLRB No. 132, 68 LRRM 1265 (1968); Red-More Corp., 164 NLRB 638, 65 LRRM 1155 (1967), *reaff'd*, 169 NLRB 426, 67 LRRM 1203 (1968), *enf'd*, 418 F.2d 890 (9th Cir. 1969).

72. Meatcutters, Local 576 v. Allen, 298 F. Supp. 985 (W.D. Mo. 1969), *aff'd*, 423 F.2d 267 (8th Cir. 1970). In considering court review, council should be aware of the doctrine that the courts accord the Board broad discretion in unit determinations and will reverse only when the Board oversteps the law. Chemical Workers v. Pittsburgh Plate Glass, __ U.S. __ (Nos. 70-32 and 70-39, decided Dec. 8, 1971), *affirming* 427 F.2d 936 (6th Cir. 1970).

73. NLRB Statements of Procedure § 101.21(d), 29 C.F.R. § 101.21(d) (1971).

74. NLRB Rules & Regulations § 102.67(j), 29 C.F.R. § 102.67(j) (1971). The Board also may remand for further evidence.

75. For representative annual statistics, see 1966 ABA Lab. Rel. Section, Ann. Comm. Rep. 228.

76. NLRB Rules and Regulations § 102.67(h), 29 C.F.R. § 102.67(h) (1971).

77. Kircher, *Yardstick for More Effective Organizing*, The American Federationist (March 1969), in 70 LRR 340.

78. G. Smith, *The Shattered Dream* (1970).

79. N. Y. Times, Nov. 4, 1964.

80. Hollywood Ceramics Co., 140 NLRB 221, 51 LRRM 1600 (1962). For circuit court approval, see cases cited in note 8 of *Bausch & Lomb Inc. v. NLRB*, __ F.2d __, 78 LRRM 2648, 2652 (2d Cir., Nos. 71-1044, 71-1227, decided Oct. 22, 1971). *See also,* Cross Baking Co. v. NLRB, __ F.2d __, 78 LRRM 3059 (1st Cir., No. 71-1185, decided Dec. 2, 1971), *denying enforcement to* 191 NLRB No. 9, 77 LRRM 1753 (1971).

81. LMRA § 101.8(c), 29 U.S.C. § 158(c) (1964).

82. 192 NLRB No. 88, 77 LRRM 1923 (1971).

83. *Id.* at 77 LRRM 1926. *But see,* Hineline's Meat Plant, Inc., 193 NLRB No. 135, 78 LRRM 1387 (1971), wherein the Board set aside the

election because the employer told the employees of a proposed profit sharing plan which had been decided upon prior to the filing of the petition. In a dissenting opinion, however, Chairman Miller stated:

> "The result of the majority decision here is to require that employees be kept ignorant of a benefit which the employer had legitimately decided to provide, and which employees might well want to take into account in deciding whether or not they desired to be represented by a union. I see no policy reason which compels that predetermined benefits be thus hidden from employee view." 77 LRRM at 1388.

84. Thomas Prods. Co. Div. of Thomas Indus., 167 NLRB 732, 733, 66 LRRM 1147 (1967), *motion for reconsideration denied,* 169 NLRB 706, 67 LRRM 1237 (1968).

85. 77 NLRB 577, 22 LRRM 1057 (1948).

86. 145 NLRB 888, 55 LRRM 1068 (1964).

87. This proposition will vary, however, according to the particular court of appeals in which review or enforcement is sought and the particular three member panel assigned to the case.

88. Excelsior Underwear Inc., *supra* note 60, at 1240.

89. P. R. Mallory & Co. v. NLRB, 389 F.2d 704, 707 n. 3 (7th Cir. 1967), *enforcing in part* 162 NLRB 1404, 64 LRRM 1207 (1967).

CHAPTER VII

CAMPAIGN WINDUP

The employer should anticipate the Direction of Election. He should previously have prepared a calendar of events and activities, and drafts of employee communications. The following is an example of the first week of such a calendar. Additional weeks appear subsequently.

FOUR WEEKS TO GO

Monday	Tuesday	Wednesday	Thursday	Friday
°Receipt of NLRB Decision				°Excelsior List Submitted
°Supervisory Meeting	°Handout		°Handout	°NLRB Conference
°Speech To All Employees				
°Home Mailing		°Home Mailing	°Home Mailing	°Bulletin Board Notice

On Monday, the following activities will take place:

9 A.M.: Receipt of Decision and Direction of Election

10 A.M.: Supervisory meeting held. Decision is read and discussed. Throughout the next four weeks, frequent, unscheduled, supervisory meetings are held. Their agenda, format and purpose were discussed in Chapters III and IV.

11 A.M.: Speech to all employees.

3 P.M.: Letter mailed to homes of all employees, including supervisors.

SPEECH TO ALL EMPLOYEES

<u>MONDAY</u>

       I have asked you to come to this meeting this morning so that we can discuss our future - your's, your family's, your company's.

       I am sure that all of you are aware that unions have been trying to organize our company for quite a while. A couple of months ago, a union representative demanded that we recognize his union as the representative of our employees. We refused. We believe that you should have a right to vote in secret as to whether or not you want a union. Therefore, we filed a petition with the National Labor Relations Board to provide for such a secret vote.

       This morning we received notification from the Board, directing an election. It will be held later this month. Between now and then, you will have to decide for yourself whether or not you are better off with or without a union. Your decision will affect your future and I am deeply concerned about your making the right decision. I want to make my position crystal clear to you. I am strongly opposed to a union in our company.

       I have been asked whether we would have to agree to what the union asks if it should win the election. While we would negotiate in good faith with the union, we would not have to agree to anything that is improper or unreasonable.

       I have also been asked whether, if the union won, the end result would be more or less benefits. The answer is simple. Everything is negotiable. This means that you could end up with higher wages that you have been receiving in the past, the same amount, or less. The same thing would be true of fringe benefits, such as health insurance.

       It is unfortunate that unions very often make fancy promises to employees during the pre-election period. Promises are cheap when you don't have to deliver.

       We all know that a union sometimes strikes to force a company to do something to which it wouldn't agree voluntarily. We try to know the hardship that can occur by a strike, as we read about it in our papers every day. What you may not know is that a company can lawfully, permanently replace employees who engage in an economic strike. Its only obligation is to place employees on a preferential hiring list and to hire from this list if and when openings occur.

The union will ask you to vote for it and suggest that if you want to change your mind, you can vote it out any time you want to. Don't fall for that line. It is easier to get married than to get divorced. And with the union, it is easier to get one in than to get rid of one.

I know that you are too intelligent to vote on mere promises. You will vote on the facts. One indisputable fact is that last year you received liberal pay increases, family hospitalization coverage, an additional paid holiday, and accumlated sick leave benefits. You achieved these improvements without a strike and without one day's lost pay, or dues payment.

What do you know about this union? Have you read its constitution? As a union member, you would be bound to follow every rule in this constitution. Have you learned how costly joining the union is? Of course, you would pay dues every month. But have you learned yet about assessments, reinstatement fees, and fines?

Lastly, I would like to talk to you about our philosophy. We provide steady work, opportunities to get ahead and recognition for a job well done. We constantly make improvements because we know that a loyal group of employees is necessary to our success. We have a reputation as being one of the best places to work. We have worked hard to develop this reputation. We are proud of it. We want to keep it that way.

All of us want the better things in life for ourselves and our families. I believe that our record has shown that this can be achieved without a union. Sharing the rewards of our progress is a fundamental principle which we follow.

I will be talking to you again and writing to you about these topics. I am sure you will agree, after considering all the facts, that you are better off without a union. If you have any questions, I will be available after the meeting to discuss them with you. Thank you.

HOME MAILING

<u>MONDAY</u>

Dear Fellow Employee:

        We have just received notification from the National
Labor Relations Board, directing an election. The date has not
yet been agreed upon, but will be set shortly. Now we are all
faced with a very serious decision which can have far reaching
effects on our jobs and our families.

        In the coming weeks we will be talking and writing to
you about the important issues involved in this election. We urge
you to consider these facts carefully when you vote on election day.

        During the time our company has been here, our policy
has been one of fairness to you and to our customers. Our growth
and improvements in wages, benefits and working conditions are
proof of this. We must be fair to you so that you will continue to
produce quality products; we must be fair to our customers to insure
a continued demand for our products.

        These organizers have made promises - big promises. This
is all rather foolish because, as everyone knows, the union can make
a lot of promises but delivering on them is another matter. Only
your company can deliver. However, the law is such that the union
can make these promises to you at this time, but your company may not.
So beware of this union tactic.

        We feel that our employees know of our efforts to treat
them fairly. We are convinced that you and your families are better
off without a union. We hope you will agree and vote against union
representation on election day.

                            Sincerely,

                            General Manager

HANDOUT

<u>TUESDAY</u>

<u>DID YOU KNOW</u>....

That although you are a law-abiding free American citizen, you may have to stand trial before a kangaroo court of the union?

Here are some of the offenses listed in the union's constitution.

"Violation of any of the provisions of this Constitution...or by-laws or rules of the local union."

"Advocating or attempting to bring about the withdrawal from the International Union of any... member or group of members."

"Slandering or...wronging a member of the International Union."

"Using abusive language or disturbing the peace or harmony of any meeting..."

These are a few of the offenses that you can be tried and fined for. Why give away your personal freedom?

PERSONNEL DEPARTMENT

HOME MAILING

<u>WEDNESDAY</u>

Dear Fellow Employee:

At our plant gate yesterday, the union distributed a leaf-
let in which it discussed how it will back up its demands at our
company.

In other words, the union is stating that it can fulfill
its promises by the use of force. This is absolutely untrue.
While the union can make promises and threaten to force us to do
things, it is the company which pays your wages and provides you
with benefits.

I think you should know some facts about what the union
<u>cannot do</u> to your company, and some of the things they <u>can do</u> to <u>you.</u>

First, let's look at what it <u>cannot</u> force your company
to do:

1. It cannot force the company to agree to any
    proposal that the company is unwilling or
    unable to meet.

2. It cannot increase any wages or benefits unless
    the company feels it is in its best interest to
    do so.

3. It cannot guarantee job security or furnish you
    a day's work or a day's pay.

Now let's look at what it <u>can</u> "force" employees to do:

1. It can force the employees to pay dues each and
    every month where there is a union shop clause
    in the contract.

2. It can force members to stand trial and pay fines
    for violation of any of the provisions of the
    "book of rules" (Constitution).

3. It can force members to pay assessments whenever
    the union treasury requires more money.

Consider the many advantages and benefits you now enjoy.
These have been provided without a union. Consider the many
disadvantages of union membership. When you do, I am sure you will
vote "NO".

Sincerely,

General Manager

HANDOUT

THURSDAY

TO ALL EMPLOYEES:

DID YOU KNOW
That the Union has the authority to assess its members whenever it runs short of funds or needs additional money to support union projects. These projects may include money for striking members at other plants, support for political candidates favored by the union or money to pay the expenses and salaries of union officials.

DID YOU KNOW
That in some locals of the Union they collect more from assessments of members than from any other source. One local of the Union assessed its members over $15,000 last year. The following is part of the Union's financial statement.

LABOR ORGANIZATION ANNUAL REPORT
LM - 2
STATEMENT OF RECEIPTS AND DISBURSEMENTS

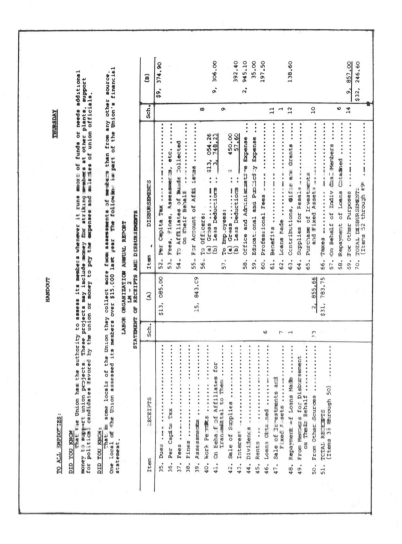

Item	RECEIPTS	Sch.	(A)	Item	DISBURSEMENTS	Sch.	(B)
35.	Dues		$13,085.00	52.	Per Capita Tax		$9,374.90
36.	Per Capita Tax			53.	Fees, Fines, Assessments, etc.		
37.	Fees			54.	To Affiliates of Funds Collected On Their Behalf		
38.	Fines			55.	For Account of Affiliates	8	
39.	Assessments		15,843.09	56.	To Officers:		
40.	Work Permits				(a) Gross $13,054.26		
41.	On Behalf of Affiliates for Transmittal to Them				(b) Less Deductions .. 3,748.23		9,306.00
42.	Sale of Supplies			57.	To Employees:	9	
43.	Interest				(a) Gross 450.00		392.40
44.	Dividends				(b) Less Deductions .. 57.60		
45.	Rents	6		58.	Office and Administrative Expense		2,945.10
46.	Loans Obtained	7		59.	Educational and Publicity Expense		35.00
47.	Sale of Investments and Fixed Assets	1		60.	Professional Fees		197.50
48.	Repayment of Loans Made			61.	Benefits	11	
49.	From Members for Disbursement on Their Behalf			62.	Loans Made	1	
50.	From Other Sources	13	2,855.66	63.	Contributions, Gifts and Grants	12	138.60
51.	TOTAL RECEIPTS (Items 35 through 50)		$31,783.75	64.	Supplies for Resale		
				65.	Purchase of Investments and Fixed Assets	10	
				66.	Taxes		
				67.	On Behalf of Indiv. Members	6	
				68.	Repayment of Loans Obtained		
				69.	For Other Purposes	14	9,857.00
				70.	TOTAL DISBURSEMENTS (Items 52 through 69)		$32,246.60

HOME MAILING

<u>THURSDAY</u>

Dear Fellow Employee:

Enclosed with this letter is a bill you might receive if you became a member of the union.

This bill is an obligation you could assume if you vote to place yourself under the control of the union. Part of the bill is for the monthly dues you would have to pay. Recently the union increased the dues required from its members. This obligation could be increased again at any time.

Part of the bill is for an initiation fee that you would be required to pay to join the union.

Part of the bill is for fines that could be levied against you by the union for failure to attend union meetings - or refusing to march in picket lines - or simply as "discipline" for not following union orders.

These are a few of the ways the union takes a large part of your pay check. If the union gets in, you could receive a monthly bill from it for the rest of your working life.

Vote against the union, don't waste your money.

Sincerely,

encl.   General Manager

BILL

The United Workers of America

John Doe
Any Company
Any City, U.S.A.

UNION BANK ACCOUNT (no money back guarantee if we don't deliver on our promises)

DUES	$ 5.00
Initiation Fee	$ 25.00
Fines	$ 500.00
Strike Fund Assessment	$ 10.00
Other Special Assessments	$ 5.00

PAYMENT DUE AFTER JOINING

AUTHORS' NOTE:

1. Care should be exercised to insert accurate figures in the bill.

2. Some employers prefer to dramatize the cost of union member-
    ship by a deduction from the paycheck equivalent to the
    amount of monthly union dues. The deducted amount is
    placed in a separate envelope and handed out with the
    paycheck.   Appropriate comments may be printed or typed
    on the envelope, such as: "This envelope contains $5.00
    of your money, the minimum amount the union would take
    out of your paycheck every month." For relevant Board
    decisions, see TRW, Inc., 173 NLRB 1445, 70 LRRM 1017
    (1968); Mosler Safe Co., 129 NLRB 747, 47 LRRM 1058
    (1960); Montrose Hanger Co., 120 NLRB 88, 41 LRRM 1432
    (1958). Cf. Nat'l Mobil Homes, Div. Nat'l Homes Corp.,
    186 NLRB No. 86, 75 nRRM 1477 (1970).

BULLETIN BOARD NOTICE

<u>FRIDAY</u>

<u>N O T I C E</u>

Your Company, the Union and the NLRB agreed this morning on the date for an election.

DAY & DATE: Friday, January 29.

TIME: 8 A.M. to 9 A.M. and 3 P.M. to 4 P.M.

PLACE: Stock Room.

WHO VOTES: All production and maintenance employees employed at this plant, including group leaders.

Regardless of whether you signed a card for the union, you can vote in secret as you now feel.

Think for yourself - VOTE "NO."

General Manager

THREE WEEKS TO GO

Monday	Tuesday	Wednesday	Thursday	Friday
	°Bulletin Board Notice			
		°Handout	°Handout	°Handout
°Home Mailing		°Home Mailing		

HOME MAILING

Dear Fellow Employee:

I wrote to you last week about union fines. They are used as you
know, by unions to punish members for violating union-made rules.
The following are actual cases in which union members have been fined
by their unions:

REASONS	AMOUNT OF FINE
A union member attended church instead of a union meeting.	$ 5.00
A union member exceeded union-set production quotas.	100.00
A union member filed unfair labor practice charges against the union.	450.00
A union member informed the company that a fellow employee union member had violated a company rule.	500.00
A union member made derogatory remarks about the union and its officials.	1,000.00
A union member refused to join a strike.	2,000.00

Sincerely,

General Manager

AUTHORS' NOTE:

$ 5.00	N. Y. Times, May 5, 1962; Cleveland Press, May 4, 1962.
100.00	Scofield v. NLRB, 393 U. S. 995 (1969).
450.00	Local 925, Operating Eng'rs, 148 NLRB 674, 57 LRRM 1012 (1964).
500.00	Communications Workers Local 5795, 192 NLRB No. 85, 77 LRRM 1827 (1971).
1,000.00	Teamsters Local 25, Case No. 1-CB-748 (TXD, Nov. 8, 1962), 51 LRR 282 (1962).
2,000.00	Pressmen's Local 60, 190 NLRB No. 38,77 LRRM 1199 (1971).

BULLETIN BOARD NOTICE

<u>TUESDAY</u>

<u>DID YOU KNOW</u>....

That the Union Constitution provides for the "prompt" payment
of your assessments and fines in order to remain in good standing:

Article XI, Section 2

> "A member shall...continue to pay all
> dues, assessments and fines or other
> obligations promptly when due in order
> to be and remain in good standing."

The Union certainly wants and needs your money badly.

What "other obligations" is the Union referring to? Is
it special collections to help strikers at some other plant?

HANDOUT

<u>WEDNESDAY</u>

<u>FACTS TO CONSIDER</u>

Last week we distributed an extract from the Union's financial report which it must file with the government. We noted that new income was **derived** from dues and assessments. Now let's look at how this money was spent.

1. It paid over $ 9,000 to the International Union.

2. It paid over $13,000 to local officers.

3. It spent over $ 9,000 for "other purposes."

<u>Yet, the union reported spending nothing "On Behalf of Individual Members."</u>

It looks like this union is in no position to do anything for anyone, except itself. It needs your money so that it can continue to pay salaries, expense accounts, and spend money for "other purposes."

HOME MAILING

Dear Fellow Employee:

There are many complex rules and regulations which a member of
the union must obey. You would have to live under these rules, and
it is important that you fully understand a member's obligations.

What happens if the union feels that a member has violated some
provision of the Constitution? The Constitution states:

Article XXV, Section B

"If a member of this Union is charged with committing
an offense against the by-laws or the general good
and welfare of his local or of the Union, he shall
be given a fair trial."

How does the trial come about?

* Any member of the union can bring charges against a
  member.

* At this trial you can be represented only by another
  union member. You cannot use an outside attorney to
  represent you.

Some of the many charges that could be brought against you are:

* Crossing a union picket line.

* Failure to perform picket duty during a strike.

* Dissension or insubordination.

* Attempting to get rid of the union.

Violation of the Constitution can result in "Fines, Suspension or
Expulsion."

There is no reason for you to subject yourself to Trial and Penalty
because you displease the union. Vote NO.

Sincerely,

General Manager

HANDOUT

<u>THURSDAY</u>

Fellow Employee:

       You received a leaflet at the gate this morning from the Union which contains statements which are either absolutely false or only half-true.

       1) They claim that you have no pension plan -- YOU KNOW BETTER. ALL OF US HAVE A COPY OF THE BOOKLET DESCRIBING THE <u>FREE</u> COMPANY PENSION PLAN.

       2) They claim that our sick leave plan is the minimum required by law -- WE ALL KNOW THAT WE ARE COVERED BY THE <u>BEST</u> ACCIDENT AND SICKNESS PROGRAM IN THE COMMUNITY.

       3) They claim that "in all other organized plants" all benefits are fully paid by the company -- AT THOSE OTHER COMPANIES THE UNION EMPLOYEES PAY A PORTION OF THEIR INSURANCE PREMIUMS, JUST AS WE DO.

       4) They state that there are 19 million union members in our country -- WHY DON'T THEY TELL US ABOUT THE 63 MILLION AMERICAN WORKERS WHO ARE <u>NOT</u> MEMBERS OF A UNION?

       5) They claim that there will be no strike without your approval -- WHY PUT YOURSELF IN A POSITION WHERE YOU HAVE TO MAKE SUCH A CHOICE?

       6) They claim that they will put more money in your pocket -- BUT WE ALL KNOW THEY CAN'T GUARANTEE ANY MORE MONEY. THEY <u>CAN</u> GUARANTEE THAT YOU WILL PAY DUES AND ASSESSMENTS.

       7) The Union now admits that they have a <u>"Trial Committee"</u> to hand out "justice" -- HOW MUCH DOES THIS "JUSTICE" COST? IS THE COST A FINE OF $10.00, $20.00, $50.00, or $500.00?

       Their leaflet shows the kind of "truth" that you can expect. Why put your future in the hands of union bosses who will say anything to get your money?

Sincerely,

General Manager

HANDOUT

<u>FRIDAY</u>

<u>DID YOU KNOW....</u>

      Being in a union in many respects is like being in the Army. You are told what to do and, if you refuse, you are punished. For example, the following news item appeared on the first page of the New York Times:

<u>UNION ORDERS 8,500 TO PARADE OR PAY</u>

"Approximately 8,500 union painters decorators and paperhangers have been ordered to participate in next Monday's Labor Day parade here or be subject to fines.

The members of District Council 9 of the Painters, Decorators and Paperhangers Union have been told that the council designated the occasion as a mandatory picketing day in accordance with its bylaws and that any member who failed to report for a place in the parade would be fined. The members of the union were informed of the decision by postcard. The message from the council prescribed the parade uniform for its members."

      What happens to members who refuse to parade? Is a fine imposed? The following Letter to the Editor appeared in the New York Daily News.

<u>ONE WORKER'S UNION</u>

"Brooklyn: My union gave us notices to march in the Labor Day parade. I had to refuse because I had to attend my grandfather's birthday celebration, so I was fined $30. When I objected to the fine, my employer had to suspend me for two weeks' layoff for insubordination to union officials. I was fined another $20. for objecting to that. I then managed to get hold of a restricted mimeographed copy of our union bylaws. It stated that fines of union members become the property of union officials, so our union officials have managed to make a profit of about $3,000. for their Labor Day efforts. Nice, maybe, for a down-payment on a girl friend's apartment?"

Need anymore be said? When you vote <u>NO UNION</u> - you vote <u>NO FINES.</u>

TWO WEEKS TO GO

Monday	Tuesday	Wednesday	Thursday	Friday
*Bulletin Board Notice				
	*Handout		*Handout	
*Small Group Meetings	*Small Group Meetings	*Small Group Meetings	*Small Group Meetings	*Small Group Meetings
*Home Mailing		*Home Mailing		*Home Mailing

NOTE: The format for small group meetings is discussed in Chapter III.

BULLETIN BOARD NOTICE

MONDAY

THE UNION SAYS	THE FACTS
THE UNION STATES THAT IN ORDER TO CALL A STRIKE 2/3 OF THE LOCAL MEMBERSHIP HAVE TO APPROVE THE STRIKE ACTION.	THE UNION'S CONSTITUTION - Page 82, ARTICLE 49, SECTION 1 - "Whenever any difficulty arises within the jurisdiction of any local Union within the shop involved, between its members and any employer or employees, growing, out of reduction in wages, a shorter work day or other changes in the conditions of employment, the Local Union involved shall call a meeting of all members to decide whether the proposed changes shall be accepted or rejected. The majority vote of those present and voting on the question shall decide. If, as a result of this decision, a strike vote is decided upon, the Local Union Executive Board shall notify all members, and it shall require a two-thirds (2/3) vote by secret ballot of those voting to declare a strike."

HOME MAILING   MONDAY

Dear Fellow Employee:

      Most of you have never been involved in a strike. We hope
you never will be . It is a terrible and terrifying experience. The
unions know this. Therefore, they carefully instruct their organizers
what to do during a strike. One union has prepared a "STRIKE MANUAL"
for use by their officials in conducting a strike. It is worth
reading. Many of the comments in the manual provide food for thought.

First: The manual advises the union officials:

        "NEVER, NEVER predict a short strike. Always speak in
        terms of a long strike."

Second: The manual suggests that a special assessment be collected
        before a strike starts. It reads:

        "MAKE FINANCIAL PREPARATIONS IN ADVANCE." "Recommend to
        the membership that a special assessment be levied and
        that members begin arranging their personal finances so
        that they can hold out over a long stretch."

Third: The manual suggests that other union members be asked to
        contribute:

        "GET WEEKLY DONATIONS FROM MEMBERS WORKING."

Fourth: The manual discusses what happens if a striker finds a
        job during the strike:

        "When a man is excused from picket duty to do outside work,
        one condition should be that he contribute a given percent-
        age of his earnings to the strike fund."

Fifth: But, what happens when the strike fails as many do? The
        manual advises that the strikers should be told:

        "PRESERVE THE UNION." "Better to go back to work for poor
        conditions and keep the union intact than to stay out in-
        definitely and see the union fall to pieces."

      We are not suggesting that if the union would win, which is
unlikely, that a strike would be inevitable. However, when we read
strike manuals such as this, and know the history of the union, we
are very much concerned about the possible consequences. We ask
that you consider all the facts before you vote. VOTE NO.

                    Sincerely yours,

                    General Manager

HANDOUT

"WIN A TV SET CONTEST"

All you have to do is guess the amount of the largest
fine ever imposed on a member of the union and the length of time
of the longest strike called by the union.

The union says they do not fine members. They also deny
their reputation for strikes. But we all know different. What may
not be known is just how big the fines can be and how long the strikes
san last.

All you have to do is tear off the entry blank below and
write in your guess. The winner will be judged on the basis of the
entry coming closest in both categories. In case of a tie, there
will be a drawing for the winner.

Each person may make one entry. Boxes in which to deposit
your entry will be located in the cafeteria and by the time clock.

A portable TV set will be the winner's prize. Be sure to
keep your numbered receipt. Do not sign your name. The Contest
will close a week from today.

****

No. 1	RECEIPT NO. 1
I believe the largest fine ever levied against a member of this Union was $_____.	Retain this numbered receipt so that you may claim your prize if your entry wins. The winning number will be posted on the bulletin boards next Wednesday
The longest strike lasted _____ days.	

AUTHOR'NOTE.

The Board has held that contests and campaign devices are lawful.

    a. $84.00 of groceries raffled off, as dramatization of
cost of annual dues. Buzza-Cardozo, 77 NLRB No. 38,
71 LRRM 1390 (1969). But see, Electro-Voice,Inc., 191
NLRB No. 96, 77 LRRM 1436 (1971) (Miller, C., at 77 LRRM
1437 n.2.).

    b. Anti-Union Coloring Book. Employer offered cash prize to
children of employees who completed pictures. Great Lakes
Screw Corp., 164 NLRB 149, 65 LRRM 1236 (1967); enforcement
denied on other grounds, 409 F. 2d. 375 (7th Cir. 1969).

    c. T.V. set offered as prize in raffle as encouragement to
vote. Tunica Mfg. Co., 182 NLRB No. 111, 76 LRRM 1535 (1970);

Austin Concrete Works, Inc., 132 NLRB 184, 48 LRRM 1330 (1961).

HOME MAILING

<u>WEDNESDAY</u>

Dear Fellow Employee:

You and your wife or husband are cordially invited to attend a special Employee's Dinner Meeting to be held next week on Thursday evening starting at 6 P.M.

Important announcements of special significance to all employees and their families will be made immediately following the dinner. The program will be concluded at 9:00 P.M.

Tickets are enclosed.

Sincerely,

Encl.

General Manager

AUTHOR'S NOTE:

An employer may not hold a mandatory meeting with employees on company premises within 24 hours of the election. Peerless Plywood Co., 107 NLRB 427, 33 LRRM 1151 (1953). However, an election-eve employee meeting may be held off the premises, after work, if attendance is voluntary. It is permissible to provide a free meal on such occasion. Fasion Fair, Inc., 157 NLRB 1645, 61 LRRM 1575 (1966); Lloyd A. Fry Roofing Co., 123 NLRB 86, 43 LRRM 1391 (1959); Zeller Corp., 115 NLRB 762, 37 LRRM 1399 (1956).

THURSDAY

Handout

YOUR PERSONAL

STRIKE COST COMPUTER

PERIOD	TAKE HOME PAY	YOU LOSE	YOU ARE PAYING FOR										
			0¢	1¢	2¢	3¢	4¢	5¢	6¢	7¢	8¢	9¢	10¢
			To Get It Back It Will Take You										
THREE WEEKS	$80	$240	Never	11Yrs 28Wks	5Yrs 40Wks	3Yrs 44Wks	2Yrs 46Wks	2Yrs 16Wks	1Yr 48Wks	1Yr 34Wks	1Yr 23Wks	1Yr 14Wks	1Yr 8Wks
	$85	$255	Never	12Yrs 12Wks	6Yrs 6Wks	4Yrs 5Wks	3Yrs 3Wks	2Yrs 23Wks	2Yrs 2Wks	1Yr 39Wks	1Yr 28Wks	1Yr 19Wks	1Yr 12Wks
	$90	$270	Never	12Yrs 50Wks	6Yrs 25Wks	4Yrs 17Wks	3Yrs 12Wks	2Yrs 31Wks	2Yrs 8Wks	1Yr 44Wks	1Yr 32Wks	1Yr 23Wks	1Yr 15Wks
	$95	$285	Never	13Yrs 36Wks	6Yrs 44Wks	4Yrs 29Wks	3Yrs 22Wks	2Yrs 38Wks	2Yrs 15Wks	1Yr 50Wks	1Yr 37Wks	1Yr 27Wks	1Yr 19Wks
	$100	$300	Never	14Yrs 22Wks	7Yrs 11Wks	4Yrs 42Wks	3Yrs 32Wks	2Yrs 46Wks	2Yrs 21Wks	2Yrs 3Wks	1Yr 42Wks	1Yr 31Wks	1Yr 23Wks
	$105	$315	Never	15Yrs 7Wks	7Yrs 29Wks	5Yrs 2Wks	3Yrs 40Wks	3Yrs 1Wk	2Yrs 27Wks	2Yrs 8Wks	1Yr 46Wks	1Yr 35Wks	1Yr 26Wks
	$110	$330	Never	15Yrs 45Wks	7Yrs 48Wks	5Yrs 15Wks	3Yrs 50Wks	3Yrs 9Wks	2Yrs 33Wks	2Yrs 13Wks	1Yr 51Wks	1Yr 39Wks	1Yr 30Wks
	$115	$345	Never	16Yrs 30Wks	8Yrs 15Wks	5Yrs 27Wks	4Yrs 7Wks	3Yrs 16Wks	2Yrs 39Wks	2Yrs 19Wks	2Yrs 3Wks	1Yr 43Wks	1Yr 34Wks

HOME MAILING

Dear Fellow Employee:

On Monday I quoted from portions of one union's strike manual. Now let's look at a specific case - a strike by the Chemical Workers at one of the companies it represents.

The strike started on October 31st. Over 1,000 employees walked out and did not return to work until December 26th - a period of <u>56 days</u>. The lost wages during the strike was enormous. Hospitalization and life insurance benefits were terminated during the walkout.

What did the employees gain? Not a thing. They received exactly the same general increase at the end of the strike as was offered by the company before the strike. An even more tragic result of the strike was the fact that over 100 employees never returned to work when it was settled.

A strike of 56 days is not long as far as Chemical Workers' strikes go. It is a relatively short one. Enclosed is an article from the Chemical Workers own newspaper describing a strike which was then in its <u>8th month</u>.

As we said before, if the union wins here, which is unlikely, we would negotiate in good faith. However, we are always concerned about the possibility of strikes.

Consider this: Have you ever heard of a strike at a company which did not have a union? Let's not take a chance. <u>Vote NO.</u>

Sincerely,

General Manager

THE INTERNATIONAL CHEMICAL WORKER, MARCH, 1968

Local 703 Members On Strike

Copper Strike In 8th Month; Local 703 Still Pickets Plant

July 15, 1967 was a hot, dusty day in Ajo, Ariz., as the 200 members of ICWU Local 703 joined some 60,000 copper workers across the nation in striking against sub-standard working conditions.

Today, it is still hot and dusty in Ajo and Local 703 is still "hitting the bricks" as the nation's copper 'barons' continue to refuse to bargain fairly. Local 703 is on strike against the giant Phelps-Dodge Corp., one of the nation's largest producers of copper.

As the strike enters its eighth month, little progress has been made on the basic issues . . . money, seniority, job seniority and common expiration dates . . . although negotiations have begun once again.

ONE WEEK TO GO

Monday	Tuesday	Wednesday	Thursday	Friday
	*Vote Demonstration and Sample Ballot Handout		*Dinner and Speech To All Employees	Election Day
*Home Mailing		*Home Mailing		

HOME MAILING

Dear Fellow Employee:

On Friday, the National Labor Relations Board will hold
an election among our production and maintenance employees. For
the last few days a Notice of Election has been posted on your
bulletin boards. Department schedules also have been posted and
you will be reminded of your proper time to vote on the morning
of the election. We thought you might like to know a few additional
details concerning the election procedures:

1. The voting booths will be set up so as to
    insure that your vote can be cast in absolute
    secrecy. An NLRB representative will be
    present to conduct and supervise the balloting.
    In addition, there will be present at the voting
    locations two observers designated by the Union
    and two observers designated by the Company.

2. We consented to the holding of the election on
    Company premises and Company time in order to
    insure the largest possible turnout.

3. The voting procedure required that you go to the
    table at which the NLRB representative and the
    observers are sitting, give your name, take into
    the voting booth the ballot given you by the NLRB
    representative, mark it with an "X" and then
    deposit it in the ballot box.

4. The outcome of the election will be determined by
    the majority of those actually voting, and not by
    a majority of those who have a right to vote.
    For example, there are about 500 employees eligible
    to vote in the election. If only 100 of you vote,
    only 51 'yes' votes would mean the Union wins the
    right to bargain for 500 people.

5. Regardless of whether you have signed a union card -
    joined the union - or otherwise indicated your
    preference for the union - you have not committed
    yourself until you have actually marked your ballot
    and deposited it in the ballot box. You are
    completely free to vote as your conscience and
    reasoning dictate.

6. As you may have noted in looking at the NLRB's notice of election, the ballot, which will be provided by the NLRB clearly gives you two choices. You are to choose between "no" Union or the Union. You are to indicate your choice by placing an "X" in the appropriate box. THE COMPANY URGES YOU TO PLACE YOUR "X" IN THE BOX MARKED "NO."

NO

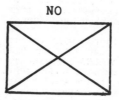

7. <u>Do Not</u> mark your ballot with a check mark. <u>Do not</u> sign your name. <u>Do not</u> place other marks on the ballot. If you do so, it may not be counted. Place your "X" squarely within the box indicating your choice. If you should accidentally spoil your ballot, ask the NLRB representative to give you another one.

8. Be sure and vote.

Sincerely yours,

General Manager

Three Days to Go

There are now only three days remaining. Employees may be thinking about the mechanics of voting. If they have never voted in an NLRB election they may be apprehensive.

Familiarity with the voting procedure will dispel any apprehension or mystery. A simulated vote demonstration is an excellent way of doing this. (See pages 158-159.) It may be presented to either one large employee group or a number of small groups. Role playing is used with employees assuming the roles of the NLRB agent, the company observers, the union observers and the voter. The company representative explains each step of the voting procedure, using the Board election notice and sample ballot.

A voting demonstration provides the employer with an opportunity to emphasize the importance of voting. An explanation of the procedure in marking the ballot minimizes the possibility of void ballots.

A voting demonstration also provides an occasion for the distribution of a sample ballot prepared by the company. It should not bear any markings, although there may be editorial material surrounding it. [Allied Elec. Prods., 109 NLRB 1270, 34 LRRM 1538 (1954).]

Communicating with employees through a vote demonstration often provides an opportunity to inject some levity at a usually tense time in the campaign.

TEXT OF "VOTE DEMONSTRATION"

I have written you several times about the vote that
will finally come about on Friday. When you arrive home
this afternoon there should be a letter from me concerning
the actual voting procedure. It summarizes what we will
be discussing at this meeting. The procedure is not very
complicated.

Now, I'd like you to join me in a little "role playing."
I need three volunteers. How about you, Joe, you, John, and
you, Mary. Mary, you act as the NLRB representative. Please
sit at the table where the sign says "NLRB." John, you be the
Company observer. Please sit where the sign says "Company
Observer." Joe, you will be the union observer. Please sit
in front of the sign stating "Union Observer." You will note
that Mary is in the middle. John and Joe are going to help
the NLRB representative to make sure that everyone who is
eligible will receive a ballot to vote. I need two more
observers who will stand by the ballot box and the voting
booth to see that everything goes okay. O.K. Now, I need
one more volunteer - Margaret, how about you? Will you please
act the part of the "voter?"

As you know, the balloting will be from 8 to 9 A.M. and
3 to 4 P.M. The NLRB representative will come in early with
a brand new ballot box. He will open it up and will demonstrate that there is nothing in it. (Hold up a cardboard box
with a slot). The Labor Board is very particular to see that
everything is honest and above board. (Start to tape the box).
First this is what he will do. He will assemble the ballot
box only after it has been examined, and before any vote is
cast so that everyone can be sure it is not stuffed.

Margaret, you are the first in line to vote. You state
your name to Mary. It will be checked against a list of those
eligible to vote. This has been prepared by the Company from
its payroll. Now Margaret will be given a ballot (hold up
sample ballot taken from the election notice) - just like this
ballot. This is marked "sample." The ballot you get on Friday
will be about this size but probably a different color.

The real observers will receive instructions from the Labor
Board man on Friday. They may raise questions about whether
someone seeking to vote is an employee or is eligible to vote.
That person nevertheless will get a ballot and will vote under
challenge. The challenged ballot is voted in secret like the
other ballots, but it is first put into an envelope. The
envelope is sealed, and then it is put into the ballot box.
Then, after the election, if there are enough challenged
ballots to change the results, the challenges to these ballots
are either withdrawn or the Labor Board decides whether the
person should have voted.

I want to emphasize one very important point about marking the ballot. (Show sample ballot). If you want the union, mark an "X" in the left box; if you do <u>not</u> want a union, mark an "X" in the right box, marked "No." (Demonstrate by pointing to the sample ballot).

Do not put any mark on the ballot, except an "X". If you do, it may be disqualified and thrown out. Don't write "hell no" for example - if you don't want the union, as one employee did in an election. Just put an "X", in the NO box. If your vote is not counted, it would be the same as not voting. Let me explain that. There are about 500 employees eligible to vote. If only 100 vote, 51 votes will decide for everybody. So please vote. If you make a mistake or have any questions about voting ask the NLRB man. He will help you.

You will see that we have constructed a booth with a drop cloth curtain and a shelf. We will probably use this actual booth in the election, although sometimes the Labor Board representative will bring along a portable one. We will have a pencil in the booth. Now, take the ballot into the booth. Go ahead Margaret, no one is in there.

After you mark the ballot in the booth, you fold the ballot over just once, with the "X" marked on the inside. Don't curl it into a little ball. Just fold it over once; come out now - and put it into the ballot box. Margaret - where are you? You can come out now, Margaret!

As you can see, your vote is a secret one and known only to you. Don't let anyone tell you otherwise. The polls are closed at 4 P.M. Then the ballot box will be opened. You can come back down here if you like. The ballots will be taken out by the NLRB representative and counted. The results will be known right then and there.

We have prepared a sample ballot for you to keep. It is exactly like the one on the Notice of Election - in fact, it is a reproduction of it. Look it over. If you have any questions, please feel free to ask your supervisor or come directly to me.

Well folks that's it. See you at the dinner tomorrow night. How about a big hand for our volunteers.

TUESDAY

HANDOUT

BE SURE TO VOTE

DATE: January 29th

TIME: 8-9 AM; 3-4 PM

PLACE: Stockroom

UNITED STATES OF AMERICA
National Labor Relations Board
OFFICIAL SECRET BALLOT

SAMPLE

FOR CERTAIN EMPLOYEES OF

Do you wish to be represented for purposes of collective bargaining by -

MARK AN "X" IN THE SQUARE OF YOUR CHOICE

YES	NO
☐	☐

DO NOT SIGN THIS BALLOT. Fold and drop in ballot box.
If you spoil this ballot return it to the Board Agent for a new one.

YOUR X IN THIS
SQUARE WILL MEAN
YOU DO NOT WANT
THIS UNION

HOME MAILING

<u>WEDNESDAY</u>

Dear Fellow Employee:

As you know, on Friday an election will be held to determine whether or not you wish to be represented by the Union.

The basic issue you will be voting on is a choice between continuing to work under the philosphy and policies which have been our cornerstone over the years, or abandoning it and substituting instead the unknown policies of outside union officials.

We believe that an employee, regardless of job, deserves to be treated with dignity and respect. We also believe in fair wages for every employee. In addition, we believe that all employees should share in the profits of the company. Operating under this philosophy we pay better than average wages and have a generous profit-sharing plan.

We further believe that an employee is entitled to peace of mind with regard to his family's needs in the event of misfortune. And we believe that an employee should have adequate time off to enjoy a fuller life. Consequently, we provide a liberal fringe benefit program that includes hospital and surgical coverage, group life insurance, pensions, profit sharing, paid holidays, and extended vacations.

We sincerely hope you will reject this bid by the Union for your membership - and your dues. We respectfully ask for your support. Ours has been a sincere effort over the years to make your company the finest possible place to work. We will continue our efforts. You can help us - and help yourself - by voting NO.

Sincerely,

General Manager

SPEECH TO ALL EMPLOYEES

<u>THURSDAY</u>

I hope you have had a pleasant dinner. Now I would like
to speak to you about a serious matter - The election tomorrow.

The question you will have to decide for yourself is
whether you are better off with or without a union. Please do
not let anyone else make this decision for you. It is one of the
most important decisions you will ever have to make.

I truly believe that each person is an individual and
wants to be treated as an individual and not as one of the crowd.
We have tried to develop a feeling of informal atmosphere, to
have the kind of plant where people enjoy coming to work every day.

I am concerned that a Union in this plant would change
all this. Instead of cooperation, there would be bickering and dis-
harmony. Many union plants become a battleground, an armed camp
with everyone suspicious of everyone else and there is a loss of a
spirit of cooperation.

We have provided you with information about the union
so you may make a better decision. We sent you facts concerning its
constitution. We told you about its fines and assessments. We
reported on a few of its lengthy strikes. But we only touched
the surface.

The Union has made many promises using a prepared
"Sales Talk". It is the same in every plant. The Union always
says that they can get better benefits, better working conditions,
and higher wages if you will only vote for them. This is only
propaganda.

Compare our record. We promised an improved hospital
plan and we delivered. We promised an additional holiday and
we delivered. We promised an improved wage schedule and we
delivered. When we promise something we deliver, because we have
the means to do so. The Union does not.

I don't want to take up your time this evening with a
long after dinner speech. You know how I feel. I have confidence
in your good judgment. Have a pleasant evening. Thank You.

CHAPTER VIII

ELECTION DAY AND AFTER

The day of the election has finally arrived. It is not a day for campaigning. Everything that could be said has been said.

PRE-ELECTION CONFERENCE

The Board representative will have scheduled a pre-election conference, immediately before the election. He appears at the company premises at the appointed time. The union representatives also appear at the same time. Arrangements should be made for their arrival so they may be escorted to the location of the conference. Otherwise, they may be inclined to wander through the plant. The conference is held either in an office, conference room, or the polling area.

Ordinarily it is agreed in advance that each side will have one or two observers to assist in the balloting. The Board representative requests that the observers be called; he will then instruct them in their duties. Written instructions for observers will have been previously sent along with forms for their designation.

Now the list of eligible employees is reviewed. It is the same list previously mailed to the Board for the union's use pursuant to the *Excelsior* decision. If the union had reason to believe that the list was incomplete, it will have raised this objection when it first received the list from the Board. If the matter was not then resolved, the union may wish to renew its objection at this time.

Employees who have resigned or have been discharged are not permitted to vote. Their names are stricken from the list. If, however, a person claims that he has been discharged because of his union activities, he will be given a ballot. He will then vote, but his ballot will be challenged by the Board agent or the employer-observer. To vote under these circumstances, it is not necessary for the discharged employee to have previously filed an unfair labor practice charge.[1]

Employees engaged in an economic strike are eligible to vote, provided the election is conducted within twelve months after the commencement of the strike.[2]

The Board representative will inspect the voting area. Some regional offices provide portable aluminum booths with drop cloth attached. In other instances, the employer cooperates by erecting sufficient booths to accommodate the number of employees voting. The Board provides the ballot box. The Board agent will construct the ballot box from its collapsed form and will secure all the edges after exhibiting it to the observers.

It is now a few minutes before the opening of the polls. All but the observers are asked to leave. Neither managerial nor supervisory personnel or union representatives may remain in or near the voting area,[3] nor may they act as observers.[4]

CONDUCTING THE ELECTION

If a person appears to vote whose name is not on the list of eligible voters or who is unknown, he will be challenged either by an observer or by the Board representative. Names are sometimes challenged, despite their appearance on the list. For example, an employee may be challenged if a union observer claims that he is a supervisor.

Challenged voters will receive a ballot and an envelope into which it is placed. The envelope contains a perforated stub. The Board agent writes on the stub the name of the voter, the reason for the challenge, and the party challenging. The voter then places the envelope, with ballot inside, in the ballot box along with the other ballots.

The polls remain open until the hour set for closing since, usually, there are some people who show up at the last minute if they show up at all. When the closing time arrives the observers are asked to sign a "Certification on Conduct of Election." (See Facsimile No. 26, page 166.) The parties thereby certify that the balloting was conducted fairly, that all eligible voters were given an opportunity to cast their ballots in secret, and that the ballot box was protected in the interest of a fair and secret vote.

One caution: the Board agent is instructed to obtain the signatures of the observers attesting to the fair conduct of the election upon the closing of the polls. This usually is done before counsel has had an opportunity to consult with the employer observers to ascertain whether there were any improprieties. Therefore, counsel may instruct the company observers in advance not to sign until he returns to the voting area. In this way, the observer can advise him if anything happened during the voting. Counsel can then evaluate whether anything untoward occurred. For example, there may have been disturbances in the voting area,[5] prolonged conversations between union observers and voters,[6] or, a failure of the Board representative to seal the ballot box.[7] The observer's certification that the election was conducted fairly could preclude the raising of such objections.

After the polls are closed, the Board representative will empty the ballot box in the presence of the observers and all others attending. There are no prohibitions on those who may attend. The principals of the parties, of course, are present.

FACSIMILE No. 26

UNITED STATES OF AMERICA
NATIONAL LABOR RELATIONS BOARD

CERTIFICATION ON CONDUCT OF ELECTION

Name of employer .... Case No. ....

Date of election .... Place ....

    The undersigned acted as agents of the Regional Director and as authorized observers, respectively, in the conduct of the balloting at the above time and place.

    WE HEREBY CERTIFY that such balloting was fairly conducted, that all eligible voters were given an opportunity to vote their ballots in secret, and that the ballot box was protected in the interest of a fair and secret vote.

For   For the Regional Director,   Region

_____   _____

_____   _____

_____   _____

_____   _____

For   For

_____   _____

_____   _____

_____   _____

_____   _____

COUNTING THE BALLOTS

There is now high tension in the air. During the past four weeks, the union and company have engaged in intensive campaigning. Now they are face to face. Will the efforts have been in vain? One side must lose. Notwithstanding one's earlier confidence, there can never be certainty until the ballots are counted.

Then, one by one, the ballots are opened. "YES—NO—YES—NO—NO—NO," and so on. The observers will keep their count on forms supplied by the Board. The roles are reversed, with the union observer counting the "NO" votes and the company observer counting the "YES" votes. The observers are instructed to advise the Board agent when a total of 50 is reached in the ballots being counted.

Finally, there are no ballots remaining to be opened. A sigh of relief sometimes is heard. The results are announced. Smiles appear on some faces, frowns on others. The election is over.

The total "YES" and "NO" votes are then summarized on a tally of ballots form. (See Facsimile No. 27, page 168.) The number of eligible voters is listed, although this figure is not significant because it is a majority of those who vote that counts. The number of votes cast for and against the union is entered. (Note that the sixth item of Facsimile No. 27, page 168, does *not* read votes cast *for* the employer!) The number of challenged ballots is counted and entered. These figures should equal the total number of names checked off the eligibility list by the observers.

If the challenged ballots are not sufficient in number to affect the outcome, they are not the subject of any determination and are later destroyed. If they are sufficient in number to affect the outcome, the Board representative will attempt to obtain agreement of the parties to open the ballots or to withdraw the challenges. If this fails, formal Board procedures come into play.[8]

FACSIMILE No. 27

UNITED STATES OF AMERICA

NATIONAL LABOR RELATIONS BOARD

Case No. ....

Date issued ....

Type of election (Check one):

☐ Consent Agreement

☐ Stipulation

☐ Board Direction

☐ RD Direction

☐ 8(b)(7)

TALLY OF BALLOTS

The undersigned agent of the Regional Director certifies that the results of the tabulation of ballots cast in the election held in the above case, and concluded on the date indicated above, were as follows:

1. Approximate number of eligible voters............................ _____

2. Void ballots.. _____

3. Votes cast for .... _____

4. Votes cast for .... _____

5. Votes cast for .... _____

6. Votes cast against participating labor organization(s)............................ _____

7. Valid votes counted (sum of 3, 4, 5, and 6)..................................... _____

8. Challenged ballots .... _____

9. Valid votes counted plus challenged ballots (sum of 7 and 8)................ _____

10. Challenges are (not) sufficient in number to affect the results of the election.

11. A majority of the valid votes counted plus challenged ballots (Item 9) has (not) been cast for:

....

For the Regional Director

....

The undersigned acted as authorized observers in the counting and tabulating of ballots indicated above. We hereby certify that the counting and tabulating were fairly and accurately done, that the secrecy of the ballots was maintained, and that the results were as indicated above. We also acknowledge service of this tally.

For   For

....

....

....

For   For

....

....

....

If the vote is a tie and there are no challenges, Item 11 of the tally of ballots will state that a majority of valid votes has *not* been cast for the union. In other words, a tie vote represents a victory for the employer. If there are challenges and, after they are resolved, the vote is a tie, the employer again has prevailed. After the Board agent has completed filling out the tally of ballots form, the observers are asked to sign it. Usually there is no reason for their not doing so.

Once the tally of ballots has been signed, the election is over. The Board representative reassembles the voting booth, picks up the empty box, collects his papers and ballots and leaves. The union and employer representatives shake hands. The union representative often is an old hand at his business. He has won and lost many elections. He usually will not express any words of bitterness at having lost. He may part with the words, sometimes half muttered: "See you next year," or "You'll be hearing from us." Sometimes, from his reaction, counsel may discern whether he intends to file objections.

TWO-UNION CONTEST

We have assumed that the employer is faced with organizing by one union. On occasion, there are two unions contending for representation rights. The proceedings involved in arranging for an election are the same, except for the placement of the two unions on the ballot. Usually, the unions agree on the ballot placement; sometimes, however, it is decided by a flip of a coin.[9] The "neither" designation is in the center position. When faced with two unions, the employer may express a preference between them, or for neither of them in his employee communications.[10]

In a two union election, if none of the three choices receives a majority of the votes cast, a second election must be held. This is called a runoff election. The two choices receiving the largest and second largest number of votes participate in the runoff election. Thus, the vote may be between the two unions, or may be for or against one of the unions. Only one such runoff election may be held.[11]

The procedures involved in the holding of the runoff election are similar to that of the original election. This time, of course, there is no "neither" choice. There is one anomaly. It may occur in a two-union runoff. Should each of the two unions receive the same number of votes, neither will have won.[12] The result is the same as if a majority of employees had voted against representation.

OBJECTIONS AND CHALLENGED BALLOTS

There are two types of objections. A party may file objections either to "the conduct of the election," or to "conduct affecting the results of the election."

Let us assume that the Board representative permitted electioneering in the voting area. This supports an objection to the *conduct of the election.* Let us assume also that the employer distributed a facsimile ballot with an "X" marked in the "NO" box. That supports an objection to *conduct affecting the results of the election.*

Within five days after the tally of ballots has been furnished to the parties by the regional director, objections to the conduct of the election or to conduct affecting the results of the election may be filed by any of the parties.[13] The objections must be in writing and supported by a short statement of the reasons therefor. The five day time limit is strictly applied and must be observed even though there are enough challenged ballots outstanding to affect the numerical results of the vote.[14] If objections are not filed with the regional director by the close of business on the fifth day (Saturdays and Sundays are not counted [15]), a later attempt to file them will be unavailing.[16]

If no objections are filed within the five day period, and if ballots which may have been challenged are insufficient in number to affect the results, the regional director will issue one of two types of certification. If the union has won the election, he will mail a certification of representative to the parties. (See Facsimile No. 28, page 172.) If the union has lost the election, he mails a certification of the results. (See Facsimile No. 29, page 173.) The proceeding is thereupon closed.[17]

Where objections are filed, the regional director will notify the other party. (See Facsimile No. 30, page 174.) However, the party filing the objections is responsible for serving a copy on the other party. The Board rule requires that this be done immediately. The party whose conduct is objected to is requested to advise the regional director of his answer to the objections.

Certain employer conduct will automatically void an election, if a timely objection is filed. Examples are distributing a marked ballot, as described above;[18] speaking to a massed assembly of employees on working time and on the premises, within 24 hours prior to the opening of the polls;[19] electioneering within the polling area;[20] and, failing to submit the *Excelsior* list.[21] It should be noted that these transgressions are not unfair labor practices.

An unfair labor practice alleged in the form of an objection, may be the basis for upsetting an election when the conduct complained of occurred between the time the petition was filed and the date the election was held.[22] However, not every unfair labor practice will void an election. The Board may decide that the conduct, although technically unlawful, was not of sufficient gravity to influence employee votes.[23] In evaluating employer conduct, the Board is guided by Section 8(c) of the Act. Conduct not constituting either threats or promises will not cause an election to be set aside,[24] absent some other basis such as a gross misrepresentation of a substantial matter.[25]

FACSIMILE No. 28

RC-RM-RD

UNITED STATES OF AMERICA
NATIONAL LABOR RELATIONS BOARD

Type of Election

☐ CONSENT AGREEMENT
☐ STIPULATION
☐ BOARD DIRECTION
☐ RD DIRECTION
☐ 8 (b) (7)

Case No.

CERTIFICATION OF REPRESENTATIVE

An election having been conducted in the above matter by the undersigned Regional Director of the National Labor Relations Board in accordance with the Rules and Regulations of the Board; and it appearing from the Tally of Ballots that a collective bargaining representative has been selected; and no objections having been filed to the Tally of Ballots furnished to the parties, or to the conduct of the election, within the time provided therefor;

Pursuant to authority vested in the undersigned by the National Labor Relations Board, IT IS HEREBY CERTIFIED that

has been designated and selected by a majority of the employees of the above-named Employer, in the unit described below, as their representative for the purposes of collective bargaining, and that, pursuant to Section 9 (a) of the Act as amended, the said organization is the exclusive representative of all the employees in such unit for the purposes of collective bargaining with respect to rates of pay, wages, hours of employment, and other conditions of employment.

UNIT:

Signed at
On the   day of   19

On behalf of

NATIONAL LABOR RELATIONS BOARD

_____
Regional Director for   Region
National Labor Relations Board

FACSIMILE No. 29

RC-RM-RD

UNITED STATES OF AMERICA

NATIONAL LABOR RELATIONS BOARD

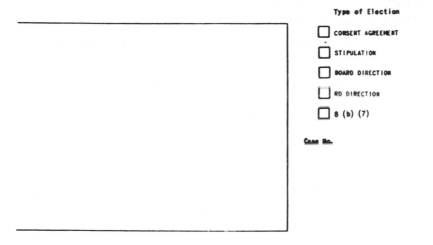

Type of Election

- [ ] CONSENT AGREEMENT
- [ ] STIPULATION
- [ ] BOARD DIRECTION
- [ ] RD DIRECTION
- [ ] 8 (b) (7)

Case No.

CERTIFICATION OF RESULTS OF ELECTION

An election having been conducted in the above matter by the undersigned Regional Director of the National Labor Relations Board in accordance with the Rules and Regulations of the Board; and it appearing from the Tally of Ballots that no collective bargaining representative has been selected; and no objections having been filed to the Tally of Ballots furnished to the parties, or to the conduct of the election, within the time provided therefor;

Pursuant to authority vested in the undersigned by the National Labor Relations Board,

IT IS HEREBY CERTIFIED that a majority of the valid ballots has not been cast for any labor organization appearing on the ballot, and that no such organization is the exclusive representative of all the employees, in the unit herein involved, within the meaning of Section 9(a) of the National Labor Relations Act.

Signed at
On the   day of   , 19

_____   _____
Regional Director for   Region
National Labor Relations Board

FACSIMILE No. 30

NATIONAL LABOR RELATIONS BOARD

REGION 29

16 Court Street

Brooklyn, New York 11201

Telephone -- 596-3535

Re:

Case No.

Gentlemen:

Objections have been filed to the election in the above matter. Under the Board's Rules and Regulations, the party filing the objections is required to serve a copy on you.

Five days after receipt of this letter you are requested to furnish this office with a statement setting forth your answer and particulars concerning each of the items enumerated in the objections.

Very truly yours,

Samuel M. Kaynard
Regional Director

Studies of Voting Behavior

The Board has set aside thousands of elections based upon its determination that certain conduct coerced voters. Yet, the question of what influences employees in how they vote has never been examined scientifically.[26]

Two law professors, recognizing this deficiency, have undertaken such a study. Since they planned to interview employees who had voted in NLRB elections, they requested the NLRB to furnish them with *Excelsior* lists of names and addresses of employees in 35 elections.[27] The Board refused and the professors brought an action under the Freedom of Information Act.

In ordering the Board to provide the lists, the U.S. Court of Appeals for the District of Columbia observed that the Board "in over 30 years has itself never engaged in the kind of much needed systematic empirical effort to determine the dynamics of an election campaign or the type of conduct which actually has a coercive impact."[28] It is not clear, however, notwithstanding the court's comment, that the Board has the statutory authority to engage in such studies.

If the number of challenged ballots may affect the outcome of the election, the regional director notifies the parties. (See Facsimile No. 31, page 176.) He attaches to the notice a list of names of the individuals challenged, their job titles, by whom challenged, and the reason for the challenge.

The party making the challenge is given five days within which to supply substantiating evidence. The other party is asked to state its position within the same time limits and to submit factual support.

INVESTIGATIVE PROCEDURE

Let us consider the situation where an election is held pursuant to a decision and direction of election after a representa-

FACSIMILE No. 31

NATIONAL LABOR RELATIONS BOARD
REGION _____

                                       Date

                                       Telephone --

                Re:

                Case No.

Gentlemen:

      In the recent election conducted in the above matter, the challenged ballots cast affect the outcome of the election. Attached hereto is a list of the names of individuals challenged, their job titles, by whom challenged, and the reason for the challenge.

      The party having made the challenge is requested, within five days from the receipt of this letter, to supply supporting evidence substantiating the basis for the challenge. Other parties in interest are requested, within the same period of time, to state their positions with respect to the eligibility or ineligibility of the challenged voters, and in addition to submit factual information or evidence bearing on the reason for the challenge.

      Please note the following contingencies and be guided accordingly.

        (1)   Where the challenged voter's name was not included on the eligibility list, the Employer is requested to supply the basis for the failure to include the name on the list.

        (2)   Where a challenge has been made by the Board for any reason other than the absence of the voter's name from the list, all parties are requested to submit, within the same period of time, their positions with respect to the challenge.

Your prompt cooperation will expedite the disposition of this matter

                          Very truly yours,

                          Regional Director

tion hearing. The regional director investigates the challenges and/or objections. During the course of his investigation he discovers other improper conduct which was not included within the objections. He has the discretion to set the election aside on this conduct alone.[29] He may do so on the basis of an administrative investigation without holding a formal hearing.[30] However, if he believes that substantial and material issues exist which can be resolved only after a hearing, he will notice the issues for hearing before a hearing officer. The hearing may include both challenges and objections.[31]

The hearing officer in these proceedings may be directed by the regional director to prepare a report to resolve the issues of credibility and to make findings of fact and recommendations as to the disposition of the issues.[32] (This is in contrast to the initial hearing on unit determination where the hearing officer may not make recommendations.)

The parties may file exceptions, with a supporting brief, to the hearing officer's report. If no exceptions are filed, the regional director decides the matter forthwith.[33] If exceptions are filed, the regional director will decide the matter upon the entire record as developed at the hearing.[34] An aggrieved party may then request Board review in Washington.[35] The criteria for doing so is the same as in a request for review of the regional director's decision in the basic representation proceeding. (See Chapter VI, page 118.)

If the regional director or the Board in Washington rules that some or all of the challenges were not valid, the ballots will be counted. The identifying stubs are removed. The envelopes are shuffled in order to eliminate any possibility of identifying the voter.[36] (Of course, if there is only one challenged ballot to be opened, the secrecy is destroyed.) They are then opened and counted. A revised tally is issued and the results are certified, provided there are no objections pending.

Where objections are pending, the results will not be certified until they are resolved. Determinations of challenges and objections are made simultaneously in the usual case.

GRANTING BENEFITS

The period between the filing of objections and their final resolution often is more difficult for an employer than during the preceding period. From the time the petition was filed up to the election, his employees could understand a moratorium on wage increases or benefits. They could accept the fact that any wage increase or improvement in benefits would be looked upon by the government as a bribe. But now the election is over, why the holdup? Time slips by after the indeterminate election. The pressure on the employer to do something increases.

What is he to do? There is a possible second election coming. If he grants benefits, he may be interfering with it. If he does not, he also may be charged with interfering with it.

The law on this subject should be carefully reviewed before counselling the employer. We state here only general rules, derived from a potpourri of cases. There are variations and exceptions, depending upon the particular factual circumstances. It should first be noted that even though the balloting is over, the representation proceeding is still pending. The Board has stated:

> An election under Board auspices to determine a majority bargaining representative does not consist solely of the physical balloting of the employees in the appropriate unit. Necessarily, the vote of the employees and the validity of the election itself must await the Board's post election investigation of objections. . . .[37]

The rules concerning the granting or withholding of benefits at this time are the same as when the first election was pending. An employer should proceed as he generally acted before a union entered the picture. The Act is violated when an employer confers or withholds benefits, if it can be established that his course of action is prompted by the union's presence.[38]

An example of the Board's application of this rule involved a company engaged in mining and distributing industrial sands. It had lost an election in one of its plants. It had been its custom to grant increases to the employees of its unorganized plant shortly after it negotiated an increase with a union at one of its other plants. After the election, the employer filed objections and, while they were pending, gave the employees their anticipated increase. The Board held that the increase was given to influence the employees' vote in the event the employer's objections resulted in a rerun election. The Board relied upon the Trial Examiner's finding that a local newspaper and radio station carried stories announcing the increase. The Board held that the increase was unlawful.[39]

WITHHOLDING BENEFITS

Similarly, the withholding of a customary wage increase because of the pendency of an election may be unlawful. A rubber manufacturer had always accorded its unrepresented print shop employees the same annual wage increase which it negotiated with the union representing its production employees. In 1969, however, it withheld the increase until after the election among the unrepresented employees in order to avoid an appearance of attempting to influence the election. The employer indicated that "the increase was being withheld . . . temporarily pending the election in order to avoid an appearance of an attempt to influence the election." [40]

The Board set aside the election, stating:

> . . . neutrality is not maintained by an announced withholding of a wage increase because of a pending

Board-conducted election. It is well settled that the employer's legal duty is to proceed as he would have done had the union not been on the scene.[41]

Thus it can be seen that the granting or withholding of benefits, while an election or certification of results is pending, although not unlawful *per se* [42] does involve serious risks, calling for the best advice counsel can give. If the employer grants benefits, he must be careful that his action may not be held to be union-related either by word or conduct. Similarly, if he withholds benefits he should not relate his conduct to the pending election. With the union looking over his shoulder, an employer must be prepared to defend whichever course he takes. With competent advice and a blend of caution and courage, ultimate success will be achieved.

RERUN ELECTIONS

When the regional director or the Board "sets aside" an election, there will be a second or rerun election. Statistics reveal that in most instances a rerun election is won by the original winner.[43]

The same processes are followed in a rerun election. A conference is held as to the time and place.

New notices are posted. Again, the parties appeal to the electorate for their vote. This time, however, there is an additional issue—the fact that the employer or the union has engaged in conduct which caused the Board to void the first election.

Where the election is set aside, based upon the union's objections, the union will seek to make capital of the employer's transgression. The employer may rejoin by pointing out that notwithstanding the union's objections, a majority of the employees did express themselves against union representation. He may call the union a "sore loser." He may express the reasons why the employees should again reject the union. He, of course, avoids repeating the conduct which gave rise to the union's valid objections.

Conversely, if the union has won the election, and it is set aside on the employer's objections, the employer has his second chance. He may decide to dramatize the union's improper conduct which led to the new election. He redoubles his efforts.

IF THE UNION WINS

Suppose the unlikely happens. Nothwithstanding the employer's efforts, the union wins the contest. It is certified as the collective bargaining agent. What should be the employer's course of action?

Of course he feels let down, but that should not lead to scorn, retribution, or hatred. His conduct during the contest has schooled him. He is still the pilot of his company, even though he will have to deal with shop stewards.

The first action the employer should take is to write his employees, formally acknowledging the outcome of the election, and stating what the future holds. Then he must study his obligations in bargaining. Where and when shall he meet with the union? How shall he conduct himself? Should he be a participant? Should counsel sit with him at the bargaining table? Shall he counterpropose? Shall he resist the check-off of dues? May he assert as a principle that he does not wish to compel anyone to join any organization?

He enters a new world of maneuver, semantics and forensic combat. He must resist the temptation to yield on things that "cost no money." He will make the best possible deal. That does not mean giving the least in wage grants. It *does mean* retaining managerial control and discipline and the right to uninterrupted work.

The union is now the representative of the employees. The employer may not bargain with them in groups or individually in derogation of the rights given the union by law. However, he can still meet and communicate with them, without intervention of the union, providing he does not negotiate or adjust grievances.[44]

The making of a contract and living with it is the subject for another book. What the authors do urge is that the same effort that was put into the election be put into winning the peace. Having opened up the gates of communication, the employer should keep them open. He should strive to keep the good will of his employees. He should keep them informed of company plans and the progress of his negotiations with the union. He should not abandon the relationship he has built. There may come a day when he may need his employees' support.

It is said that an employer who has a union has a partner in his business. His halcyon days are over. Every year or two, there will be demands and crises. With some unions, there will be no further contact until the next round of negotiations. With others, the turmoil will be constant. Grievances and confrontation will be his daily diet.

In the overwhelming majority of cases, this will be his last election. He will learn to live with his union, as do the employers of some 19 million employees.

IF THE UNION LOSES

If the employer has done his utmost, it is likely that the union will not obtain a majority of the votes. The employer will be wrapped in the glow of victory. Many employers write letters to their employees to express their appreciation. (See Facsimile No. 32, page 183.)

FACSIMILE No. 32

Dear Fellow Employee:

The NLRB election is over, and a majority of you decided against the union. I want to thank you sincerely for your support. We interpret the result as a strong mandate for the continuance of the policies which have made our company such a fine place to work in.

With this election behind us, let's look to the future. Our mutual goals must be high: high morale, high efficiency, high co-operation and high quality. By working together our company can grow and furnish better jobs for all of us, and greater rewards to our families.

Thanks again for your support. You may be assured we will make every effort to justify it.

Sincerely,

General Manager

Improved benefits and wage increases may now be granted, preferably if they meet some past time table or other rationale. On occasion, the precipitous grant of wage increases and improved benefits (even after the certification of results) has been held unlawful as fulfillment of promises made during the contest.[45] Careful study, however, should yield a viable formula to quench the employees' drought.

Now that the election is over, the employer feels safe for a year. He has been told there may not be another election for twelve months.[46] The union, he surmises, has folded its tent and has walked away—forever, he hopes.

The twelve month rule does not give complete insulation. If the defeated union or some other labor organization signs up a majority of the employees, it is not barred from action under the Act.[47] The union may charge the employer with a refusal to bargain. If the union can meet the *Gissel* criteria, it may be well on the way toward an order to bargain.

An employer should not be lulled into a false sense of security. Twelve months move by quickly. Employees do not easily forget the campaign assertions. The union, too, will not forget. It will hover over the plant, ready to exploit the employer's mistakes.

The employer's vigilance must be perpetual. He was awakened from his lethargy, and has prevailed. For that he should be grateful, but he must continue to communicate. The talks, the explanations, the group meetings, the home mailings, and the supervisory program must not be laid aside.

Conclusion

We have suggested in this book steps toward a wholesome employee relationship. Although we have not mentioned the golden rule, what has been outlined is its most important ingredient. Give employees guidance and trust, and they will trust you. Speak to them and they will speak to you. Listen to them and they will listen to you. Follow these precepts and there need never be another contest.

NOTES TO CHAPTER VIII

1. Alabaster Lime Co., 190 NLRB No. 113, 77 LRRM 1200 (1971).

2. LMRA § 101.9(c)(3), 29 U.S.C. § 159(c)(3) (1964).

3. NLRB Field Manual § 11318.3. *See also,* Star Expansion Indus. Corp., 170 NLRB No. 47, 67 LRRM 1400 (1968); Milchem, Inc., 170 NLRB No. 46, 67 LRRM 1395 (1968).

4. Worth Food Mkt. Stores, Inc., 103 NLRB 259, 31 LRRM 1527 (1953).

5. Diamond State Poultry Co., 107 NLRB 3, 33 LRRM 1043 (1953).

6. Milchem, Inc., *supra* note 3.

7. Austill Waxed Paper Co., 169 NLRB 1109, 67 LRRM 1366 (1968); Tidelands Marine Servs., 116 NLRB 1222, 38 LRRM 1444 (1956).

8. NLRB Rules & Regulations § 102.69, 29 C.F.R. § 102.69 (1971).

9. NLRB Field Manual § 11306.4.

10. Stewart Warner Corp., 102 NLRB 1153, 31 LRRM 1396 (1953).

11. NLRB Rules & Regulations § 102.70(a), 29 C.F.R. § 102.70(a) (1971).

12. *Id.* at § 102.70(d), 29 C.F.R. § 102.70(d) (1971).

13. *Id.* at § 102.69(a), 29 C.F.R. § 102.69(a) (1971).

14. *Id.*

15. *Id. at* § 102.114, 29 C.F.R. § 102.114 (1971).

16. Van Tran Elec. Corp. v. NLRB, __ F.2d __, 78 LRRM 2575 (6th Cir., No. 71-1054, decided Oct. 18, 1971), *enforcing* 187 NLRB No. 89, 76 LRRM 1148 (1970); Wilson-Sinclair Co., 191 NLRB No. 62, 77 LRRM 1438 (1971).

17. NLRB Rules & Regulations § 102.69(b), 29 C.F.R. § 102.69(b) (1971).

18. Allied Elec. Prods., 109 NLRB 1270, 34 LRRM 1538 (1964). *But see,* Vernon Convalescent Center Co., 194 NLRB No. 67, 78 LRRM 1673 (1971); Rett Electronics, Inc., 169 NLRB 1111, 67 LRRM 1461 (1968).

19. Peerless Plywood Co., 107 NLRB 427, 33 LRRM 1151 (1953).

20. Milchem, Inc., *supra* note 3.

21. Ponce Television Corp., 192 NLRB No. 20, 77 LRRM 1622 (1971).

22. Goodyear Tire & Rubber Co., 138 NLRB 453, 51 LRRM 1070 (1962); Idea Elec. & Mfg. Co., 134 NLRB 1275, 49 LRRM 1316 (1961).

23. Tennessee Handbags, Inc., 179 NLRB No. 161, 82 LRRM 1576 (1969); West Texas Equip. Co., 142 NLRB 1538, 53 LRRM 1249 (1963). *Cf.* Kutsher's Country Club Corp., 192 NLRB No. 154, 78 LRRM 1104 (1971), where the Board noted that "the criteria applied in determining whether certain conduct interfered with an election are not identical to the criteria applied in determining whether an unfair labor practice has been committed." 78 LRRM 1104 at n. 2.

24. Bostitch Div. of Textron, Inc., 176 NLRB No. 47, 71 LRRM 1241 (1969). Board affirms Trial Examiner's decision certifying results of election. The Trial Examiner held that employer's speech and letters were protected by Section 8(c). Board decision contains full text of both speech and letters.

25. Hollywood Ceramics Co., 140 NLRB 221, 51 LRRM 1600 (1962).

26. See Appendix E: Lewis, *Gissel Packing: Was The Supreme Court Right?*, 56 A.B.A.J. 877 (1970), and authorities cited therein. *See also,* Samoff, *NLRB Elections: Uncertainty and Certainty,* 117 U. Pa. L. Rev. 228, 251 (1968): "No one can say with any assurance what impels workers to vote one way or another." It would appear that the only study ever made as to the factors influencing employee choice in a Board election involved employees in a single election at one retail store. Brotslaw, *Attitude of Retail Workers Toward Union Organization,* 18 Lab. L. J. 149 (1967).

27. Goldberg & Getman, *Voting Behavior In NLRB Elections: Preliminary Observations On An Empirical Study,* 23 NYU Conf. on Labor 115 (1970).

28. Getman v. NLRB, __ F.2d __, 78 LRRM 2101, 2105 (D.C. Cir., No. 71-1097, decided August 31, 1971), *affirming* __ F.Supp. __, 77 LRRM 3063 (D.D.C. No. 2349-70, decided January 21, 1971), *application for stay denied,* __ U.S. __, 78 LRRM 2100 (No. A-109, decided July 27, 1971).

29. Pure Chem Corp., 192 NLRB No. 88, 77 LRRM 1925 (1971).

30. NLRB Rules & Regulations § 102.69(c), 29 C.F.R. § 102.69(c) (1971).

31. *Id.*

32. *Id.* at § 102.69(d), 29 C.F.R. § 102.69(d) (1971).

33. *Id.*

34. *Id.* at §§ 102.69(c) & (d), 29 C.F.R. §§ 102.69(c) & (d) (1971).

35. *Id.* at § 102.69(c), 29 C.F.R. 102.69(c) (1971).

36. NLRB Field Manual § 11378.

37. Ralph Printing & Lithographing Co., 158 NLRB 1353, 1354 n. 3, 62 LRRM 1233 (1966), *modified on other grounds,* 379 F.2d 687 (8th Cir. 1967). Announcement of benefits the day after the election, but prior to the date the union filed objections, held unlawful.

38. Great Atlantic & Pacific Tea Co., 166 NLRB 27, 29 n. 1, 65 LRRM 1489 (1967).

39. Pennsylvania Glass Sand Corp., 172 NLRB No. 54, 70 LRRM 1281 (1968), *enf'd sub nom.,* Teamsters Local 992 v. NLRB, 427 F.2d 582 (D.C. Cir. 1970).

40. Gates Rubber Co., 182 NLRRB No. 15, 74 LRRM 1049 (1970).

41. *Id.* at 74 LRRM 1049. *Cf.* Uarco, Inc., 169 NLRB 1153, 67 LRRM 1341 (1968).

42. Gen. Indus. Electronics Co., 152 NLRB 1029, 59 LRRM 1238 (1965); Champion Pneumatic Mach. Co., 152 NLRB 300, 59 LRRM 1089 (1965).

43. NLRB v. Gissel Packing Co., 395 U.S. 575, 611 n. 30 (1969).

44. Ingraham Indus., 178 NLRB No. 89, 72 LRRM 1248 (1969). *Cf.* LMRA § 101.9(a), 29 U.S.C. § 159(a) (1964). In *Barberton Citizens Hosp. Co.,* 57 LA 604 (1971), the arbitrator held that the hospital did not violate its contract with the union by establishing an employee communication committee since it was not used as a substitute for the union's grievance machinery.

45. Shelby Mfg. Co., 155 NLRB 464, 473, 60 LRRM 1345 (1965), *modified on other grounds,* 390 F.2d 595 (6th Cir. 1968); Northwest Eng'r Co., 148 NLRB 1136, 1145, 57 LRRM 1116 (1964), *amended on other grounds,* 158 NLRB 624, 62 LRRM 1089 (1966), *aff'd sub nom.,* Steelworkers v. NLRB, 376 F.2d 770 (D.C. Cir. 1967).

46. LMRA §101.9(c)(3), 29 U.S.C. § 159(c)(3) (1959).

47. Conren, Inc.,156 NLRB 592, 61 LRRM 1090 (1966), *enf'd,* 368 F.2d 173 (7th Cir. 1966), *cert. denied,* 386 U.S. 974 (1967).

APPENDICES

APPENDIX A

PUBLICATIONS ON PERSONNEL ADMINISTRATION

The following publications are commended to the attorney or employer who seeks background information in the field of personnel administration.

Personnel, American Management Association, Inc., 135 W. 50th St., New York City, New York 10020.
Bi-Monthly. $12.00 per year.

Personnel Administration, Society for Personnel Administration, 485 National Press Building, Washington, D. C. 20004.
Bi-Monthly. $10.00 per year.

The Personnel Administrator, American Society for Personnel Administration, 52 East Bridge St., Berea, Ohio 44017.
Bi-Monthly. $8.00 per year.

Personnel Journal, The Personnel Journal, Inc., 100 Park Avenue, Swarthmore, Pennsylvania 19081.
Monthly. $12.00 per year.

APPENDIX B

A BRIEF HISTORY OF THE LABOR MOVEMENT

I. The Early Beginnings (1776–1869)

In this country, unions began as fraternal, benevolent associations, primarily interested in providing members or their families with financial aid in the event the wage-earner became incapacitated or died. They were composed of skilled artisans.

About the time of the adoption of the Constitution, craft unions began to appear in the major cities. Carpenters, shoemakers, and printers formed craft unions in Philadelphia, New York and Boston. While retaining benevolent aims, these organizations also sought higher wages, minimum rates, shorter hours, institution of apprenticeship programs and what would become known as the "closed shop," *i.e.*, hiring solely from union ranks.

It was not coincidence that craft groups should be the first to seek protection through collective action. Members of the crafts were highly skilled. In an age when nearly all goods were still manufactured by hand, tailors, bakers, carpenters and shoemakers possessed vast economic power. Moreover, their limited number made concerted activity administratively possible.

The printers, one of the early organized craft groups, deserve special mention. The nature of their work promoted a high degree of literacy among the craftsmen. Since books, pamphlets and newspapers constituted the "media" of the day (and for over a century thereafter), printers were in an advantageous position to absorb new ideas, including the concept of concerted activity, as they were expressed in publications. At the turn of the nineteenth century, the printers in Philadelphia and New York, following the lead of the Philadelphia shoemakers, entered into collective bargaining with their respective employers.

The techniques employed by unions in those early days foreshadowed those which would be used with effect later. A "sympathy" strike was called in Philadelphia in 1799 by shoe workers to support bootmakers in that city. 1805 saw the creation of a permanent shoemakers' strike fund in New York. Four years later these same shoemakers engaged in a multi-employer strike, perhaps the first of its kind.

The internal operations of unions began to take shape at this time, too. "Tramping Committees" and unpaid representatives gave way to paid "walking delegates," the forerunners of the modern business agent. These men would go from shop to shop enlisting new people and generally attending to the welfare of members.

We do not mean to imply that unions assumed their present form overnight. Not at all. First, these early organizational efforts were uniformly confined to local areas. The union member in New York had virtually no connection with his counterpart in Philadelphia. Even within the local community, a union could seldom boast that it represented all the members of its craft.

The reason for the limited sphere of union operations lay with the local market economy of the time. National markets had not yet arisen. With the growth of a nationwide transportation system and communications network, the tentacles of unionization also would grow. That would come in the middle of the nineteenth century.

Unions of this early period lacked the coercive characteristics of their descendants. The closed shop and the union shop (where a new employee had to become a union member to remain employed) were almost unknown. These were voluntary associations wherein members decided upon a "price list" and agreed not to work for less. Legal sanctions against dissenters were lacking.

In addition, the workers' organizations lacked permanency. They were formed to gain particular economic ends, such as a ten-hour day, or to combat immediate threats, such as wage cuts. After the objective was achieved, the organization declined. That the Typographical Society of New York City Printers was able to remain in existence for over ten years (1794–1804), may be regarded as exceptional.

One agency which hastened the fall of many unions at this time was the courts. Early in the eighteenth century, an English court in *Rex. v. Journeymen Tailors of Cambridge*, 8 Mod. 10 (1721), held that the combination of workers to compel employers to raise wages was a common law conspiracy. This doctrine found fast acceptance in the courts of the new American republic. In 1806, members of the Philadelphia Federal Society of Journeymen Cordwainers were tried on conspiracy charges. Found guilty, the union was fined and became bankrupt. It disbanded soon after. Other unions also met this fate.

Finally, the nature of union action did not strongly resemble that which is apparent today. Though collective bargaining had begun, it was by no means common. Labor conflict, which is now institutionalized in widespread, organized work stoppages, took a different form then. Individual protest was more common: high turnover, absenteeism, sabotage and irregular hours evidenced workers' displeasure. Collective protests, such as they were, were more spontaneous, and frequently chaotic and violent.

The 1820's saw the onset of the industrial revolution in earnest, and with it, various social and economic ills. Rising prices in the middle of the decade gave impetus to organizing activity. So, too, did the general malaise engendered among workers by adjustment to the factory system and urban life. In 1828, the Mechanics' Union of Trade Associations in Philadelphia initiated the first of several workingmen's political parties.[1] Late in the same year, depression gripped the country, which led to still greater cohesion among workingmen and demand for political action. The political aims of labor were "intended to improve labor morale rather than its economic position."[2]

By the mid 1830's the movement for the 10-hour day was in full swing. The demand for the shorter work day was strongly linked to the utopian demand for "mental cultivation."[3] The General Trades Union was organized in Boston in January 1834 to achieve this demand. Labor had become emboldened by the prosperity of the period and the demands for its services had given it power. Strikes ensued, but almost none were successful. Predictably, "by October [1835] it was reported that no one was left in the Union but the president." "A main cause of the decay of the Union, was the enthusiasm with which workingmen were turning to politics."[4]

The Mechanics' Union of Trade Associations, mentioned previously, represented a significant advance in labor organization. It was an association of a number of Philadelphia unions and may properly be considered the prototype of the "city central labor council." Boston, New York and Baltimore spawned similar centrals. The urban market was expanding and labor sought to keep pace.

In 1834, at the behest of the General Trades Union of Boston, the "National Trades Union" held its first national convention in New York. This was the first effort to have a nationwide labor organization. The NTU was a loose confederation; it had no authority over member unions. But it did provide members with a forum to exchange ideas and lent some semblance of common purpose.

The NTU was no stronger than its constituents. The depression of 1837 proved devastating. The union was consumed in the economic holocaust. Along with it went various craft unions which had arisen in the middle thirties.

March 1842, marked a milestone in the history of organized labor. In that month and year, Chief Justice Shaw of the Massachusetts Supreme Court, rendered his famous decision in *Commonwealth v. Hunt*. This case struck down the common law conspiracy doctrine. Shaw found, first, that combination, of itself, is not criminal. The legal status of the combination depends upon its purpose. Second, he found the avowed purpose of the combination in question, to withhold work from master bootmakers employing non-union labor, is also not criminal:

> We cannot perceive, that it is criminal
> for men to agree together to exercise
> their own acknowledged rights, in such
> manner as best to subserve their own
> interests.[5]

With this landmark decision, the law began to turn in favor of the workingman.

The decade preceding the Civil War saw the resuscitation of the labor movement and the birth of the national union. What gave rise to this creature?

As before, the growth of organized labor paralleled the growth of commercial markets. The early 19th century marked the era of canal building, and with canals came barges. They provided the first real economical means for profitably transporting quantities of goods within the country. The settlers' westward trek had opened up the great Mississippi River network. By the 1850's, a brisk trade had developed along the banks of the Ohio and other tributaries. Most significant, however, was the growth of the railroads. More than any other factor, they contributed to the growth of national markets for goods. National unions were close behind.

These unions were craft unions: The Typographical Union (1850), Stonecutters (1853), Hat Finishers (1854), Molders and Machinists (1857). They were concentrated in the industrialized, urban North. The manpower shortage caused by the Civil War augmented union strength, and by 1870 their number had increased to thirty-two.

The national labor organizations were not very large, each included perhaps a few thousand members, skilled men who had ample bargaining power on their own. But they had permanency. While their fortunes might wax and wane with industrial cycles, they would endure.

The forces which had militated for the National Trades Union were at work again. Immediately following the Civil War, in 1866, the National Labor Union was formed. Like its predecessor, it became distracted with political and social manipulation. Like its predecessor, it shortly became defunct.

2. The Knights of Labor (1869–1917)

Despite its pompous name, the Noble Order of the Knights of Labor had modest beginnings. Founded by Uriah S. Stephens in 1869, it initially served as a small local union of Philadelphia garment workers, but growth came rapidly for the Knights. From an estimated 10,000 members in the first year of its existence, its ranks swelled to over 700,000 by 1886, the height of its power. What is surprising about this growth is that until 1878 the organization was conducted as a secret society.

The Knights differed from predecessor organizations, particularly the National Labor Union. It opened its membership to all workers, not just craftsmen. It would exclude no one on the basis of race, creed, nationality or sex. Local assemblies of the organization reflected this cross-section of the work force.

The Knights were idealistic. They sought to replace capitalism with cooperatives. With harmful competition eliminated, workers would be able to partake in the fruits of their labors.

Specifically, the Knights championed the eight-hour day, equal pay for equal work by women, the abolition of child and convict labor, the public ownership of utilities and the establishment of cooperatives.

The Knights did not advocate violence. They stressed, rather, education and political action. As they saw it, the evil in society was concentrated in the financial power of banks. Enlightened law-making could eliminate the evil. Consequently, strikes against individual employers were not to be encouraged; they would be non-productive.

The idealism which so typified the Knights proved its undoing. By not attending to the immediate economic aspirations of its members, by concentrating too much on political action and long-term social reform, it provoked an internal leadership crisis. Those leaders favoring vigorous trade union activity rebelled against the aims of the Knights. This led to a series of strikes and culminated in a successful strike against the Gould railway interests in 1885.

The Knights had reached their apogee. Craftsmen who had never felt very comfortable with the Knights turned to the newly formed American Federation of Labor. 1886 also witnessed the Chicago Haymarket Riot. In the wake of this anarchist tragedy, the Knights drew most of the blame. The Knights never recovered from those blows. By 1890, membership had plummeted to 100,000, and they had ceased to be a power in the labor movement. The Noble Order finally expired in 1917.

3. The American Federation of Labor (1886–1935)

Samuel Gompers was a key personality in the history of the labor movement. He was president of the Cigar Makers International Union, a strong craft union. He would have none of the idealistic Knights of Labor, who embraced all labor, skilled and unskilled. In 1881, he journeyed to Pittsburgh, where leaders of eight national unions, similarly disposed, created the Federation of Organized Trades and Labor Unions (FOTLU).

These men reasoned that unskilled labor diluted the bargaining power of skilled workers, and was therefore a threat to the latter's economic progress. Egalitarianism was proper in its place, but should not interfere with sound business judgment essential to a strong labor movement.

In December 1886, several large craft unions met in Columbus, Ohio, and formed a new organization: the American Federation of Labor. By coincidence or design, FOTLU was in convention in Columbus at the same time. It agreed to join the Federation.

The AF of L decided early upon fundamental principles which would characterize organized labor for half a century. Basically, they were:

> • Each member national union would have full autonomy. The Federation would not try to usurp the authority of intra-union leadership.
>
> • A strike fund would be created from a tax imposed upon the members of the national unions; strikes would be regarded as an ultimate weapon and would be used judiciously.
>
> • An Executive Council would charter new unions and resolve jurisdictional disputes.
>
> • Organization would be on the basis of craft, and would cut across industry lines.
>
> • The Federation and its member nationals would refrain from active political participation: there would be no "Labor Party." But the Federation encouraged a

policy of rewarding office-holders and candidates favorable to its cause and opposing those who were hostile.

• Lastly, the AF of L would oppose government interference with employment conditions. It did not want minimum wage laws or other regulations. Except in cases where the interests of craft workers as a group were in question, it was staunchly conservative in outlook.

By 1892, AF of L membership had reached 250,000. The 1890's was a period of economic depression, however, and so growth and power did not manifest themselves. In 1898, when the economy had recovered, all organized labor represented less than 3% of the non-agricultural work force of 17 million.

The turn of the century saw a marked increase in organized labor's strength. "Nourished by the spread of German and British labor theories, business prosperity, and rising prices, encouraged by 'progressive' politicians and social reformers, AF of L unions scored a five-fold increase in membership between 1898 and 1904." [6]

The AF of L's growth in the years preceding the First World War cannot be attributed to wage gains obtained by unions. On the contrary, the purchasing power for workers actually fell during these years. What, then, was the explanation?

Cochran and Miller offer the following:

Collective action by labor had roots far more complex than simple questions of wages or hours. Men whose necessary feeling of self-importance, of belonging to some meaningful or responsive social structure, had been weakened by submergence in great impersonal factories and urban slums responded eagerly to opportunities for restoring themselves through group activity. Labor unions were but a part of the mass movement into clubs, lodges, and fraternal orders. Working for the union and empowering the delegates to do battle with the boss was a reassertion of the individual's power over his environment. The mutual benefit policies of the unions gave a feeling of security in the face of industrial accidents and seasonal unemployment, while union socials, dances, picnics, and lectures offered stimulating leisure time activity.[7]

Employers did not ignore this rapid growth. While industrial giants could effectively combat unionism unassisted, smaller firms were fearful that increased wage costs through unionism would make them non-competitive. A national employer association was needed, and so was created the National Association of Manufacturers.

The NAM undertook an intensive educational campaign, concentrating on smaller cities. Not only was the national growth of the AF of L stopped, but the Federation actually began to lose members in certain areas.

The AF of L, in consequence, turned to political action, generally at the state level. The NAM countered with its own lobbying. For a time, the NAM was highly successful. The success was due mainly to the ministrations of its chief lobbyist, James A. Emery. From 1902 to 1912 almost all bills proposed by the AF of L for the regulation of working conditions were killed in committee.

The courts, too, were hostile to labor. In the "Danbury Hatters" case,[8] the Supreme Court held that a union could be liable under the Sherman Act for restraint of trade. The Court imposed damages of almost a quarter of a million dollars upon the union for its secondary boycott. The common law doctrines of civil conspiracy and inducement of breach of contract also persisted in many state and federal court decisions. Injunctions issued apace. Equity courts quickly enjoined conduct which they regarded as harmful or dangerous, as well as unlawful.

Notwithstanding such adversity, the Federation grew. By 1917, it could claim two and one-half million members; by 1920, over four million. Significant in fostering this growth was the passage of the Clayton Act which reversed the anti-labor judicial trend.[9] Section 6 of the Act explicitly excluded labor organizations from the scope of the anti-trust laws. Significant, too, was the formal recognition extended unions by an agency of the federal government, the National War Labor Board. Mainly, however, by relaxing its standards to include unions other than strictly craft groups, the AF of L contributed to its own expansion. At the same time, there were countervailing influences to union growth.

> [E]mployers were discovering that nine hours work under good conditions might produce more than ten, that fatigue might be profitably lessened by rest periods, be cut by pleasanter working conditions. They discovered that even expensive welfare work, if intelligently carried on, might pay dividends.[10]

By the mid-twenties, personnel departments had sprung up in many companies. Their purpose was simple: to obtain and maintain a satisfied and satisfactory work force. Picnics, parties and contests abounded. Congeniality was the order of the day, the practice of paternalism, the norm.

Welfare work, profit sharing and stock distribution plans became prominent. These slowed unionism, but the most important factor in halting union growth was company-sponsored unionism.

We have mentioned that the National War Labor Board gave legal sanction to unions during the First World War. Rather than be faced with outside unions coming in, many large companies led by General Electric decided to form their own unions. Surprisingly, Samuel Gompers approved of the idea. He thought that this was a first step toward trade unionism. By 1919, he realized his mistake, but by then it was too late.

Company unionism flourished for the next decade. Many years later Gompers' mistaken assessment would prove correct.

AF of L unions foundered. Membership dropped to three and one-half million during the recession of the early twenties. It remained at this level for the rest of the decade despite the return to prosperity. The great crash of 1929 only caused a further reduction in membership of a quarter of a million.

4. Congress Enacts Laws (1926–1935)

The Railway Labor Act was passed in 1926. It required employers to bargain collectively and to avoid discrimination against employees for joining a union. The Act also provided for settlement of railway labor disputes through mediation, voluntary arbitration, and fact finding boards.

The election of 1932 ushered in Franklin D. Roosevelt and the New Deal. "Although critics stamped the Roosevelt administration a 'labor government,' the New Dealers had far less interest in labor than in the farmer." [11]   Nevertheless, labor had a sufficient number of friends in high places to insure passage of the Norris-LaGuardia Act (1932), a pre-New Deal measure.[12]   The National Industrial Recovery Act (1933) [13] provided for NRA codes guaranteeing the right of employees to organize and bargain collectively through representatives of their own choosing without interference, restraint or coercion by employers.[14]   The year 1935 saw the passage of the National Labor Relations (Wagner) Act,[15] the Bituminous Coal Conservation (Guffey) Act [16] and the Federal Social Security Act.[17] The climate had changed for widening welfare legislation and for support and extension of unionism.

Unfortunately for the American Federation of Labor, the nature of unionism had also changed. While the traditional craft unions made substantial gains, industrial unions made the most dramatic impact. Whole companies and industries were unionized by "organizing committees." The AF of L did not

know where to place these new organizations in its existing
craft structure. It resolved the problem by chartering them directly from the Federation as federal labor unions.

5. The CIO and the House Divided (1935–1955)

The charters which the AF of L granted to the new industrial unions were limited. Where possible, the parent Executive Council would carve out existing craft units and distribute them to traditional craft members. This practice weakened
the industrial unions but their complaints fell on deaf ears.

The 1935 AF of L convention in Atlantic City brought matters to a head. A year before in San Francisco, under the
prodding of John L. Lewis, president of the United Mine
Workers, the convention had endorsed in principle the organization of workers into industrial unions. But it was a Pyrrhic
victory for industrial unionists, for the AF of L Executive Council stubbornly refused to alter its practice of issuing watered-
down charters.

A "Committee for Industrial Organization (CIO)," later the
"Congress of Industrial Organization" was formed a few weeks
after the convention. It consisted of several industrial unions.[18]
Its stated purpose was to promote the organization of mass production and unorganized industries. The CIO attempted to
persuade the AF of L to foster industrial unionism within its
structure. However, in January 1936, the AF of L Executive
Council asked the CIO to disband. The Committee refused
and much wrangling followed. Eventually, all the members of
the Committee, with the exception of the ILGWU, were expelled from the AF of L amidst charges of "dual unionism."

The competition between the AF of L and CIO stimulated
union growth. Beginning in 1938, under the impetus of the
rival federations, union membership showed a steady increase,
reaching close to 11 million at the time of America's entry into
World War II.

The CIO made most headway in the mass-production industries. Unionization of the steel and automobile industries were its first and major achievements. In 1937, General Motors agreed to recognize the United Automobile Workers. In the same year, U. S. Steel recognized the Steel Workers Organizing Committee. Workers in rubber, oil, textiles and electrical appliance industries also were drawn into the CIO camp. 1937 was a banner year for organized labor. The National Labor Relations Act was held to be constitutional by the U. S. Supreme Court in the landmark case of *NLRB v. Jones and Laughlin Steel Corp.*[19]

By 1945, the CIO had approximately six and one-half million members, almost as many as the AF of L.

World War II produced generally an era of labor-management cooperation. Wages and prices were regulated by the government. Peaceful labor relations were encouraged by the National War Labor Board.

The National War Labor Board's "Little Steel Formula" in 1942, sought to hold wages in line by establishing a maximum limit on general increases. The Wage Stabilization Act of 1942 authorized the President to stabilize wages and salaries.[20] To compensate for this check, workers were granted increased "fringe benefits," for example, paid vacations and holidays, shift differentials and insurance and pension plans. World War II thus was largely responsible for unions' increased interest in fringes as an alternative means of compensation.

With the restraints of war lifted in 1945, the perhaps inevitable reaction set in. Overtime was cut; to preserve workers' wartime earning levels, many unions made large wage demands. Crippling strikes took place in the oil, automobile, steel and coal industries. Inflationary pressures and the dislocation caused by a return to a peacetime economy contributed to many other strikes throughout 1946. Strike idleness reached an all-time high.

During the late thirties public opinion had been sympathetic to labor in its frequently bloody confrontations with management. Now, public displeasure became manifest: a conservative Congress was sent to Washington in the 1946 elections.

In 1947, the Taft-Hartley Act was enacted as a result of Labor's postwar restlessness.[21] Although Labor vehemently opposed its passage, giving rise to a new episode of feverish union political activity, Congress passed it over a Presidential veto. By the terms of the Act, labor unions as well as employers could be found guilty of unfair labor practices. Still more difficult for unions to accept was the much-despised Section 14(b), which explicitly permitted states to enact "right-to-work" laws.[22]

The CIO was confronted with another problem at this time: communism. Communist sympathies had been tolerated among labor leaders since the inception of the CIO. Indeed, during the 1930's, leftist leanings were considered fashionable. By the late 1940's, however, the communists' parroting of the Moscow "party line" became an acute embarrassment to the labor movement. This was especially so in view of mounting public hostility to organized labor and the impending "Red Scare." Between 1949–1950, therefore, eleven unions within the CIO were expelled for communist domination.

In the early 1950's, William Green of the AF of L, and Philip Murray, of the CIO, died. Their deaths marked the passing of the "inevitability" of two federations. George Meany and Walter Reuther, the new leaders, were more amenable to reconciliation.

6. Reconciliation (1955–1968)

In 1953, the two federations took a major step towards reunion. At their respective conventions, the AF of L and the CIO approved a no-raiding agreement to extend for two years from January 1, 1954. It was binding only upon those member unions which ratified it. Nevertheless, major obstacles to reunification had been overcome, on paper at least.

Two years later, on December 5, 1955, formal merger took place. Over 16 million workers, more than 85% of all union membership, were now under one roof. The new organization was called the "American Federation of Labor and Congress of Industrial Organizations (AFL–CIO)." Its officers were drawn from the executive ranks of the preexisting federations. Significantly, the constitution of the new organization accommodated the interests of industrial unions, which, it will be recalled, was a major point of dispute in the 1930's.

The remainder of the decade was notable for the increasing attention given to the problem of corruption and racketeering in the labor movement. As early as 1953, the AF of L had revoked the 60 year-old charter of the International Longshoremen's Association, claiming that the ILA was rife with corruption. A new longshoremen's union was chartered and a bitter dispute followed. The longshoremen remained loyal to the old organization, however, and in 1954 it was certified as bargaining agent for the dock workers by the NLRB.

In the first year of its existence, the AFL–CIO continued the scrutiny of member unions' practices. The Ethical Practices Committee recommended that three unions show cause why they should not be suspended because of domination by "corrupt" influences in the administration of employee welfare funds.[23] In 1957, the AFL–CIO convention took stronger action. It expelled the Teamsters, Bakery Workers and Laundry Workers, and thus reduced its ranks by over 1½ million. These unions had failed to comply with the AFL–CIO Executive Council's recommendation for corrective action. The Distillery Workers were continued on probation. The United Textile Workers and the Allied Industrial Workers were restored to good standing.

The internal problems of the AFL–CIO did not escape notice in Washington. In 1958, the Senate Select Committee on Improper Activities in the Labor or Management Field (The McClellan Committee) began conducting hearings. The results of the Committee's efforts were embodied in the Welfare

and Pension Plans Disclosure Act, passed in 1958.[24]   The Act
established extensive reporting requirements, set standards for
administering union funds and amended the Taft-Hartley Act.

In 1959, the Labor-Management Reporting and Disclosure
Act was signed into law.[25]   This Act provided protection for
union members, and provided for financial reports by unions,
certain employers, labor relations consultants and unions in
trusteeship.   It also amended the Taft-Hartley Law with respect
to the jurisdiction of the National Labor Relations Board and
placed limitations on secondary boycotts and picketing.

The 1960's marked an increased union interest in white collar
employees.   For many years, organized labor ignored office,
professional and public employees.   Now it became clear that
unions would have to step up their efforts to organize these
employees to maintain their strength.   Blue collar jobs were de-
creasing.   Teachers and other civil servants became a target of
organizational campaigns.   The right of public employees to
bargain collectively and to strike became paramount issues.

7. The New Schism (1968–   )

Walter Reuther was dissatisfied with the "complacency" of
the AFL–CIO, and with George Meany. Reuther was convinced
that the AFL–CIO was not doing enough: unionization was not
keeping pace with the growth of the labor force; more had to
be accomplished in areas of health, education, old-age security,
and unemployment; steps had to be taken to combat racism;
the fight for urban renewal had to be carried forward. In short,
Reuther believed a total program for social action was necessary.
He did not envision one forthcoming from the assertedly
undemocratic leadership of the AFL–CIO under George Meany.
He stated:

> [T]he AFL–CIO, in policy and program, too often con-
> tinues to live with the past. It advances few new ideas
> and lacks the necessary vitality, vision, imagination and

social invention to make it equal to the challenging problems of a changing world.[26]

Reuther initiated the schism by withholding the UAW's per capita tax from the AFL–CIO unless and until some action was taken on a special "reform" convention demanded by the UAW. On May 15, 1968, the Auto Workers were suspended for failing to pay the tax for three months.

In July, the UAW formally disaffiliated from the AFL–CIO. Soon after, it joined with the outcast International Brotherhood of Teamsters to form the Alliance for Labor Action (ALA). The avowed purpose of the ALA was to organize the unorganized, particularly in the South.

The following year, the Chemical Workers Union joined the ALA, adding its 90,000 members to the more than 3½ million comprising the UAW and Teamsters membership. The Chemical Workers were promptly expelled from the AFL-CIO.[27] In 1970, the National Council, Distributive Workers of America, formerly District 65, and other local unions of the R.W.D.S.U. joined the ALA. New membership from this source swelled ALA ranks by approximately 50,000.[28]

Following the death of Reuther in May 1970, there was increasing speculation that the UAW might rejoin the AFL–CIO.[29] There was also speculation that, with James Hoffa no longer President, the way was open for the Teamsters to return to the "house of labor." However, at the time of this writing, neither event has occurred.

NOTES TO APPENDIX B

1. John R. Commons and Associates, *History of Labor in the United States* 108-231.

2. A. Schlesinger, Jr., *The Age of Jackson* 134 (1945).

3. *Id.* at 167.

4. *Id.*

5. 4 Metcalf 119, 130 (1842).

6. K. C. Cochran and W. Miller, *The Age of Enterprise* 234 (1961).

7. *Id.* at 235.

8. Loewe v. Lawlor, 208 U.S. 274 (1908).

9. Clayton Act § 6, 15 U.S.C. § 17 (1964).

10. Cochran and Miller, *supra* note 6, at 245.

11. W. E. Leuchtenberg, *Franklin D. Roosevelt and The New Deal* 35 (6th ed. 1965).

12. 29 U.S.C. §§ 101-115 (1964).

13. Act of June 16, 1933, Ch. 90, 48 Stat. 195.

14. Title I of this Act was declared unconstitutional in *Schechter Poultry Co. v. U.S.*, 295 U.S. 495 (1935).

15. National Labor Relations Act, Ch. 372, 49 Stat. 449 (1935), as amended, 29 U.S.C. § 151 *et seq.* (1964).

16. Act of August 30, 1935, Ch. 824, 49 Stat. 991.

17. Social Security Act, Ch. 531, 49 Stat. 620 (1935), as amended, 42 U.S.C. § 301 *et seq.* (1964).

18. Amalgamated Clothing Workers; International Ladies Garment Workers; United Textile Workers; International Union of Mine, Mill and Smelter Workers; International Association of Oil Field, Gas Well and Refinery Workers. These were later joined by United Automobile Workers; United Rubber Workers; Amalgamated Association of Iron, Steel and Tin Workers; and Federation of Flat Glass Workers. U.S. Bureau of Labor Statistics, Dept. of Labor, Bull. No. 1000, *A Brief History of the American Labor Movement* (1970).

19. 301 U.S. 1 (1937).

20. Act of October 10, 1942, Ch. 578, 56 Stat. 765.

21. Labor Management Relations Act (Taft-Hartley Act), 29 U.S.C. § 141 *et seq.* (1964).

22. Taft-Hartley Act § 14(b), 29 U.S.C. § 164(b) (1964).

23. The Allied Industrial Workers; The Laundry Workers; and The Distillery Workers.

24. 29 U.S.C. § 301 *et seq.* (1964).

25. 29 U.S.C. §§ 153, 158-160, 164, 186, 187, 401 *et seq.* (1964).

26. 1967 BNA Lab. Rel. Yearbook 356, 359.

27. However, in May 1971 the AFL–CIO Executive Council approved the reaffiliation of the Chemical Workers Union. 75 LRR 75, 76.

28. In July 1971 it was reported that the UAW and the Teamsters were suspending their respective monthly dues payments of $65,000 and $100,000 to the ALA. On January 25, 1972, the ALA was dissolved. N.Y. Times, Jan. 25, 1972, at 39, col. 6.

29. 74 LRR 124, 125.

APPENDIX C

Text of Labor Management Relations Act, 1947, as Amended by Public Law 86–257, 1959*

[Public Law 101—80th Congress]

AN ACT

To amend the National Labor Relations Act, to provide additional facilities for the mediation of labor disputes affecting commerce, to equalize legal responsibilities of labor organizations and employers, and for other purposes.

Be it enacted by the Senate and House of Representatives of the United States of America in Congress assembled,

SHORT TITLE AND DECLARATION OF POLICY

SECTION 1. (a) This Act may be cited as the "Labor Management Relations Act, 1947."

(b) Industrial strife which interferes with the normal flow of commerce and with the full production of articles and commodities for commerce, can be avoided or substantially minimized if employers, employees, and labor organizations each recognize under law one another's legitimate rights in their relations with each other, and above all recognize under law that neither party has any right in its relations with any other to engage in acts or practices which jeopardize the public health, safety, or interest.

It is the purpose and policy of this Act, in order to promote the full flow of commerce, to prescribe the legitimate rights of both employees and employers in their relations affecting commerce, to provide orderly and peaceful procedures for preventing the interference by either with the legitimate rights of the other, to protect the rights of individual employees in their relations with labor organizations whose activities affect commerce, to define and proscribe practices on the part of labor and management which affect commerce and are inimical to the general welfare, and to protect the rights of the public in connection with labor disputes affecting commerce.

TITLE I—AMENDMENT OF NATIONAL LABOR RELATIONS ACT

SEC. 101. The National Labor Relations Act is hereby amended to read as follows:

FINDINGS AND POLICIES

SECTION 1. The denial by some employers of the right of employees to organize and the refusal by some employers to accept the procedure of collective bargaining

---

*Section 201(d) and (e) of the Labor-Management Reporting and Disclosure Act of 1959 which repealed Section 9(f), (g), and (h) of the Labor Management Relations Act, 1947, and Section 505 amending Section 302(a), (b), and (c) of the Labor Management Relations Act, 1947, took effect upon enactment of Public Law 86–257, September 14, 1959. As to the other amendments of the Labor Management Relations Act, 1947, Section 707 of the Labor-Management Reporting and Disclosure Act provides :

The amendments made by this title shall take effect sixty days after the date of the enactment of this Act and no provision of this title shall be deemed to make an unfair labor practice, any act which is performed prior to such effective date which did not constitute an unfair labor practice prior thereto.

lead to strikes and other forms of industrial strife or unrest, which have the intent or the necessary effect of burdening or obstructing commerce by (a) impairing the efficiency, safety, or operation of the instrumentalities of commerce; (b) occurring in the current of commerce; (c) materially affecting, restraining, or controlling the flow of raw materials or manufactured or processed goods from or into the channels of commerce, or the prices of such materials or goods in commerce; or (d) causing diminution of employment and wages in such volume as substantially to impair or disrupt the market for goods flowing from or into the channels of commerce.

The inequality of bargaining power between employees who do not possess full freedom of association or actual liberty of contract, and employers who are organized in the corporate or other forms of ownership association substantially burdens and affects the flow of commerce, and tends to aggravate recurrent business depressions, by depressing wage rates and the purchasing power of wage earners in industry and by preventing the stabilization of competitive wage rates and working conditions within and between industries.

Experience has proved that protection by law of the right of employees to organize and bargain collectively safeguards commerce from injury, impairment, or interruption, and promotes the flow of commerce by removing certain recognized sources of industrial strife and unrest, by encouraging practices fundamental to the friendly adjustment of industrial disputes arising out of differences as to wages, hours, or other working conditions, and by restoring equality of bargaining power between employers and employees.

Experience has further demonstrated that certain practices by some labor organizations, their officers, and members have the intent or the necessary effect of burdening or obstructing commerce by preventing the free flow of goods in such commerce through strikes and other forms of industrial unrest or through concerted activities which impair the interest of the public in the free flow of such commerce. The elimination of such practices is a necessary condition to the assurance of the rights herein guaranteed.

It is hereby declared to be the policy of the United States to eliminate the causes of certain substantial obstructions to the free flow of commerce and to mitigate and eliminate these obstructions when they have occurred by encouraging the practice and procedure of collective bargaining and by protecting the exercise by workers of full freedom of association, self-organization, and designation of representatives of their own choosing, for the purpose of negotiating the terms and conditions of their employment or other mutual aid or protection.

DEFINITIONS

Sec. 2. When used in this Act—

(1) The term "person" includes one or more individuals, labor organizations, partnerships, associations, corporations, legal representatives, trustees, trustees in bankruptcy, or receivers.

(2) The term "employer" includes any person acting as an agent of an employer, directly or indirectly, but shall not include the United States or any wholly owned Government corporation, or any Federal Reserve Bank, or any State or political subdivision thereof, or any corporation or association operating a hospital, if no part of the net earnings inures to the benefit of any private shareholder or individual, or any person subject to the Railway Labor Act, as amended from time to time, or any labor organization (other than when acting as an employer), or anyone acting in the capacity of officer or agent of such labor organization.

(3) The term "employee" shall include any employee, and shall not be limited to the employees of a particular employer, unless the Act explicitly states otherwise, and shall include any individual whose work has ceased as a consequence of, or in connection with, any current labor dispute or because of any unfair labor practice, and who has not obtained any other regular and substantially equivalent employment, but shall not include any individual employed as an agricultural laborer, or in the domestic service of any family or person at his home, or any individual employed by his parent or spouse, or any individual having the status of an independent contractor, or any individual employed as a supervisor, or any individual employed by an employer subject to the Railway Labor Act, as amended from time to time, or by any other person who is not an employer as herein defined.

(4) The term "representatives" includes any individual or labor organization.

(5) The term "labor organization" means any organization of any kind, or any agency or employee representation committee or plan, in which employees participate and which exists for the purpose, in whole or in part, of dealing with employers concerning grievances, labor disputes, wages, rates of pay, hours of employment, or conditions of work.

(6) The term "commerce" means trade, traffic, commerce, transportation, or communication among the several States, or between the District of Columbia or any Territory of the United States and any State or other Territory, or between any foreign country and any State, Territory, or the District of Columbia, or within the District of Columbia or any Territory, or between points in the same State but through any other State or any Territory or the District of Columbia or any foreign country.

(7) The term "affecting commerce" means in commerce, or burdening or obstructing commerce or the free flow of commerce, or having led or tending to lead to a labor dispute burdening or obstructing commerce or the free flow of commerce.

(8) The term "unfair labor practice" means any unfair labor practice listed in section 8.

(9) The term "labor dispute" includes any controversy concerning terms, tenure or conditions of employment, or concerning the association or representation of persons in negotiating, fixing, maintaining, changing, or seeking to arrange terms or conditions of employment, regardless of whether the disputants stand in the proximate relation of employer and employee.

(10) The term "National Labor Relations Board" means the National Labor Relations Board provided for in section 3 of this Act.

(11) The term "supervisor" means any individual having authority, in the interest of the employer, to hire, transfer, suspend, lay off, recall, promote, discharge, assign, reward, or discipline other employees, or responsibly to direct them, or to adjust their grievances, or effectively to recommend such action, if in connection with the foregoing the exercise of such authority is not of a merely routine or clerical nature, but requires the use of independent judgment.

(12) The term "professional employee" means—

(a) any employee engaged in work (i) predominantly intellectual and varied in character as opposed to routine mental, manual, mechanical, or physical work; (ii) involving the consistent exercise of discretion and judgment in its performance; (iii) of such a character that the output produced or the result accomplished cannot be standardized in relation to a given period of time; (iv) requiring knowledge of an advanced type in a field of science or learning customarily acquired by a prolonged course of specialized intellectual instruction and study in an institution of higher learning or a hospital, as distinguished from a general academic education or from an apprenticeship or from training in the performance of routine mental, manual, or physical processes; or

(b) any employee, who (i) has completed the courses of specialized intellectual instruction and study described in clause (iv) of paragraph (a), and (ii) is performing related work under the supervision of a professional person to qualify himself to become a professional employee as defined in paragraph (a).

(13) In determining whether any person is acting as an "agent" of another person so as to make such other person responsible for his acts, the question of whether the specific acts performed were actually authorized or subsequently ratified shall not be controlling.

NATIONAL LABOR RELATIONS BOARD

SEC. 3. (a) The National Labor Relations Board (hereinafter called the "Board") created by this Act prior to its amendment by the Labor Management Relations Act, 1947, is hereby continued as an agency of the United States, except that the Board shall consist of five instead of three members, appointed by the President by and with the advice and consent of the Senate. Of the two additional members so provided for, one shall be appointed for a term of five years and the other for a term of two years. Their successors, and the successors of the other members, shall be appointed for terms of five years each, excepting that any individual chosen to fill a vacancy shall be appointed only for the unexpired term of the member whom he shall succeed. The President shall designate one member to serve as Chairman of the Board. Any member of the Board may be removed by the President, upon notice and hearing, for neglect of duty or malfeasance in office, but for no other cause.

(b) The Board is authorized to delegate to any group of three of more members any or all of the powers which it may itself exercise. The Board is also authorized to delegate to its regional directors its powers under section 9 to determine the unit appropriate for the purpose of collective bargaining, to investigate and provide for hearings, and determine whether a question of representation exists, and to direct an election or take a secret ballot under subsection (c) or (e) of section 9 and certify the results thereof, except that upon the filing of a request therefor with the Board by any interested person, the Board may review any action of a regional director delegated to him under this paragraph, but such a review shall not, unless specifically ordered by the Board, operate as a stay of any action taken by the regional director. A vacancy in the Board shall not impair the right of the remaining members to exercise all of the powers of the Board, and three members of the Board shall, at all times, constitute a quorum of the Board, except that two members shall constitute a quorum of any group designated pursuant to the first sentence hereof. The Board shall have an official seal which shall be judicially noticed.

(c) The Board shall at the close of each fiscal year make a report in writing to Congress and to the President stating in detail the cases it has heard, the decisions it has rendered, the names, salaries, and duties of all employees and officers in the employ or under the supervision of the Board, and an account of all moneys it has disbursed.

(d) There shall be a General Counsel of the Board who shall be appointed by the President, by and with the advice and consent of the Senate, for a term of four years. The General Counsel of the Board shall exercise general supervision over all attorneys employed by the Board (other than trial examiners and legal assistants to Board members) and over the officers and employees in the regional offices. He shall have final authority, on behalf of the Board, in respect of the investigation of charges and issuance of complaints under section 10, and in respect of the prosecution of such complaints before the Board, and shall have such other duties as the Board may prescribe or as may be provided by law. In case of a vacancy in the office of the General Counsel the President is authorized to designate the officer or employee who shall act as General Counsel during such vacancy, but no person or persons so designated shall so act (1) for more than forty days when the Congress is in session unless a nomination to fill such vacancy shall have been submitted to the Senate, or (2) after the adjournment *sine die* of the session of the Senate in which such nomination was submitted.

SEC. 4. (a) Each member of the Board and the General Counsel of the Board shall receive a salary of $12,000* a year, shall be eligible for reappointment, and shall not engage in any other business, vocation, or employment. The Board shall appoint an executive secretary, and such attorneys, examiners, and regional directors, and such other employees as it may from time to time find necessary for the proper performance of its duties. The Board may not employ any attorneys for the purpose of reviewing transcripts of hearings or preparing drafts of opinions except that any attorney employed for assignment as a legal assistant to any Board member may for such Board member review such transcripts and prepare such drafts. No trial examiner's report shall be reviewed, either before or after its publication, by any person other than a member of the Board or his legal assistant, and no trial examiner shall advise or consult with the Board with respect to exceptions taken to his findings, rulings, or recommendations. The Board may establish or utilize such regional, local, or other agencies, and utilize such voluntary and uncompensated services, as may from time to time be needed. Attorneys appointed under this section may, at the direction of the Board, appear for and represent the Board in any case in court. Nothing in this Act shall be construed to authorize the Board to appoint individuals for the purpose of conciliation or mediation, or for economic analysis.

(b) All of the expenses of the Board, including all necessary traveling and subsistence expenses outside the District of Columbia incurred by the members or employees of the Board under its orders, shall be allowed and paid on the presentation of itemized vouchers therefor approved by the Board or by any individual it designates for that purpose.

SEC. 5. The principal office of the Board shall be in the District of Columbia, but it may meet and exercise any or all of its powers at any other place. The Board may, by one or more of its members or by such agents or agencies as it may designate, prosecute any inquiry necessary to its functions in any part of the United States. A member who participates in such an inquiry shall not be disqualified from subsequently participating in a decision of the Board in the same case.

SEC. 6. The Board shall have authority from time to time to make, amend, and rescind, in the manner prescribed by the Administrative Procedure Act, such rules and regulations as may be necessary to carry out the provisions of this Act.

RIGHTS OF EMPLOYEES

SEC. 7. Employees shall have the right to self-organization, to form, join, or assist labor organizations, to bargain collectively through representatives of their own choosing, and to engage in other concerted activities for the purpose of collective bargaining or other mutual aid or protection, and shall also have the right to refrain from any or all of such activities except to the extent that such right may be affected

---

*Pursuant to Public Law 90–206, 90th Congress, 81 Stat. 644, approved December 16, 1967, and in accordance with Section 225(f)(ii) thereof, effective in 1969, the salary of the Chairman of the Board shall be $40,000 per year and the salaries of the General Counsel and each Board member shall be $38,000 per year.

by an agreement requiring membership in a labor organization as a condition of employment as authorized in section 8(a)(3).

UNFAIR LABOR PRACTICES

SEC. 8. (a) It shall be an unfair labor practice for an employer—

(1) to interfere with, restrain, or coerce employees in the exercise of the rights guaranteed in section 7;

(2) to dominate or interfere with the formation or administration of any labor organization or contribute financial or other support to it: *Provided*, That subject to rules and regulations made and published by the Board pursuant to section 6, an employer shall not be prohibited from permitting employees to confer with him during working hours without loss of time or pay;

(3) by discrimination in regard to hire or tenure of employment or any term or condition of employment to encourage or discourage membership in any labor organization: *Provided*, That nothing in this Act, or in any other statute of the United States, shall preclude an employer from making an agreement with a labor organization (not established, maintained, or assisted by any action defined in section 8(a) of this Act as an unfair labor practice) to require as a condition of employment membership therein on or after the thirtieth day following the beginning of such employment or the effective date of such agreement, whichever is the later, (i) if such labor organization is the representative of the employees as provided in section 9(a), in the appropriate collective-bargaining unit covered by such agreement when made, and (ii) unless following an election held as provided in section 9(e) within one year preceding the effective date of such agreement, the Board shall have certified that at least a majority of the employees eligible to vote in such election have voted to rescind the authority of such labor organization to make such an agreement: *Provided further*, That no employer shall justify any discrimination against an employee for non-membership in a labor organization (A) if he has reasonable grounds for believing that such membership was not available to the employee on the same terms and conditions generally applicable to other members, or (B) if he has reasonable grounds for believing that membership was denied or terminated for reasons other than the failure of the employee to tender the periodic dues and the initiation fees uniformly required as a condition of acquiring or retaining membership;

(4) to discharge or otherwise discriminate against an employee because he has filed charges or given testimony under this Act;

(5) to refuse to bargain collectively with the representatives of his employees, subject to the provisions of section 9(a).

(b) It shall be an unfair labor practice for a labor organization or its agents—

(1) to restrain or coerce (A) employees in the exercise of the rights guaranteed in section 7: *Provided*, That this paragraph shall not impair the right of a labor organization to prescribe its own rules with respect to the acquisition or retention of membership therein; or (B) an employer in the selection of his representatives for the purposes of collective bargaining or the adjustment of grievances;

(2) to cause or attempt to cause an employer to discriminate against an employee in violation of subsection (a)(3) or to discriminate against an employee with respect to whom membership in such organization has been denied or terminated on some ground other than his failure to tender the periodic dues and the initiation fees uniformly required as a condition of acquiring or retaining membership;

(3) to refuse to bargain collectively with an employer, provided it is the representative of his employees subject to the provisions of section 9(a);

(4) (i) to engage in, or to induce or encourage any individual employed by any person engaged in commerce or in an industry affecting commerce to engage in, a strike or a refusal in the course of his employment to use, manufacture, process, transport, or otherwise handle or work on any goods, articles, materials, or commodities or to perform any services; or (ii) to threaten, coerce, or restrain any person engaged in commerce or in an industry affecting commerce, where in either case an object thereof is:

(A) forcing or requiring any employer or self-employed person to join any labor or employer organization or to enter into any agreement which is prohibited by section 8(e);

(B) forcing or requiring any person to cease using, selling, handling, transporting, or otherwise dealing in the products of any other producer, processor, or manufacturer, or to cease doing business with any other person, or forcing or requiring any other employer to recognize or bargain with a labor organization as the representative of his employees unless such labor organization has been certified as the representative of such employees under the provisions of section 9: *Provided,* That nothing contained in this clause (B) shall be construed to make unlawful, where not otherwise unlawful, any primary strike or primary picketing;

(C) forcing or requiring any employer to recognize or bargain with a particular labor organization as the representative of his employees if another labor organization has been certified as the representative of such employees under the provisions of section 9;

(D) forcing or requiring any employer to assign particular work to employees in a particular labor organization or in a particular trade, craft, or class rather than to employees in another labor organization or in another trade, craft, or class, unless such employer is failing to conform to an order or certification of the Board determining the bargaining representative for employees performing such work:

Provided, That nothing contained in this subsection (b) shall be construed to make unlawful a refusal by any person to enter upon the premises of any employer (other than his own employer), if the employees of such employer are engaged in a strike ratified or approved by a representative of such employees whom such employer is required to recognize under this Act: *Provided further,* That for the purposes of this paragraph (4) only, nothing contained in such paragraph shall be construed to prohibit publicity, other than picketing, for the purpose of truthfully advising the public, including consumers and members of a labor organization, that a product or products are produced by an employer with whom the labor organization has a primary dispute and are distributed by another employer, as long as such publicity does not have an effect of inducing any individual employed by any person other than the primary employer in the course of his employment to refuse to pick up, deliver, or transport any goods, or not to perform any services, at the establishment of the employer engaged in such distribution;

(5) to require of employees covered by an agreement authorized under subsection (a)(3) the payment, as a condition precedent to becoming a member of such organization, of a fee in an amount which the Board finds excessive or discriminatory under all the circumstances. In making such a finding, the Board shall consider, among other relevant factors, the practices and customs of labor organizations in the particular industry, and the wages currently paid to the employees affected;

(6) to cause or attempt to cause an employer to pay or deliver or agree to pay or deliver any money or other thing of value, in the nature of an exaction, for services which are not performed or not to be performed; and

(7) to picket or cause to be picketed, or threaten to picket or cause to be picketed, any employer where an object thereof is forcing or requiring an employer to recognize or bargain with a labor organization as the representative of his employees, or forcing or requiring the employees of an employer to accept or select such labor organization as their collective bargaining representative, unless such labor organization is currently certified as the representative of such employees:

(A) where the employer has lawfully recognized in accordance with this Act any other labor organization and a question concerning representation may not appropriately be raised under section 9(c) of this Act,

(B) where within the preceding twelve months a valid election under section 9(c) of this Act has been conducted, or

(C) where such picketing has been conducted without a petition under section 9(c) being filed within a reasonable period of time not to exceed thirty days from the commencement of such picketing: *Provided,* That when such a petition has been filed the Board shall forthwith, without regard to the provisions of section 9(c)(1) or the absence of a showing of a substantial interest on the part of the labor organization, direct an election in such unit as the Board finds to be appropriate and shall certify the results thereof: *Provided further,* That nothing in this subparagraph (C) shall be construed to prohibit any picketing or other publicity for the purpose of truthfully advising the public (including consumers) that an employer does not employ members of, or have a contract with, a labor organization, unless an effect of such picketing is to induce any individual employed by any other person in the course of his employment, not to pick up, deliver or transport any goods or not to perform any services.

Nothing in this paragraph (7) shall be construed to permit any act which would otherwise be an unfair labor practice under this section 8(b).

(c) The expressing of any views, argument, or opinion, or the dissemination thereof, whether in written, printed, graphic, or visual form, shall not constitute or be evidence of an unfair labor practice under any of the provisions of this Act, if such expression contains no threat of reprisal or force or promise of benefit.

(d) For the purposes of this section, to bargain collectively is the performance of the mutual obligation of the employer and the representative of the employees to meet at reasonable times and confer in good faith with respect to wages, hours, and other terms and conditions of employment, or the negotiation of an agreement, or any question arising thereunder, and the execution of a written contract incorporating any agreement reached if requested by either party, but such obligation does not compel either party to agree to a proposal or require the making of a concession: *Provided,* That where there is in effect a collective-bargaining contract covering employees in an industry affecting commerce, the duty to bargain collectively shall also mean that no party to such contract shall terminate or modify such contract, unless the party desiring such termination or modification—

(1) serves a written notice upon the other party to the contract of the proposed termination or modification sixty days prior to the expiration date thereof, or in the event such contract contains no expiration date, sixty days prior to the time it is proposed to make such termination or modification;

(2) offers to meet and confer with the other party for the purpose of negotiating a new contract or a contract containing the proposed modifications;

(3) notifies the Federal Mediation and Conciliation Service within thirty days after such notice of the existence of a dispute, and simultaneously therewith notifies any State or Territorial agency established to mediate and conciliate disputes within the State or Territory where the dispute occurred, provided no agreement has been reached by that time; and

(4) continues in full force and effect, without resorting to strike or lockout, all the terms and conditions of the existing contract for a period of sixty days after such notice is given or until the expiration date of such contract, whichever occurs later:

The duties imposed upon employers, employees, and labor organizations by paragraphs (2), (3), and (4) shall become inapplicable upon an intervening certification of the Board, under which the labor organization or individual, which is a party to the contract, has been superseded as or ceased to be the representative of the employees subject to the provisions of section 9(a), and the duties so imposed shall not be construed as requiring either party to discuss or agree to any modification of the terms and conditions contained in a contract for a fixed period, if such modification is to become effective before such terms and conditions can be reopened under the provisions of the contract. Any employee who engages in a strike within the sixty-day period specified in this subsection shall lose his status as an employee of the employer engaged in the particular labor dispute, for the purposes of sections 8, 9, and 10 of this Act, as amended, but such loss of status for such employee shall terminate if and when he is reemployed by such employer.

(e) It shall be an unfair labor practice for any labor organization and any employer to enter into any contract or agreement, express or implied, whereby such employer ceases or refrains or agrees to cease or refrain from handling, using, selling, transporting or otherwise dealing in any of the products of any other employer, or to cease doing business with any other person, and any contract or agreement entered into heretofore or hereafter containing such an agreement shall be to such extent unenforceable and void: *Provided,* That nothing in this subsection (e) shall apply to an agreement between a labor organization and an employer in the construction industry relating to the contracting or subcontracting of work to be done at the site of the construction, alteration, painting, or repair of a building, structure, or other work: *Provided further,* That for the purposes of this subsection (e) and section 8(b)(4) (B) the terms "any employer", "any person engaged in commerce or in industry affecting commerce", and "any person" when used in relation to the terms "any other producer, processor, or manufacturer", "any other employer", or "any other person" shall not include persons in the relation of a jobber, manufacturer, contractor, or subcontractor working on the goods or premises of the jobber or manufacturer or performing parts of an integrated process of production in the apparel and clothing industry: *Provided further,* That nothing in this Act shall prohibit the enforcement of any agreement which is within the foregoing exception.

(f) It shall not be an unfair labor practice under subsections (a) and (b) of this section for an employer engaged primarily in the building and construction industry to make an agreement covering employees engaged (or who, upon their employment, will be engaged) in the building and construction industry with a labor organization of which building and construction employees are members (not established, maintained, or assisted by any action defined in section 8(a) of this Act as an unfair labor practice) because (1) the majority status of such labor organization has not been established under the provisions of section 9 of this Act prior to the making of such agreement, or (2) such agreement requires as a condition of employment, membership in such labor organization after the seventh day following the beginning of such employment or the effective date of the agreement, whichever is later, or (3) such agreement requires the employer to notify such labor organization of opportunities for employment with such employer, or gives such labor organization an opportunity to refer qualified applicants for such employment, or (4) such agreement specifies minimum training or experience qualifications for employment or provides for priority in opportunities for employment based upon length of service with such employer, in the industry or in the particular geographical area: *Provided,* That nothing in this subsection shall set aside the final proviso to section 8(a)(3) of this Act: *Provided further,* That any agreement which would be invalid, but for clause (1) of this sub-section, shall not be a bar to a petition filed pursuant to section 9(c) or 9(e).*

REPRESENTATIVES AND ELECTIONS

Sec. 9. (a) Representatives designated or selected for the purposes of collective bargaining by the majority of the employees in a unit appropriate for such purposes, shall be the exclusive representatives of all the employees in such unit for the purposes of collective bargaining in respect to rates of pay, wages, hours of employment, or other conditions of employment: *Provided,* That any individual employee or a group of employees shall have the right at any time to present grievances to their employer and to have such grievances adjusted, without the intervention of the bargaining representative, as long as the adjustment is not inconsistent with the terms of a collective-bargaining contract or agreement then in effect: *Provided further,* That the bargaining representative has been given opportunity to be present at such adjustment.

(b) The Board shall decide in each case whether, in order to assure to employees the fullest freedom in exercising the rights guaranteed by this Act, the unit appropriate for the purposes of collective bargaining shall be the employer unit, craft unit, plant unit, or subdivision thereof: *Provided,* That the Board shall not (1) decide that any unit is appropriate for such purposes if such unit includes both professional employees and employees who are not professional employees unless a majority of such professional employees vote for inclusion in such unit; or (2) decide that any craft unit is inappropriate for such purposes on the ground that a different unit has been established by a prior Board determination, unless a majority of the employees in the proposed craft unit vote against separate representation or (3) decide that any unit is appropriate for such purposes if it includes, together with other employees, any individual employed as a guard to enforce against employees and other persons rules to protect property of the employer or to protect the safety of persons on the employer's premises; but no labor organization shall be certified as the representative of employees in a bargaining unit of guards if such organization admits to membership, or is affiliated directly or indirectly with an organization which admits to membership, employees other than guards.

(c)(1) Wherever a petition shall have been filed, in accordance with such regulations as may be prescribed by the Board—

    (A) by an employee or group of employees or any individual or labor organization acting in their behalf alleging that a substantial number of

---

*Section 8(f) is inserted in the Act by subsection (a) of Section 705 of Public Law 86–257. Section 705(b) provides:

    Nothing contained in the amendment made by subsection (a) shall be construed as authorizing the execution or application of agreements requiring membership in a labor organization as a condition of employment in any State or Territory in which such execution or application is prohibited by State or Territorial law.

employees (i) wish to be represented for collective bargaining and that their employer declines to recognize their representative as the representative defined in section 9(a), or (ii) assert that the individual or labor organization, which has been certified or is being currently recognized by their employer as the bargaining representative, is no longer a representative as defined in section 9(a); or

(B) by an employer, alleging that one or more individuals or labor organizations have presented to him a claim to be recognized as the representative defined in section 9(a);

the Board shall investigate such petition and if it has reasonable cause to believe that a question of representation affecting commerce exists shall provide for an appropriate hearing upon due notice. Such hearing may be conducted by an officer or employee of the regional office, who shall not make any recommendations with respect thereto. If the Board finds upon the record of such hearing that such a question of representation exists, it shall direct an election by secret ballot and shall certify the results thereof.

(2) In determining whether or not a question of representation affecting commerce exists, the same regulations and rules of decision shall apply irrespective of the identity of the persons filing the petition or the kind of relief sought and in no case shall the Board deny a labor organization a place on the ballot by reason of an order with respect to such labor organization or its predecessor not issued in conformity with section 10(c).

(3) No election shall be directed in any bargaining unit or any subdivision within which, in the preceding twelve-month period, a valid election shall have been held. Employees engaged in an economic strike who are not entitled to reinstatement shall be eligible to vote under such regulations as the Board shall find are consistent with the purposes and provisions of this Act in any election conducted within twelve months after the commencement of the strike. In any election where none of the choices on the ballot receives a majority, a run-off shall be conducted, the ballot providing for a selection between the two choices receiving the largest and second largest number of valid votes cast in the election.

(4) Nothing in this section shall be construed to prohibit the waiving of hearings by stipulation for the purpose of a consent election in conformity with regulations and rules of decision of the Board.

(5) In determining whether a unit is appropriate for the purposes specified in subsection (b) the extent to which the employees have organized shall not be controlling.

(d) Whenever an order of the Board made pursuant to section 10(c) is based in whole or in part upon facts certified following an investigation pursuant to subsection (c) of this section and there is a petition for the enforcement or review of such order, such certification and the record of such investigation shall be included in the transcript of the entire record required to be filed under section 10(e) or 10(f), and thereupon the decree of the court enforcing, modifying, or setting aside in whole or in part the order of the Board shall be made and entered upon the pleadings, testimony, and proceedings set forth in such transcript.

(e)(1) Upon the filing with the Board, by 30 per centum or more of the employees in a bargaining unit covered by an agreement between their employer and a labor organization made pursuant to section 8(a)(3), of a petition alleging they desire that such authority be rescinded, the Board shall take a secret ballot of the employees in such unit and certify the results thereof to such labor organization and to the employer.

(2) No election shall be conducted pursuant to this subsection in any bargaining unit or any subdivision within which, in the preceding twelve-month period, a valid election shall have been held.

PREVENTION OF UNFAIR LABOR PRACTICES

SEC. 10. (a) The Board is empowered, as hereinafter provided, to prevent any person from engaging in any unfair labor practice (listed in section 8) affecting commerce. This power shall not be affected by any other means of adjustment or prevention that has been or may be established by agreement, law, or otherwise: *Provided,* That the Board is empowered by agreement with any agency of any State or Territory to cede to such agency jurisdiction over any cases in any industry (other than mining, manufacturing, communications, and transportation except where predominantly local in character) even though such cases may involve labor disputes affecting commerce, unless the provision of the State or Territorial statute applicable to the determination of such cases by such agency is inconsistent with the corresponding provision of this Act or has received a construction inconsistent therewith.

(b) Whenever it is charged that any person has engaged in or is engaging in any such unfair labor practice, the Board, or any agent or agency designated by the Board for such purposes, shall have power to issue and cause to be served upon such person a complaint stating the charges in that respect, and containing a notice of hearing before the Board or a member thereof, or before a designated agent or agency, at a place therein fixed, not less than five days after the serving of said complaint: *Provided,* That no complaint shall issue based upon any unfair labor practice occurring more than six months prior to the filing of the charge with the Board and the service of a copy thereof upon the person against whom such charge is made, unless the person aggrieved thereby was prevented from filing such charge by reason of service in the armed forces, in which event the six-month period shall be computed from the day of his discharge. Any such complaint may be amended by the member, agent, or agency conducting the hearing or the Board in its discretion at any time prior to the issuance of an order based thereon. The person so complained of shall have the right to file an answer to the original or amended complaint and to appear in person or otherwise and give testimony at the place and time fixed in the complaint. In the discretion of the member, agent, or agency conducting the hearing or the Board, any other person may be allowed to intervene in the said proceeding and to present testimony. Any such proceeding shall, so far as practicable, be conducted in accordance with the rules of evidence applicable in the district courts of the United States under the rules of civil procedure for the district courts of the United States, adopted by the Supreme Court of the United States pursuant to the Act of June 19, 1934 (U. S. C., title 28, secs. 723–B, 723–C).

(c) The testimony taken by such member, agent, or agency or the Board shall be reduced to writing and filed with the Board. Thereafter, in its discretion, the Board upon notice may take further testimony or hear argument. If upon the preponderance of the testimony taken the Board shall be of the opinion that any person named in the complaint has engaged in or is engaging in any such unfair labor practice, then the Board shall state its findings of fact and shall issue and cause to be served on such person an order requiring such person to cease and desist from such unfair labor practice, and to take such affirmative action including reinstatement of employees with or without back pay, as will effectuate the policies of this Act: *Provided,* That where an order directs reinstatement of an employee, back pay may be required of the employer or labor organization, as the case may be, responsible for the discrimination suffered by him: *And provided further,* That in determining whether a complaint shall issue alleging a violation of section 8(a)(1) or section 8(a)(2), and in deciding such cases, the same regulations and rules of decision shall apply irrespective of whether or not the labor organization affected is affiliated with a labor organization national or international in scope.

Such order may further require such person to make reports from time to time showing the extent to which it has complied with the order. If upon the preponderance of the testimony taken the Board shall not be of the opinion that the person named in the complaint has engaged in or is engaging in any such unfair labor practice, then the Board shall state its findings of fact and shall issue an order dismissing the said complaint. No order of the Board shall require the reinstatement of any individual as an employee who has been suspended or discharged, or the payment to him of any back pay, if such individual was suspended or discharged for cause. In case the evidence is presented before a member of the Board, or before an examiner or examiners thereof, such member, or such examiner or examiners, as the case may be, shall issue and cause to be served on the parties to the proceeding a proposed report, together with a recommended order, which shall be filed with the Board, and if no exceptions are filed within twenty days after service thereof upon such parties, or within such further period as the Board may authorize, such recommended order shall become the order of the Board and become effective as therein prescribed.

(d) Until the record in a case shall have been filed in a court, as hereinafter provided, the Board may at any time, upon reasonable notice and in such manner as it shall deem proper, modify or set aside, in whole or in part, any finding or order made or issued by it.

(e) The Board shall have power to petition any court of appeals of the United States, or if all the courts of appeals to which application may be made are in vacation, any district court of the United States, within any circuit or district, respectively, wherein the unfair labor practice in question occurred or wherein such person resides or transacts business, for the enforcement of such order and for appropriate temporary relief or.restraining order, and shall file in the court the record in the proceedings, as provided in section 2112 of title 28, United States Code. Upon the filing of such petition, the court shall cause notice thereof to be served upon such person, and thereupon shall have jurisdiction of the proceeding and of the question determined therein, and shall have power to grant such temporary relief or restraining order as it deems just and proper, and to make and enter a decree enforcing, modifying, and enforcing as so modified, or setting aside in whole or in part the order of the Board. No objection that has not been urged before the Board, its member, agent, or agency, shall be considered by the court, unless the failure or neglect to urge such objection shall be excused because of extraordinary circumstances. The findings of the Board with respect to questions of fact if supported by substantial evidence on the record considered as a whole shall be conclusive. If either party shall apply to the court for leave to adduce additional evidence and shall show to the satisfaction of the court that such additional evidence is material and that there were reasonable grounds for the failure to adduce such evidence in the hearing before the Board, its member, agent, or agency, the court may order such additional evidence to be taken before the Board, its member, agent, or agency, and to be made a part of the record. The Board may modify its findings as to the facts, or make new findings, by reason of additional evidence so taken and filed, and it shall file such modified or new findings, which findings with respect to questions of fact if supported by substantial evidence on the record considered as a whole shall be conclusive, and shall file its recommendations, if any, for the modification or setting aside of its original order. Upon the filing of the record with it the jurisdiction of the court shall be exclusive and its judgment and decree shall be final, except that the same shall be subject to review by the appropriate United States court of appeals if application was made to the district court as hereinabove provided, and by the Supreme Court of the United States upon writ of certiorari or certification as provided in section 1254 of title 28.

(f) Any person aggrieved by a final order of the Board granting or denying in whole or in part the relief sought may obtain a review of such order in any circuit court of appeals of the United States in the circuit wherein the unfair labor practice in question was alleged to have been engaged in or wherein such person resides or transacts business, or in the United States Court of Appeals for the District of Columbia, by filing in such court a written petition praying that the order of the Board be modified or set aside. A copy of such petition shall be forthwith transmitted by the clerk of the court to the Board, and thereupon the aggrieved party shall file in the court the record in the proceeding, certified by the Board, as provided in section 2112 of title 28, United States Code. Upon the filing of such petition, the court shall proceed in the same manner as in the case of an application by the Board under subsection (e) of this section, and shall have the same jurisdiction to grant to the Board such temporary relief or restraining order as it deems just and proper, and in like manner to make and enter a decree enforcing, modifying, and enforcing as so modified, or setting aside in whole or in part the order of the Board; the findings of the Board with respect to questions of fact if supported by substantial evidence on the record considered as a whole shall in like manner be conclusive.

(g) The commencement of proceedings under subsection (e) or (f) of this section shall not, unless specifically ordered by the court, operate as a stay of the Board's order.

(h) When granting appropriate temporary relief or a restraining order, or making and entering a decree enforcing, modifying, and enforcing as so modified, or setting aside in whole or in part an order of the Board, as provided in this section, the jurisdiction of courts sitting in equity shall not be limited by the Act entitled "An Act to amend the Judicial Code and to define and limit the jurisdiction of courts sitting in equity, and for other purposes," approved March 23, 1932 (U.S.C., Supp. VII, title 29, secs. 101–115).

(i) Petitions filed under this Act shall be heard expeditiously, and if possible within ten days after they have been docketed.

(j) The Board shall have power, upon issuance of a complaint as provided in subsection (b) charging that any person has engaged in or is engaging in an unfair labor practice, to petition any district court of the United States (including the District Court of the United States for the District of Columbia), within any district wherein the unfair labor practice in question is alleged to have occurred or wherein such person resides or transacts business, for appropriate temporary relief or restraining order. Upon the filing of any such petition the court shall cause notice thereof to be served upon such person, and thereupon shall have jurisdiction to grant to the Board such temporary relief or restraining order as it deems just and proper.

(k) Whenever it is charged that any person has engaged in an unfair labor practice within the meaning of paragraph (4)(D) of section 8(b), the Board is empowered and directed to hear and determine the dispute out of which such unfair labor practice shall have arisen, unless, within ten days after notice that such charge has been filed, the parties to such dispute submit to the Board satisfactory evidence that they have adjusted, or agreed upon methods for the voluntary adjustment of, the dispute. Upon compliance by the parties to the dispute with the decision of the Board or upon such voluntary adjustment of the dispute, such charge shall be dismissed.

(l) Whenever it is charged that any person has engaged in an unfair labor practice within the meaning of paragraph (4) (A), (B), or (C) of section 8(b), or section 8(e) or section 8(b)(7), the preliminary investigation of such charge shall be made forthwith and given priority over all other cases except cases of like character in the office where it is filed or to which it is referred. If, after such investigation, the officer or regional attorney to whom the matter may be referred has reasonable cause to believe such charge is true and that a complaint should issue, he shall, on behalf of the Board, petition any district court of the United States (including the District Court of the United States for the District of Columbia) within any district where the unfair labor practice in question has occurred, is alleged to have occurred, or wherein such person resides or transacts business, for appropriate injunctive relief pending the final adjudication of the Board with respect to such matter. Upon the filing of any such petition the district court shall have jurisdiction to grant such injunctive relief or temporary restraining order as it deems just and proper, notwithstanding any other provision of law: *Provided further,* That no temporary restraining order shall be issued without notice unless a petition alleges that substantial and irreparable injury to the charging party will be unavoidable and such temporary restraining order shall be effective for no longer than five days and will become void at the expiration of such period: *Provided further,* That such officer or regional attorney shall not apply for any restraining order under section 8(b)(7) if a charge against the employer under section 8(a)(2) has been filed and after the preliminary investigation, he has reasonable cause to believe that such charge is true and that a complaint should issue. Upon filing of any such petition the courts shall cause notice thereof to be served upon any person involved in the charge and such person, including the charging party, shall be given an opportunity to appear by counsel and present any relevant testimony: *Provided further,* That for the purposes of this subsection district courts shall be deemed to have jurisdiction of a labor organization (1) in the district in which such organization maintains its principal office, or (2) in any district in which its duly authorized officers or agents are engaged in promoting or protecting the interests of employee members. The service of legal process upon such officer or agent shall constitute service upon the labor organization and make such organizations a party to the suit. In situations where such relief is appropriate the procedure specified herein shall apply to charges with respect to section 8(b)(4)(D).

(m) Whenever it is charged that any person has engaged in an unfair labor practice within the meaning of subsection (a)(3) or (b)(2) of section 8, such charge shall be given priority over all other cases except cases of like character in the office where it is filed or to which it is referred and cases given priority under subsection (l).

INVESTIGATORY POWERS

SEC. 11. For the purpose of all hearings and investigations, which, in the opinion of the Board, are necessary and proper for the exercise of the powers vested in it by section 9 and section 10—

(1) The Board, or its duly authorized agents or agencies, shall at all reasonable times have access to, for the purpose of examination, and the right to copy any evidence of any person being investigated or proceeded against that relates to any matter under investigation or in question. The Board, or any member thereof, shall upon application of any party to such proceedings, forthwith issue to such party subpenas requiring the attendance and testimony of witnesses or the production of any evidence in such proceeding or investigation requested in such application. Within five days after the service of a subpena on any person requiring the production of any evidence in his possession or under his control, such person may petition the Board to revoke, and the Board shall revoke, such subpena if in its opinion the evidence whose production is required does not relate to any matter under investigation, or any matter in question in such proceedings, or if in its opinion such subpena does not describe with sufficient particularity the

evidence whose production is required. Any member of the Board, or any agent or agency designated by the Board for such purposes, may administer oaths and affirmations, examine witnesses, and receive evidence. Such attendance of witnesses and the production of such evidence may be required from any place in the United States or any Territory or possession thereof, at any designated place of hearing.

(2) In case of contumacy or refusal to obey a subpena issued to any person, any district court of the United States or the United States courts of any Territory or possession, or the District Court of the United States for the District of Columbia, within the jurisdiction of which the inquiry is carried on or within the jurisdiction of which said person guilty of contumacy or refusal to obey is found or resides or transacts business, upon application by the Board shall have jurisdiction to issue to such person an order requiring such person to appear before the Board, its member, agent, or agency, there to produce evidence if so ordered, or there to give testimony touching the matter under investigation or in question; and any failure to obey such order of the court may be punished by said court as a contempt thereof.

(3)*

(4) Complaints, orders, and other process and papers of the Board, its member, agent, or agency, may be served either personally or by registered mail or by telegraph or by leaving a copy thereof at the principal office or place of business of the person required to be served. The verified return by the individual so serving the same setting forth the manner of such service shall be proof of the same, and the return post office receipt or telegraph receipt therefor when registered and mailed or telegraphed as aforesaid shall be proof of service of the same. Witnesses summoned before the Board, its member, agent, or agency, shall be paid the same fees and mileage that are paid witnesses in the courts of the United States, and witnesses whose depositions are taken and the persons taking the same shall severally be entitled to the same fees as are paid for like services in the courts of the United States.

(5) All process of any court to which application may be made under this Act may be served in the judicial district wherein the defendant or other person required to be served resides or may be found.

(6) The several departments and agencies of the Government, when directed by the President, shall furnish the Board, upon its request, all records, papers, and information in their possession relating to any matter before the Board.

SEC. 12. Any person who shall willfully resist, prevent, impede, or interfere with any member of the Board or any of its agents or agencies in the performance of duties pursuant to this Act shall be punished by a fine of not more than $5,000 or by imprisonment for not more than one year, or both.

LIMITATIONS

SEC. 13. Nothing in this Act, except as specifically provided for herein, shall be construed so as either to interfere with or impede or diminish in any way the right to strike, or to affect the limitations or qualifications on that right.

---

*Section 11(3) is repealed by Sec. 234, Public Law 91–452, 91st Congress, S. 30, 84 Stat. 926, October 15, 1970. See Title 18, U.S.C. Sec. 6001, et seq.

SEC. 14. (a) Nothing herein shall prohibit any individual employed as a supervisor from becoming or remaining a member of a labor organization, but no employer subject to this Act shall be compelled to deem individuals defined herein as supervisors as employees for the purpose of any law, either national or local, relating to collective bargaining.

(b) Nothing in this Act shall be construed as authorizing the execution or application of agreements requiring membership in a labor organization as a condition of employment in any State or Territory in which such execution or application is prohibited by State or Territorial law.

(c)(1) The Board, in its discretion, may, by rule of decision or by published rules adopted pursuant to the Administrative Procedure Act, decline to assert jurisdiction over any labor dispute involving any class or category of employers, where, in the opinion of the Board, the effect of such labor dispute on commerce is not sufficiently substantial to warrant the exercise of its jurisdiction: *Provided,* That the Board shall not decline to assert jurisdiction over any labor dispute over which it would assert jurisdiction under the standards prevailing upon August 1, 1959.

(2) Nothing in this Act shall be deemed to prevent or bar any agency or the courts of any State or Territory (including the Commonwealth of Puerto Rico, Guam, and the Virgin Islands), from assuming and asserting jurisdiction over labor disputes over which the Board declines, pursuant to paragraph (1) of this subsection, to assert jurisdiction.

SEC. 15. Wherever the application of the provisions of section 272 of chapter 10 of the Act entitled "An Act to establish a uniform system of bankruptcy throughout the United States," approved July 1, 1898, and Acts amendatory thereof and supplementary thereto (U.S.C., title 11, sec. 672), conflicts with the application of the provisions of this Act, this Act shall prevail: *Provided,* That in any situation where the provisions of this Act cannot be validly enforced, the provisions of such other Acts shall remain in full force and effect.

SEC. 16. If any provision of this Act, or the application of such provision to any person or circumstances, shall be held invalid, the remainder of this Act, or the application of such provision to persons or circumstances other than those as to which it is held invalid, shall not be affected thereby.

SEC. 17. This Act may be cited as the "National Labor Relations Act."

SEC. 18. No petition entertained, no investigation made, no election held, and no certification issued by the National Labor Relations Board, under any of the provisions of section 9 of the National Labor Relations Act, as amended, shall be invalid by reason of the failure of the Congress of Industrial Organizations to have complied with the requirements of section 9(f), (g), or (h) of the aforesaid Act prior to December 22, 1949, or by reason of the failure of the American Federation of Labor to have complied with the provisions of section 9(f), (g), or (h) of the aforesaid Act prior to November 7, 1947: *Provided,* That no liability shall be imposed under any provision of this Act upon any person for failure to honor any election or certificate referred to above, prior to the effective date of this amendment: *Provided, however,* That this proviso shall not have the effect of setting aside or in any way affecting judgments or decrees heretofore entered under section 10(e) or (f) and which have become final.

EFFECTIVE DATE OF CERTAIN CHANGES*

SEC. 102. No provision of this title shall be deemed to make an unfair labor practice any act which was performed prior to the date of the enactment of this Act

*The effective date referred to in Sections 102, 103, and 104 is August 22, 1947. For effective dates of 1959 amendments, see footnote on first page of this text.

which did not constitute an unfair labor practice prior thereto, and the provisions of section 8(a)(3) and section 8(b)(2) of the National Labor Relations Act as amended by this title shall not make an unfair labor practice the performance of any obligation under a collective-bargaining agreement entered into prior to the date of the enactment of this Act, or (in the case of an agreement for a period of not more than one year) entered into on or after such date of enactment, but prior to the effective date of this title, if the performance of such obligation would not have constituted an unfair labor practice under section 8(3) of the National Labor Relations Act prior to the effective date of this title, unless such agreement was renewed or extended subsequent thereto.

SEC. 103. No provisions of this title shall affect any certification of representatives or any determination as to the appropriate collective-bargaining unit, which was made under section 9 of the National Labor Relations Act prior to the effective date of this title until one year after the date of such certification or if, in respect of any such certification, a collective-bargaining contract was entered into prior to the effective date of this title, until the end of the contract period or until one year after such date, whichever first occurs.

SEC. 104. The amendments made by this title shall take effect sixty days after the date of the enactment of this Act, except that the authority of the President to appoint certain officers conferred upon him by section 3 of the National Labor Relations Act as amended by this title may be exercised forthwith.

TITLE II—CONCILIATION OF LABOR DISPUTES IN INDUSTRIES AFFECTING COMMERCE; NATIONAL EMERGENCIES

SEC. 201. That it is the policy of the United States that—

(a) sound and stable industrial peace and the advancement of the general welfare, health, and safety of the Nation and of the best interest of employers and employees can most satisfactorily be secured by the settlement of issues between employers and employees through the processes of conference and collective bargaining between employers and the representatives of their employees;

(b) the settlement of issues between employers and employees through collective bargaining may be advanced by making available full and adequate governmental facilities for conciliation, mediation, and voluntary arbitration to aid and encourage employers and the representatives of their employees to reach and maintain agreements concerning rates of pay, hours, and working conditions, and to make all reasonable efforts to settle their differences by mutual agreement reached through conferences and collective bargaining or by such methods as may be provided for in any applicable agreement for the settlement of disputes; and

(c) certain controversies which arise between parties to collective-bargaining agreements may be avoided or minimized by making available full and adequate governmental facilities for furnishing assistance to employers and the representatives of their employees in formulating for inclusion within such agreements provision for adequate notice of any proposed changes in the terms of such agreements, for the final adjustment of grievances or questions regarding the application or interpretation of such agreements, and other provisions designed to prevent the subsequent arising of such controversies.

SEC. 202. (a) There is hereby created an independent agency to be known as the Federal Mediation and Conciliation Service (herein referred to as the "Service," except that for sixty days after the date of the enactment of this Act such term shall refer to the Conciliation Service of the Department of Labor). The Service shall be under the direction of a Federal Mediation and Conciliation Director (hereinafter referred to as the "Director"), who shall be appointed by the President by and with the advice and consent of the Senate. The Director shall receive compensation at the rate of $12,000* per annum. The Director shall not engage in any other business, vocation, or employment.

(b) The Director is authorized, subject to the civil-service laws, to appoint such clerical and other personnel as may be necessary for the execution of the functions of the Service, and shall fix their compensation in accordance with the Classification Act of 1923, as amended, and may, without regard to the provisions of the civil-service laws and the Classification Act of 1923, as amended, appoint and fix the compensation of such conciliators and mediators as may be necessary to carry out the functions of the Service. The Director is authorized to make such expenditures for supplies, facilities, and services as he deems necessary. Such expenditures shall be allowed and paid upon presentation of itemized vouchers therefor approved by the Director or by any employee designated by him for that purpose.

(c) The principal office of the Service shall be in the District of Columbia, but the Director may establish regional offices convenient to localities in which labor controversies are likely to arise. The Director may by order, subject to revocation at any time, delegate any authority and discretion conferred upon him by this Act to any regional director, or other officer or employee of the Service. The Director may establish suitable procedures for cooperation with State and local mediation agencies. The Director shall make an annual report in writing to Congress at the end of the fiscal year.

(d) All mediation and conciliation functions of the Secretary of Labor or the United States Conciliation Service under section 8 of the Act entitled "An Act to create a Department of Labor," approved March 4, 1913 (U.S.C., title 29, sec. 51), and all functions of the United States Conciliation Service under any other law are hereby transferred to the Federal Mediation and Conciliation Service, together with the personnel and records of the United States Conciliation Service. Such transfer shall take effect upon the sixtieth day after the date of enactment of this Act. Such transfer shall not affect any proceedings pending before the United States Conciliation Service or any certification, order, rule, or regulation theretofore made by it or by the Secretary of Labor. The Director and the Service shall not be subject in any way to the jurisdiction or authority of the Secretary of labor or any official or division of the Department of Labor.

FUNCTIONS OF THE SERVICE

SEC. 203. (a) It shall be the duty of the Service, in order to prevent or minimize interruptions of the free flow of commerce growing out of labor disputes, to assist parties to labor disputes in industries affecting commerce to settle such disputes through conciliation and mediation.

(b) The Service may proffer its services in any labor dispute in any industry affecting commerce, either upon its own motion or upon the request of one or more of the parties to the dispute, whenever in its judgment such dispute threatens to cause a substantial interruption of commerce. The Director and the Service are directed to avoid attempting to mediate disputes which would have only a minor effect on interstate commerce if State or other conciliation services are available to the parties. Whenever the Service does proffer its services in any dispute, it shall be the duty of the Service promptly to put itself in communication

---

*Pursuant to Public Law 90–206, 90th Congress, 81 Stat. 644, approved December 16, 1967, and in accordance with Sec. 225(f)(ii) thereof, effective in 1969, the salary of the Director shall be $40,000 per year.

with the parties and to use its best efforts, by mediation and conciliation, to bring them to agreement.

(c) If the Director is not able to bring the parties to agreement by conciliation within a reasonable time, he shall seek to induce the parties voluntarily to seek other means of settling the dispute without resort to strike, lock-out, or other coercion, including submission to the employees in the bargaining unit of the employer's last offer of settlement for approval or rejection in a secret ballot. The failure or refusal of either party to agree to any procedure suggested by the Director shall not be deemed a violation of any duty or obligation imposed by this Act.

(d) Final adjustment by a method agreed upon by the parties is hereby declared to be the desirable method for settlement of grievance disputes arising over the application or interpretation of an existing collective-bargaining agreement. The Service is directed to make its conciliation and mediation services available in the settlement of such grievance disputes only as a last resort and in exceptional cases.

SEC. 204. (a) In order to prevent or minimize interruptions of the free flow of commerce growing out of labor disputes, employers and employees and their representatives, in any industry affecting commerce, shall—

(1) exert every reasonable effort to make and maintain agreements concerning rates of pay, hours, and working conditions, including provision for adequate notice of any proposed change in the terms of such agreements;

(2) whenever a dispute arises over the terms or application of a collective-bargaining agreement and a conference is requested by a party or prospective party thereto, arrange promptly for such a conference to be held and endeavor in such conference to settle such dispute expeditiously; and

(3) in case such dispute is not settled by conference, participate fully and promptly in such meetings as may be undertaken by the Service under this Act for the purpose of aiding in a settlement of the dispute.

SEC. 205. (a) There is hereby created a National Labor-Management Panel which shall be composed of twelve members appointed by the President, six of whom shall be selected from among persons outstanding in the field of management and six of whom shall be selected from among persons outstanding in the field of labor. Each member shall hold office for a term of three years, except that any member appointed to fill a vacancy occurring prior to the expiration of the term for which his predecessor was appointed shall be appointed for the remainder of such term, and the terms of office of the members first taking office shall expire, as designated by the President at the time of appointment, four at the end of the first year, four at the end of the second year, and four at the end of the third year after the date of appointment. Members of the panel, when serving on business of the panel, shall be paid compensation at the rate of $25 per day, and shall also be entitled to receive an allowance for actual and necessary travel and subsistence expenses while so serving away from their places of residence.

(b) It shall be the duty of the panel, at the request of the Director, to advise in the avoidance of industrial controversies and the manner in which mediation and voluntary adjustment shall be administered, particularly with reference to controversies affecting the general welfare of the country.

NATIONAL EMERGENCIES

SEC. 206. Whenever in the opinion of the President of the United States, a threatened or actual strike or lock-out affecting an entire industry or a substantial part thereof engaged in trade, commerce, transportation, transmission, or communication among the several States or with foreign nations, or engaged in the production of goods for commerce, will, if permitted to occur or to continue, imperil the national health or safety, he may appoint a board of inquiry to inquire into the issues involved in the dispute and to make a written report to him within such time as he shall prescribe. Such report shall include a statement of the facts with respect to the dispute, including each party's statement of its position but shall not contain any recommendations. The President shall file a copy of such report with the Service and shall make its contents available to the public.

SEC. 207. (a) A board of inquiry shall be composed of a chairman and such other members as the President shall determine, and shall have power to sit and act in any place within the United States and to conduct such hearings either in public or in private, as it may deem necessary or proper, to ascertain the facts with respect to the causes and circumstances of the dispute.

(b) Members of a board of inquiry shall receive compensation at the rate of $50 for each day actually spent by them in the work of the board, together with necessary travel and subsistence expenses.

(c) For the purpose of any hearing or inquiry conducted by any board appointed under this title, the provisions of sections 9 and 10 (relating to the attendance of witnesses and the production of books, papers, and documents) of the Federal Trade Commission Act of September 16, 1914, as amended (U.S.C. 19, title 15, secs. 49 and 50, as amended), are hereby made applicable to the powers and duties of such board.

SEC. 208. (a) Upon receiving a report from a board of inquiry the President may direct the Attorney General to petition any district court of the United States having jurisdiction of the parties to enjoin such strike or lock-out or the continuing thereof, and if the court finds that such threatened or actual strike or lock-out—

(i) affects an entire industry or a substantial part thereof engaged in trade, commerce, transportation, transmission, or communication among the several States or with foreign nations, or engaged in the production of goods for commerce; and

(ii) if permitted to occur or to continue, will imperil the national health or safety, it shall have jurisdiction to enjoin any such strike or lock-out, or the continuing thereof, and to make such other orders as may be appropriate.

(b) In any case, the provisions of the Act of March 23, 1932, entitled "An Act to amend the Judicial Code and to define and limit the jurisdiction of courts sitting in equity, and for other purposes," shall not be applicable.

(c) The order or orders of the court shall be subject to review by the appropriate circuit court of appeals and by the Supreme Court upon writ of certiorari or certification as provided in sections 239 and 240 of the Judicial Code, as amended (U.S.C., title 29, secs. 346 and 347).

SEC. 209. (a) Whenever a district court has issued an order under section 208 enjoining acts or practices which imperil or threaten to imperil the national health or safety, it shall be the duty of the parties to the labor dispute giving rise to such order to make every effort to adjust and settle their differences, with the assistance of the Service created by this Act. Neither party shall be under any duty to accept, in whole or in part, any proposal of settlement made by the Service.

(b) Upon the issuance of such order, the President shall reconvene the board of inquiry which has previously reported with respect to the dispute. At the end of a sixty-day period (unless the dispute has been settled by that time), the board of inquiry shall report to the President the current position of the parties and the efforts which has been made for settlement, and shall include a statement by each party of its position and a statement of the employer's last offer of settlement. The President shall make such report available to the public. The National Labor Relations Board, within the succeeding fifteen days, shall take a secret ballot of the employees of each employer involved in the dispute on the question of whether they wish to accept the final offer of settlement made by their employer as stated by him and shall certify the results thereof to the Attorney General within five days thereafter.

Sec. 210. Upon the certification of the results of such ballot or upon a settlement being reached, whichever happens sooner, the Attorney General shall move the court to discharge the injunction, which motion shall then be granted and the injunction discharged. When such motion is granted, the President shall submit to the Congress a full and comprehensive report of the proceedings, including the findings of the board of inquiry and the ballot taken by the National Labor Relations Board, together with such recommendations as he may see fit to make for consideration and appropriate action.

COMPILATION OF COLLECTIVE-BARGAINING AGREEMENTS, ETC.

Sec. 211. (a) For the guidance and information of interested representatives of employers, employees, and the general public, the Bureau of Labor Statistics of the Department of Labor shall maintain a file of copies of all available collective-bargaining agreements and other available agreements and actions thereunder settling or adjusting labor disputes. Such file shall be open to inspection under appropriate conditions prescribed by the Secretary of Labor, except that no specific information submitted in confidence shall be disclosed.

(b) The Bureau of Labor Statistics in the Department of Labor is authorized to furnish upon request of the Service, or employers, employees, or their representatives, all available data and factual information which may aid in the settlement of any labor dispute, except that no specific information submitted in confidence shall be disclosed.

EXEMPTION OF RAILWAY LABOR ACT

Sec. 212. The provisions of this title shall not be applicable with respect to any matter which is subject to the provisions of the Railway Labor Act, as amended from time to time.

TITLE III

SUITS BY AND AGAINST LABOR ORGANIZATIONS

Sec. 301. (a) Suits for violation of contracts between an employer and a labor organization representing employees in an industry affecting commerce as defined in this Act, or between any such labor organizations, may be brought in any district court of the United States having jurisdiction of the parties, without respect to the amount in controversy or without regard to the citizenship of the parties.

(b) Any labor organization which represents employees in an industry affecting commerce as defined in this Act and any employer whose activities affect commerce as defined in this Act shall be bound by the acts of its agents. Any such labor organization may sue or be sued as an entity and in behalf of the employees whom it represents in the courts of the United States. Any money judgment against a labor organization in a district court of the United States shall be enforceable only against the organization as an entity and against its assets, and shall not be enforceable against any individual member or his assets.

(c) For the purposes of actions and proceedings by or against labor organizations in the district courts of the United States, district courts shall be deemed to have jurisdiction of a labor organization (1) in the district in which such organization maintains its principal offices, or (2) in any district in which its duly authorized officers or agents are engaged in representing or acting for employee members.

(d) The service of summons, subpena, or other legal process of any court of the United States upon an officer or agent of a labor organization, in his capacity as such, shall constitute service upon the labor organization.

(e) For the purposes of this section, in determining whether any person is acting as an "agent" of another person so as to make such other person responsible for his acts, the question of whether the specific acts performed were actually authorized or subsequently ratified shall not be controlling.

RESTRICTIONS ON PAYMENTS TO EMPLOYEE REPRESENTATIVES

SEC. 302. (a) It shall be unlawful for any employer or association of employers or any person who acts as a labor relations expert, adviser, or consultant to an employer or who acts in the interest of an employer to pay, lend, or deliver, or agree to pay, lend, or deliver, any money or other thing of value—

(1) to any representative of any of his employees who are employed in an industry affecting commerce; or

(2) to any labor organization, or any officer or employee thereof, which represents, seeks to represent, or would admit to membership, any of the employees of such employer who are employed in an industry affecting commerce; or

(3) to any employee or group or committee of employees of such employer employed in an industry affecting commerce in excess of their normal compensation for the purpose of causing such employee or group or committee directly or indirectly to influence any other employees in the exercise of the right to organize and bargain collectively through representatives of their own choosing; or

(4) to any officer or employee of a labor organization engaged in an industry affecting commerce with intent to influence him in respect to any of his actions, decisions, or duties as a representative of employees or as such officer or employee of such labor organization.

(b)(1) It shall be unlawful for any person to request, demand, receive, or accept, or agree to receive or accept, any payment, loan, or delivery of any money or other thing of value prohibited by subsection (a).

(2) It shall be unlawful for any labor organization, or for any person acting as an officer, agent, representative, or employee of such labor organization, to demand or accept from the operator of any motor vehicle (as defined in part II of the Interstate Commerce Act) employed in the transportation of property in commerce, or the employer of any such operator, any money or other thing of value payable to such organization or to an officer, agent, representative or employee thereof as a fee or charge for the unloading, or the connection with the unloading, of the cargo of such vehicle: *Provided*, That nothing in this paragraph shall be construed to make unlawful any payment by an employer to any of his employees as compensation for their services as employees.

(c) The provisions of this section shall not be applicable (1) in respect to any money or other thing of value payable by an employer to any of his employees whose established duties include acting openly for such employer in matters of labor relations or personnel administration or to any representative of his employees, or to any officer or employee of a labor organization, who is also an employee or former employee of such employer, as compensation for, or by reason of, his service as an employee of such employer; (2) with respect to the payment or delivery of any money or other thing of value in satisfaction of a judgment of any court or a decision or award of an arbitrator or impartial chairman or in compromise, adjustment, settlement, or release of any claim, complaint, grievance, or dispute in the absence of fraud or duress; (3) with respect to the sale or purchase of an article or commodity at the prevailing market price in the regular course of business; (4) with respect to money deducted from the wages of employees in payment of membership dues in a labor organization: *Provided*, That the employer has received from each employee, on whose account such deductions are made, a written assignment which shall not be irrevocable for a period of more than one year, or beyond the termination date of the applicable collective agreement, whichever occurs sooner; (5) with respect to money or other thing of value paid to a trust fund established by such representative, for the sole and exclusive benefit of the employees of such employer, and their families and dependents (or of such employees, families, and dependents jointly with the employees of other employers making similar payments, and their families and dependents): *Provided*, That (A) such payments are held in trust for the purpose of paying, either from principal or income or both, for the benefit of employees, their families and dependents, for medical or hospital care, pensions on retirement or death of employees, compensation for injuries or illness resulting from occupational activity or insurance to provide any of the foregoing, or unemployment benefits or life insurance, disability and sickness insurance, or accident insurance; (B) the detailed basis on which such payments are to be made is specified in a written agreement with the employer, and employees and employers are equally represented in the administration of such fund, together with such neutral persons as the representatives of the employers and the representatives of employees may agree upon and in the event the employer and employee groups deadlock on the administration of such fund and there are no neutral persons empowered to break such deadlock, such agreement provides that the two groups shall agree on an impartial umpire to decide such dispute, or in event of their failure to agree within a reasonable length of time, an impartial umpire to decide such dispute shall, on petition of either group, be appointed by the district court of the United States for the district where the trust fund has its principal office, and shall also contain provisions for an annual audit of the trust fund, a statement of the results of which shall be available for inspection by interested persons at the principal office of the trust fund and at such other places as may be designated in such written agreement; and (C) such payments as are intended to be used for the purpose of providing pensions or annuities for employees are made to a separate trust which provides that the funds held therein cannot be used for any purpose other than paying such pensions or annuities; (6) with respect to money or other thing of value paid by any employer to a trust fund established by such representative for the purpose of pooled vacation, holiday, severance or similar benefits, or defraying costs of apprenticeship or other training program: *Provided*, That the requirements of clause (B) of the proviso to clause (5) of this subsection shall apply to such trust funds; or (7) with respect to money or other thing of value paid by any employer to a pooled or individual trust fund established by such representative for the purpose of (A) scholarships for the benefit of employees, their families, and dependents for study at educational institutions, or (B) child care centers for preschool and school age dependents of employees: *Provided*, That no labor organization or employer shall be required to bargain on the establishment of any such trust fund, and refusal to do so shall not constitute an unfair labor practice:

Provided further, That the requirements of clause (B) of the proviso to clause (5) of this subsection shall apply to such trust funds.*

(d) Any person who willfully violates any of the provisions of this section shall, upon conviction thereof, be guilty of a misdemeanor and be subject to a fine of not more than $10,000 or to imprisonment for not more than one year, or both.

(e) The district courts of the United States and the United States courts of the Territories and possessions shall have jurisdiction, for cause shown, and subject to the provisions of section 17 (relating to notice to opposite party) of the Act entitled "An Act to supplement existing laws against unlawful restraints and monopolies, and for other purposes," approved October 15, 1914, as amended (U.S.C., title 28, sec. 381), to restrain violations of this section, without regard to the provisions of sections 6 and 20 of such Act of October 15, 1914, as amended (U.S.C., title 15, sec. 17, and title 29, sec. 52), and the provisions of the Act entitled "An Act to amend the Judicial Code and to define and limit the jurisdiction of courts sitting in equity, and for other purposes," approved March 23, 1932 (U.S.C., title 29, secs. 101-115).

(f) This section shall not apply to any contract in force on the date of enactment of this Act, until the expiration of such contract, or until July 1, 1948, whichever first occurs.

(g) Compliance with the restrictions contained in subsection (c)(5)(D) upon contributions to trust funds, otherwise lawful, shall not be applicable to contributions to such trust funds established by collective agreement prior to January 1, 1946, nor shall subsection (c)(5)(A) be construed as prohibiting contributions to such trust funds if prior to January 1, 1947, such funds contained provisions for pooled vacation benefits.

BOYCOTTS AND OTHER UNLAWFUL COMBINATIONS

SEC. 303. (a) It shall be unlawful, for the purpose of this section only, in an industry or activity affecting commerce, for any labor organization to engage in any activity or conduct defined as an unfair labor practice in section 8(b)(4) of the National Labor Relations Act, as amended.

(b) Whoever shall be injured in his business or property by reason of any violation of subsection (a) may sue therefor in any district court of the United States subject to the limitations and provisions of section 301 hereof without respect to the amount in controversy, or in any other court having jurisdiction of the parties, and shall recover the damages by him sustained and the cost of the suit.

RESTRICTION ON POLITICAL CONTRIBUTIONS

SEC. 304. Section 313 of the Federal Corrupt Practices Act, 1925 (U.S.C., 1940 edition, title 2, sec. 251; Supp. V, title 50, App., sec. 1509), as amended, is amended to read as follows:

SEC. 313. It is unlawful for any national bank, or any corporation organized by authority of any law of Congress to make a contribution or expenditure in connection with any election to any political office, or in connection with any primary election or political convention or caucus held to select candidates for any political office, or for any corporation whatever, or any labor organization to make a contribution or expenditure in connection with any election at which Presidential and Vice Presidential electors or a Senator or Representative in, or a Delegate or Resident Commissioner to Congress are to be voted for, or in connection with any

*Section 302(c)(7) has been added by Public Law 91-86, 91st Congress, S. 2068, 83 Stat. 133, approved October 14, 1969.

primary election or political convention or caucus held to select candidates for any of the foregoing offices, or for any candidate, political committee, or other person to accept or receive any contribution prohibited by this section. Every corporation or labor organization which makes any contribution or expenditure in violation of this section shall be fined not more than $5,000; and every officer or director of any corporation, or officer of any labor organization, who consents to any contribution or expenditure by the corporation or labor organization, as the case may be, in violation of this section shall be fined not more than $1,000 or imprisoned for not more than one year, or both. For the purposes of this section "labor organization" means any organization of any kind, or any agency or employee representation committee or plan, in which employees participate and which exists for the purpose, in whole or in part, of dealing with employers concerning grievances, labor disputes, wages, rates of pay, hours of employment, or conditions of work.

TITLE IV

CREATION OF JOINT COMMITTEE TO STUDY AND REPORT ON BASIC PROBLEMS AFFECTING FRIENDLY LABOR RELATIONS AND PRODUCTIVITY

*   *   *   *   *   *   *

TITLE V

DEFINITIONS

SEC. 501. When used in this Act—

(1) The term "industry affecting commerce" means any industry or activity in commerce or in which a labor dispute would burden or obstruct commerce or tend to burden or obstruct commerce or the free flow of commerce.

(2) The term "strike" includes any strike or other concerted stoppage of work by employees (including a stoppage by reason of the expiration of a collective-bargaining agreement) and any concerted slow-down or other concerted interruption of operations by employees.

(3) The terms "commerce," "labor disputes," "employer," "employee," "labor organization," "representative," "person," and "supervisor" shall have the same meaning as when used in the National Labor Relations Act as amended by this Act.

SAVING PROVISION

SEC. 502. Nothing in this Act shall be construed to require an individual employee to render labor or service without his consent, nor shall anything in this Act be construed to make the quitting of his labor by an individual employee an illegal act; nor shall any court issue any process to compel the performance by an individual employee of such labor or service, without his consent; nor shall the quitting of labor by an employee or employees in good faith because of abnormally dangerous conditions for work at the place of employment of such employee or employees be deemed a strike under this Act.

SEPARABILITY

SEC. 503. If any provision of this Act, or the application of such provision to any person or circumstance, shall be held invalid, the remainder of this Act, or the application of such provision to persons or circumstances other than those as to which it is held invalid, shall not be affected thereby.

U.S. GOVERNMENT PRINTING OFFICE: 1965 O—792-030

For sale by the Superintendent of Documents, U.S. Government Printing Office
Washington, D.C. 20402 - Price 20 cents

APPENDIX D

OFFICE OF LABOR-MANAGEMENT AND WELFARE-PENSION REPORTS

National Office: Location: American National Bank Bldg., 8701 Georgia Ave., Silver Spring, Maryland 20910, Tel: 301-495-4361; Mailing Address: U.S. Department of Labor, 14th and Constitution Ave., Washington, D.C. 20210.

Area Offices

Albany *
607 State Bank Bldg.,
75 State St.,
Albany, New York 12207
#472-3514

Anchorage *
214 Willholth Bldg.,
610 C St., P.O. Box 1097,
Anchorage, Alaska
#BR 8-9755

Atlanta
Peachtree Bldg., Rm. 330,
1371 Peachtree St., N.E.,
Atlanta, Ga. 30309
#526-5351

Birmingham *
Rm. 435, P.O. Bldg.,
1800 5th Ave., No.,
Birmingham, Ala. 35203
#325-3892

Boston
Rm. 1712A JFK Federal Bldg.,
Govt. Center,
Boston, Mass. 02203
#223-6736

Buffalo
Rm. 435, Federal Bldg.,
121 Ellicott St.,
Buffalo, N.Y. 14203
#842-3260

Charlotte *
Rm. 405, B.S.R. Bldg.,
316 E. Morehead St.,
Charlotte, N.C. 28202
#372-7460

Chicago
773 Federal Office Bldg.,
219 S. Dearborn St.,
Chicago, Ill. 60604
#353-7264

Area Offices

Cincinnati *
Rm. 4025, Federal Bldg.,
550 Main St.,
Cincinnati, Ohio 45202
#684-2700

Cleveland
Rm. 897, Federal Office Bldg.,
1240 E. 9th St.,
Cleveland, Ohio 44199
#522-3860

Dallas
Rms. 1005-1006,
1416 Commerce St.,
Dallas, Texas 75201
#749-2233

Denver
451 New Custom House,
721 19th St.,
Denver, Colo. 80202
#297-3203

Detroit
Rm. 1906,
Washington Blvd. Bldg.,
234 State St.,
Detroit, Mich. 48226
#226-6200

Grand Rapids *
Rm. 117,
Old Post Office Bldg.,
Ionia and Pearl Sts.,
Grand Rapids, Mich. 49502
#546-2379

Hartford *
Rm. 306, 135 High St.,
Hartford, Conn. 06101
#244-2349

Honolulu
1833 Kala Kaua Ave.,
Rm. 601,
Honolulu, Hawaii 96815
#955-0261

Houston *
Rm. 713, Federal Office Bldg.,
Fannin & Franklin Sts.,
Houston, Texas 77002
#228-4608-9

Indianapolis *
Rm. 422, Century Bldg.,
36 So. Pennsylvania St.,
Indianapolis, Ind. 46204
#633-7446

Kansas City
2503 Federal Office Bldg.,
911 Walnut St.,
Kansas City, Mo. 64106
#374-5261

Los Angeles
Rm. 7731, Federal Bldg.,
300 N. Los Angeles St.,
Los Angeles, Calif. 90012
#688-4975-6-7

Area Offices

Louisville *
Rm. 606, Republic Bldg.,
429 W. Walnut St.,
Louisville, Ky. 40202
#582-5160

Memphis *
Rm. 216, Federal Bldg.,
167 N. Main,
Memphis, Tenn. 38003
#534-3283

Miami
Rm. 1517,
51 S.W. First Ave.,
Miami, Fla. 33130
#350-5777

Minneapolis
110 Federal Courts Bldg.,
110 S. 4th St.,
Minneapolis, Minn.
#334-2591-2

Nashville
U.S. Court House Bldg.,
Rm. 786, 801 Broadway,
Nashville, Tenn. 37203
#242-8321 ext. 5438

New Orleans
204 U.S. Customs House Bldg.,
423 Canal St.,
New Orleans, La. 70130
#527-6174

New York City
233 W. 49th St.,
New York, N.Y. 10019
PLaza 7-9410

Newark
Rm. 635, Federal Bldg.,
970 Broad St.,
Newark, N.J. 07102
#645-3016

Philadelphia
5000 U.S. Courthouse Bldg.,
9th & Market Sts.,
Philadelphia, Pa. 19107
#597-4961

Pittsburgh
Rm. 2002,
Federal Office Bldg.,
1000 Liberty Ave.,
Pittsburgh, Pa. 15222
#644-2925

Portland *
Rm. 201, Federal Bldg.,
511 N.W. Broadway,
Portland, Ore. 97209
#226-3928

Puerto Rico
706 San Alberto Condominio
Bldg.,
1200 Ponce de Leon Ave.,
Santurce, P.R. 00907
#723-8790

Area Offices

St. Louis
3740 Federal Office Bldg.,
1520 Market St.,
St. Louis, Mo. 63103
#622-4691

San Francisco
9403 Federal Office Bldg.,
450 Golden Gate Ave.,
San Francisco, Calif. 94102
#556-2030

Seattle
3301 Smith Tower Bldg.,
506 Second Ave.,
Seattle, Wash. 98104
#583-5216

Tampa *
Rm. 1, 2104 S. Lois Ave.,
Tampa, Fla. 33609
#228-7342

Washington, D. C.
509 Vanguard Bldg.,
1111 20th St., N.W.,
Washington, D. C. 20210
#386-4661

* One-man office: appointment should be made in advance.

Gissel Packing:

Was the Supreme Court Right?

by Robert Lewis

The Supreme Court made bad law in the *Gissel Packing Company* case, the last labor law decision of the Court under Chief Justice Warren. The Court approved the use of authorization cards by unions to establish their representational status. If the effect of the decision is not changed by future cases, legislation will be needed.

IN JUNE OF 1969 the Supreme Court significantly changed the law of labor relations with its decision in *NLRB* v. *Gissel Packing Company*, 395 U. S. 575. In a lengthy opinion the Court approved the use of authorization cards by unions to establish their representative status. Under the new rules unions will find "the going easier". Organization by misrepresentation is now sanctioned, and the slightest misstep by an employer may result in a bargaining order.

The purpose of this commentary is to highlight the changes in the law wrought by the Court, with the hope that perhaps some day the wrong will be corrected.

Previously, an employer's subjective motivation in denying recognition to a majority union was the determinative factor as to whether the National Labor Relations Board would order bargaining. In *Gissel* the Court held that an employer's good or bad faith doubt of the union's alleged majority status is no longer relevant. Henceforth, compulsory bargaining will turn on the issue of the gravity of an employer's unfair labor practices.

Chief Justice Warren, writing for the Court, declared that "the Board announced at oral argument that it had virtually abandoned the *Joy Silk* doctrine[1] altogether. Under the board's current practice, an employer's good faith doubt is largely irrelevant. . . ."

---

1. *Joy Silk Mills* v. *NLRB*, 85 N.L.R.B. 1263, *enf'd* 185 F. 2d 732 (D. C. Cir. 1950). The Court described this doctrine as holding that "an employer could lawfully refuse to bargain with a union claiming representative status through possession of authorization cards if he had a 'good faith doubt' as to the union's majority status . . .".

Reprinted from American Bar Association Journal September 1970 Volume 56

Accordingly, the Court remanded to the board for new findings because of what it conceived to be a new approach by the board.

It must have come as a shock to the members of the National Labor Relations Board to learn that their long-employed good faith standard was now discarded. Surely, no less surprising to the board was the news that *they* had abandoned it.

It would be novel for a litigant to argue one contention in his brief to the Supreme Court and a different one orally. For a governmental agency to do so would be unprecedented. The National Labor Relations Board did not abandon its *Joy Silk* doctrine. The Court, wrong in concluding that it had, misconstrued its colloquy with the board's representative.

The board's brief in *Gissel* dealt at great length with the principles underlying its rule that "an employer confronted with a union demand to bargain may refuse if, in good faith, he doubts the union's majority status". Furthermore, stated the board in a headnote, "an employer acting in good faith is entitled to insist upon an election". Conversely, "if the employer was not acting in good faith, his refusal to bargain with a union which in fact represented a majority of the employees would be unlawful".

The board adhered to this thesis in oral argument. Associate General Counsel Dominick L. Manoli in his opening statement referred to the board's long-standing practice of premising bargaining orders on the employ-er's lack of good faith doubt of the union's majority status. He categorically denied that he was arguing differently when subsequently questioned by the Court:

> JUSTICE WHITE: The test you state in your brief is whether or not the employer has a good faith doubt about the majority status of the union and that unfair labor practice is only a material element in judging whether or not he had a good faith doubt. Now you are stating a considerably different rule now. Don't you think the rule you are stating is different?
>
> MR. MANOLI: No, I think it is the rule that we have indicated. It is the Board rule in Aaron Brothers.[2]

Mr. Manoli had an opportunity further to explain *Aaron Brothers*.[3] When he was asked whether "there had been some shift in the subtleties", he replied:

> Yes. The shift has been I think primarily in this respect, that the Board originally would say that the employer had to come forward with some objective . . . evidence to support his good faith doubt. Today the Board does not insist that he come forward objectively with evidence. In fact the Board puts the burden of proving the employer's lack of a good faith doubt, puts that burden upon the general counsel.[4]

---

2. PROCEEDINGS OF SUPREME COURT, GISSEL PACKING, oral argument at 21-22.
3. In *Aaron Brothers*, 158 N.L.R.B. 1077 (1966), the board reviewed and reaffirmed its good faith—bad faith approach. In doing so, it also reaffirmed a recent decision shifting the burden of proof to the board's general counsel to "come forward with evidence and affirmatively establish the existence of . . . bad faith". The board further stated, with recent case illustrations, that not every unfair labor practice would automatically result in a finding of bad faith and therefore a bargaining order.
4. *Supra* note 2, at 27.

Thus, the Court's statement that "under the Board's current practice, an employer's good faith doubt is largely irrelevant" is incorrect. Mr. Manoli stated unequivocally that under current practice an employer's lack of good faith is relevant, to be proved by the General Counsel. It was the Court, not the board, which "announced" a change in the law. It was the Court, not the board, which "abandoned" *Joy Silk*.

Guessing About Major or Minor Unfair Labor Practices

The Court made further changes. It announced that henceforth "the key to the issuance of a bargaining order is the commission of serious unfair labor practices that interfere with the election processes and tend to preclude the holding of a fair election". Conversely, stated the Court, when the unfair labor practices are "minor or less extensive", with minimal impact on the election machinery, a bargaining order is not warranted. In determining whether to issue a bargaining order, the board should consider "the extensiveness of an employer's unfair practices in terms of their past effect on election conditions and the likelihood of their recurrence in the future".

Thus, for the first time, the Court created "gradations of unfair labor practices". Two general categories were established, the major and the minor. Serious or extensive unfair labor practices will support a bargaining order; less serious conduct will not. The determination of the category

is to be decided by the NLRB, based upon its "expert estimate" as to the effect of the particular unfair labor practice on the election process. Reviewing courts should accord the board's choice special respect.

The Court noted that there might be an additional type of unfair labor practice—the "outrageous"—which also could result in a bargaining order. This species was suggested by Chief Judge Haynsworth in *NLRB* v. *S. S. Logan Packing Company*, 386 F. 2d 562 (4th Cir. 1967). He cautioned, however, that since the issuance of a bargaining order is an extraordinary remedy, "its use, if ever appropriate, must be reserved for extraordinary cases". This dictum was cited by the Supreme Court as showing that, on this issue, the view of the Fourth Circuit and the Court were relatively close.[5]

Split in Attitude Toward Authorization Cards

The views of the Fourth Circuit and the Supreme Court were diametrically opposite as to the reliability of authorization cards to reflect employee sentiment. It was Judge Haynsworth's opinion that "It would be difficult to imagine a more unreliable method of ascertaining the real wishes of employees

---

5. The Court's discussion of the Fourth Circuit's dictum concerning bargaining orders to remedy outrageous unfair labor practices in extraordinary cases was itself dictum. It noted that: "The only effect of our holding here is to approve the Board's use of the bargaining order in less extraordinary cases . . .".

than a 'card check' . . .".[6] He spoke of the "inclination to be agreeable" and to "avoid stands which appear to be nonconformist and antagonistic to friends and fellow employees", stating "many people, solicited alone and in private, will sign a petition and, later . . . will sign an opposing petition, in each instance out of concern for the feelings of the solicitors and the difficulty of saying 'NO.' "[7] He criticized the unsupervised solicitation of cards accompanied by misrepresentations such as: "We need these cards to get an election. You believe in the democratic process, don't you? Do you want to deny people the right to vote?"[8]

The Supreme Court, while acknowledging the inferiority of cards to a secret ballot election, nevertheless rejected these arguments. It was the Court's view that when an employer has impeded the election process by committing serious unfair labor practices, "cards may be the most effective —perhaps the only—way of assuring employee choice". Notwithstanding occasional abuses "arising out of misrepresentations by union organizers" as to the card's purpose, it was the Court's view that employees should be bound by the clear language of what they sign. "There is nothing inconsistent in handing an employee a card that says the signer authorizes the union to represent him and then telling him that the card will probably be used first to get an election."

This explanation may not be inconsistent, but it is misleading. If all the employee hears is that an election will be sought, a misrepresentation occurs when he is not advised that the card may be used to prevent an election from ever being held or that the card can be used after an election to cancel out his vote.

In reliance on *Gissel,* the board has held that a union solicitor's misrepresentation to an employee that a majority of his fellow workers have signed previously does not invalidate his card, even though he testifies that he would not have signed if he had known the truth.[9] Thus, the law today permits— indeed, encourages—organization by misrepresentation.

The Court in *Gissel* disposed of all arguments challenging the use of cards. In answering the contention that "employees cannot make an informed choice because the card drive will be over before the employer has had a chance to present his side of the unionization issues", the Court responded that "[n]ormally . . . the union will

6. Echoing this sentiment was Judge Medina, who stated: "This 'representation' card business is an abomination." *Schwarzenbach-Huber Company* v. *NLRB,* 408 F. 2d 236 (2d Cir. 1969).

7. Compare: "Social scientists have testified that the most intense coercion which can be directed at most people in our conformist society is the threat of social ostracism by their peer groups." Affeldt, *Bargaining Orders Without An Election,* 57 KY. L. J. 151, 167 (Winter 1968-1969).

8. It is a matter of public record that these views largely contributed to labor's opposition to Judge Haynsworth's nomination as a member of the Supreme Court. For example, see BUTCHER WORKMAN, December, 1969: "The Amalgamated Meat Cutters' battle against Haynsworth was instigated by his decision in the *Logan Packing* case."

9. *Marie Phillips, Inc.,* 178 N.L.R.B. 53 (1969).

inform the employer of its organization drive early", enabling the employer to reply before the union obtains its majority.

This reasoning is fallacious. It is not normally the practice of unions to give employers notice that it is organizing. Most campaigns begin *sub rosa*. Frequently, the first notice to the employer is the receipt of a request for recognition, after the union has achieved its majority. This is particularly true in small bargaining units, where, according to the Court, election cases most often arise.[10] Even when the employer becomes aware of the union's drive prior to its achieving majority status, it has had no opportunity to communicate with those who have already signed.

The Court in *Gissel Packing* acknowledged that authorization cards were an "admittedly inferior" procedure, but it said it had chosen the procedure because it better reflected employee sentiment than an election conducted concomitant with employer unfair labor practices. This thesis is open to challenge.

Employee Reactions to Employer Actions

It has never been proved to what extent, if any, unfair labor practices influence a voter's choice in a National Labor Relations Board election.

The fact is that an enormous number of Board doctrines are based upon untested suppositions. We have had twenty-five years and more of litigation about organizing activities on and off

company property but little data on how employees react to various devices. We simply do not know what makes an employee feel fear in an election situation.[11]

Derek C. Bok, Dean of the Harvard Law School, has argued that there is an inadequate understanding of voting behavior and the nature of the election process itself.[12] As support he quoted, to use his words, "one of the most careful studies in the field", which recited:

Despite the universal interest in what has influenced our elections, interpretation has scarcely risen above the simplest impressionism. The explanations offered for an electoral result are astonishingly varied; they depend typically on the slenderest evidence, and disagreements are commonplace even among knowledgeable observers.[13]

Dean Bok concluded that in NLRB elections "it is difficult to determine how much protection the voters actually need in reaching their decision —or to determine the circumstances in which they are coerced or interfered with . . .".

---

10. See, for example, *Aaron Brothers, supra* note 3, at 1085; *NLRB v. Century Broadcasting Corporation,* 419 F. 2d 771 (8th Cir. 1969); *Oxco,* 171 N.L.R.B. 70 (1968).
11. Address by Professor Merton C. Bernstein before a meeting of the Section of Labor Relations Law of the American Bar Association, August 11, 1969. 71 L.R.R.M. 585, 591.
12. Bok, *The Regulation of Campaign Tactics in Representation Elections Under the National Labor Relations Act,* 78 HARV. L. REV. 38, 40 (1964).
13. CAMPBELL, CONVERSE, MILLER & STOKES, THE AMERICAN VOTER 523 (1960).

Notwithstanding the absence of empirical studies, the Court in *Gissel* instructed the board to determine whether a particular unfair labor practice "probably" prevents the holding of a fair election. It is questionable whether unfair labor practices can be graded as to their probable impact on a prospective election without engaging in pure guesswork.

Dean Bok apparently would disagree with the Court's statement that the Board's *expertise* permits it to "estimate . . . the effects on the election process of unfair labor practices of varying intensity". He refers to "inferences of 'coercion' or 'interference' drawn by officials far removed from the heat of the election campaign" and states that "the problems in drawing such inferences are substantial, and they do not disappear with greater familiarity and experience". As an example, he cites the discharge of a union sympathizer and states: "Although this tactic can often frustrate a union drive, any experienced organizer knows that a discriminatory discharge may rally the voters against the employer instead of frightening them into submission. A few organizers have even provoked a discharge deliberately for this reason."

Similarly, he argues that employer threats and other appeals to fear and emotion may cause employees, because of resentment, to vote against, rather than for, the employer.

Why Unions with Card Majorities Lose

The problem the Court grappled with in *Gissel* was what causes a union with a pre-election card majority nevertheless to lose the election. It concluded that it is usually the employer's unfair labor practices.

Unions with pre-election card majorities lose elections, not because of employer unfair practices, but because the cards were signed without conviction.[14] When an employer subsequently presents his employees with cogent, factual arguments against unionization, the union's ephemeral majority evaporates.

In its last labor law decision, the Warren Court sought to resolve the authorization card controversy with a lasting epitaph. Instead, it made bad law. Unless the result is changed by the Burger Court, legislation is urgently needed. The effort to accomplish this should be unceasing.

---

14. Lewis, *The Use and Abuse of Authorization Cards in Determining Union Majority*, 16 LAB. L. J. 434 (1965); *Refusal To Recognize Charges Under Section 8(a) (5) of the NLRB: Card Checks and Employee Free Choice*, 33 U. CHI. L. REV. 387, 390 (Winter 1966); Lewis, *NLRB Again Stretches Joy Silk's Tenuous Fabric*, 18 LAB. L. J. 222 (1967); McGuiness, *Are Union Authorization Cards Consistent with Employee Freedom of Choice?* N. Y. U. 21ST CONF. LABOR 313, 324-325 (1968).

Often cards are signed by employees who cannot read or write English, or after having consumed alcoholic beverages. These cards are valid under the board's shockingly loose rules. *NLRB* v. *American Art Industries, Inc.*, 415 F. 2d 1223 (5th Cir. 1969); *Morse Chain Company*, 175 N.L.R.B. 98 (1969); *Mid-State Beverages*, 153 N.L.R.B. 135 (1965) (8-12 bottles of beer).

APPENDIX F

NLRB v. GISSEL PACKING CO.

OCTOBER TERM, 1968.

NATIONAL LABOR RELATIONS BOARD v. GISSEL PACKING CO., INC., ET AL.

CERTIORARI TO THE UNITED STATES COURT OF APPEALS FOR THE FOURTH CIRCUIT.

No. 573. Argued March 26, 1969.—Decided June 16, 1969.*

In Nos. 573 and 691, Unions waged organizational campaigns, obtained authorization cards from a majority of employees in the appropriate bargaining units, and demanded recognition by the employers. The employers refused to bargain, on the ground that the cards were inherently unreliable, and carried out vigorous antiunion campaigns. In one instance the Union did not seek a representation election, but filed unfair labor practice charges against the employer; in a second, an election sought by the Union was not held because of unfair labor practice charges filed by the Union as a result of the employer's antiunion campaign; and in the third, an election petitioned by the Union and won by the employer was set aside by the National Labor Relations Board (NLRB) because of the employer's pre-election unfair labor practices. In each instance the NLRB found that the Union had obtained valid authorization cards from a majority of the employees in the bargaining unit and was thus entitled to represent the employees for bargaining purposes, and that the employer's refusal to bargain, in violation of § 8 (a) (5) of the National Labor Relations Act, was motivated, not by a "good faith" doubt of the Union's majority status, but by a desire to gain time to dissipate that status. The NLRB ordered the employers to stop their unfair labor practices, offer reinstatement and back pay to employees discriminatorily discharged, and to bargain with the Unions on request. The Court of Appeals for the Fourth Circuit upheld the NLRB's findings as to violations of §§ 8 (a) (1) and (3) but declined to enforce the orders to bargain, holding that the Taft-Hartley amendments to the Act withdrew the NLRB's

---

*Together with No. 691, *Food Store Employees Union, Local No. 347, Amalgamated Meat Cutters & Butcher Workmen of North America, AFL–CIO* v. *Gissel Packing Co., Inc.*, also on certiorari to the same court, argued March 26, 1969, and No. 585, *Sinclair Co.* v. *National Labor Relations Board*, on certiorari to the United States Court of Appeals for the First Circuit, argued March 26–27, 1969.

245

authority to order an employer to bargain under § 8 (a)(5) on the basis of cards, in the absence of NLRB certification, unless the employer knows, independently of the cards, that there is in fact no representation dispute. The court held that the cards were so inherently unreliable that their use gave the employer an automatic, good faith claim that such a dispute existed, for which an election was necessary. In No. 585, after the Union announced to the employer that it held authorization cards from a majority of the bargaining unit, and the employer claimed it had a good faith doubt of majority status, the Union petitioned for an election. From the time the employer first learned of the Union's drive until the election, the company's president talked and wrote to the employees. The NLRB stated that the communications "reasonably tended to convey . . . the belief or impression that selection of the Union in the forthcoming election could lead [the Company] to close its plant, or to the transfer of the weaving production, with the resultant loss of jobs to the wire weavers," and constituted a violation of § 8 (a)(1). The NLRB set aside the election because the employer "interfered with the exercise of a free and untrammeled choice in the election," found that the Union had a valid card majority when it demanded recognition and that the employer declined recognition in order to gain time to dissipate that majority status in violation of § 8 (a)(5). The employer was ordered to bargain on request. The Court of Appeals for the First Circuit sustained the NLRB's findings and enforced its order. *Held:*

1. To obtain recognition as the exclusive bargaining representative under the Act, a union has not been required, prior to or since the Taft-Hartley amendments, to obtain certification as a winner of an NLRB election; it can establish majority status by possession of cards signed by a majority of the employees authorizing the union to represent them for bargaining purposes. Pp. 595–600.

2. Authorization cards can adequately reflect employee desires for representation and the NLRB's rules for controlling card solicitation are adequate safeguards against union misrepresentation and coercion where the cards are clear and unambiguous on their face. Pp. 601–610.

(a) The NLRB's rule set forth in *Cumberland Shoe Corp.,* 144 N. L. R. B. 1268, that an unambiguous authorization card will be counted unless it is proved that the employee was told that the card was to be used *solely* to obtain an election, should not be applied mechanically. Pp. 607–609.

(b) An employer is not obligated to accept a card check as proof of majority status under the NLRB's current practice, and he is not required to justify his insistence on an election by making his own investigation of employee sentiment and showing affirmative reasons for doubting the majority status. Not every employer unfair labor practice will necessarily support a bargaining order. Pp. 609–610.

3. The issuance of a bargaining order is an appropriate remedy where an employer who has rejected a card majority has committed unfair labor practices which have made the holding of a fair election unlikely, or which have undermined a union's majority, caused an election to be set aside, and made the holding of a fair rerun election unlikely. Pp. 610–616.

(a) In fashioning a remedy the NLRB can consider the extensiveness of an employer's unfair practices in terms of their past effect on election conditions and the likelihood of their recurrence in the future, and if it finds that the possibility of erasing the effects of past practices and of ensuring a fair election (or a fair rerun) by the use of traditional remedies is slight and that employee sentiment once expressed through cards would be better protected by a bargaining order, such order should issue. Pp. 614–615.

(b) Because the NLRB's findings in Nos. 573 and 691 were based on its former practice of phrasing its findings in terms of an employer's good or bad faith doubts of a union's majority status, these cases are remanded for proper findings. Pp. 615–616.

4. An employer's free speech right to communicate with his employees is firmly established and cannot be infringed by a union or by the NLRB, and § 8 (c) merely implements the First Amendment by requiring that the expression of "any views, argument or opinion" shall not be "evidence of an unfair labor practice," so long as such expression contains "no threat of reprisal or force or promise of benefit" in violation of § 8 (a)(1). Pp. 616–620.

(a) An assessment of the precise scope of employer expression must be made in the context of its labor relations setting, and an employer's rights cannot outweigh the equal rights of the employees to associate freely, as those rights are embodied and protected in the Act. Pp. 617–618.

(b) An employer may communicate to his employees any of his general views on unionism and his specific views about a particular union, as long as there is no "threat of reprisal or force or promise of benefit." He may predict the precise effects he believes unionization will have on his company, if the prediction is based on objective fact to convey his belief as to demonstrably probable consequences beyond his control or to convey a management decision already arrived at to close the plant in case of unionization. Pp. 618–619.

(c) In No. 585 the NLRB correctly found that the communications were cast as a threat of retaliatory action and not as a prediction of "demonstrable economic consequences." P. 619.

No. 585, 397 F. 2d 157, affirmed; Nos. 573 and 691, 398 F. 2d 336, 337, and 339, reversed and remanded.

Dominick L. Manoli argued the cause for petitioner in No. 573. With him on the brief were *Solicitor General Griswold, Peter L. Strauss, Arnold Ordman,* and *Norton J. Come. Albert Gore* argued the cause for petitioner in No. 691. With him on the brief was *Joseph M. Jacobs. Edward J. Simerka* argued the cause for petitioner in No. 585. With him on the brief was *Eugene B. Schwartz.*

John E. Jenkins, Jr., argued the cause and filed briefs for Gissel Packing Co., Inc., respondent in Nos. 573 and 691. *Lewis P. Hamlin, Jr.,* argued the cause and filed a brief for General Steel Products, Inc., et al., respondents in No. 573. *Fred F. Holroyd* argued the cause for Heck's, Inc., respondent in No. 573. With him on the brief was *Charles E. Hurt. Lawrence G. Wallace* argued the cause for respondent in No. 585. On the brief were *Solicitor General Griswold, Dominick L. Manoli,* and *Messrs. Strauss, Ordman,* and *Come.*

Briefs of *amici curiae* in Nos. 573 and 691 were filed by *J. Albert Woll, Laurence Gold,* and *Thomas E. Harris* for the American Federation of Labor & Congress of Industrial Organizations, and by the Associated Builders & Contractors, Inc. Briefs of *amici curiae* in No. 585 were filed by *Lambert H. Miller* for the National Association of Manufacturers; by *Harry L. Browne* for the American Retail Federation; and by *Stanley E. Tobin* for the Mechanical Specialties Co., Inc.

Mr. Chief Justice Warren delivered the opinion of the Court.

These cases involve the extent of an employer's duty under the National Labor Relations Act to recognize a union that bases its claim to representative status solely on the possession of union authorization cards, and the steps an employer may take, particularly with regard to the scope and content of statements he may make, in legitimately resisting such card-based recognition. The specific questions facing us here are whether the duty to bargain can arise without a Board election under the Act; whether union authorization cards, if obtained from a majority of employees without misrepresentation or coercion, are reliable enough generally to provide a valid, alternate route to majority status; whether a bargaining order is an appropriate and authorized remedy where an employer rejects a card majority while at the same time committing unfair labor practices that tend to undermine the union's majority and make a fair election an unlikely possibility; and whether certain specific statements made by an employer to his employees constituted such an election-voiding unfair labor practice and thus fell outside the protection of the First Amendment and § 8 (c) of the Act, 49 Stat. 452, as amended, 29 U. S. C. § 158 (c). For reasons given below, we answer each of these questions in the affirmative.

I.

Of the four cases before us, three—*Gissel Packing Co., Heck's Inc.,* and *General Steel Products, Inc.*—were consolidated following separate decisions in the Court of Appeals for the Fourth Circuit and brought here by the National Labor Relations Board in No. 573. Food Store Employees Union, Local No. 347, the petitioning Union in *Gissel,* brought that case here in a separate petition in No. 691. All three cases present the same legal issues in similar, uncomplicated factual settings that can be briefly described together. The fourth case, No. 585 (*Sinclair Company*), brought here from the Court of Appeals for the First Circuit and argued separately, presents many of the same questions and will thus be disposed of in this opinion; but because the validity of some of the Board's factual findings are under attack on First Amendment grounds, detailed attention must be paid to the factual setting of that case.

Nos. 573 and 691.

In each of the cases from the Fourth Circuit, the course of action followed by the Union and the employer and the Board's response were similar. In each case, the Union waged an organizational campaign, obtained authorization cards from a majority of employees in the appropriate bargaining unit, and then, on the basis of the cards demanded recognition by the employer. All three employers refused to bargain on the ground that authorization cards were inherently unreliable indicators of employee desires; and they either embarked on, or continued, vigorous antiunion campaigns that gave rise to numerous unfair labor practice charges. In *Gissel*, where the employer's campaign began almost at the outset of the Union's organizational drive, the Union (petitioner in No. 691), did not seek an election, but instead filed three unfair labor practice charges against the employer, for refusing to bargain in violation of § 8 (a)(5), for coercion and intimidation of employees in violation of § 8 (a)(1), and for discharge of Union adherents in violation of § 8 (a)(3).[1] In *Heck's* an elec-

---

[1] At the outset of the Union campaign, the Company vice president informed two employees, later discharged, that if they were caught talking to Union men, "you God-damned things will go." Subsequently, the Union presented oral and written demands for recognition, claiming possession of authorization cards from 31

tion sought by the Union was never held because of nearly identical unfair labor practice charges later filed by the Union as a result of the employer's antiunion campaign, initiated, after the Union's recognition demand.[2]

---

of the 47 employees in the appropriate unit. Rejecting the bargaining demand, the Company began to interrogate employees as to their Union activities; to promise them better benefits than the Union could offer; and to warn them that if the "union got in, [the vice president] would just take his money and let the union run the place," that the Union was not going to get in, and that it would have to "fight" the Company first. Further, when the Company learned of an impending Union meeting, it arranged, so the Board later found, to have an agent present to report the identity of the Union's adherents. On the first day following the meeting, the vice president told the two employees referred to above that he knew they had gone to the meeting and that their work hours were henceforth reduced to half a day. Three hours later, the two employees were discharged.

[2] The organizing drive was initiated by the employees themselves at Heck's Charleston warehouses. The Union first demanded recognition on the basis of 13 cards from 26 employees of the Company's three Charleston warehouses. After responding "No comment" to the Union's repeated requests for recognition, the president assembled the employees and told them of his shock at their selection of the Union; he singled out one of the employees to ask if he had signed an authorization card. The next day the Union obtained the additional card necessary to establish a majority That same day, the leading Union supporter (the employee who had first established contacts with the Union and had solicited a large number of the cards) was discharged, and another employee was interrogated as to his Union activities, encouraged to withdraw his authorization, and warned that a Union victory could result in reduced hours, fewer raises, and withdrawal of bonuses. A second demand for recognition was made two days later, and thereafter the president summoned two known Union supporters to his office and offered them new jobs at higher pay if they would use their influence to "break up the union."

The same pattern was repeated a year later at the Company's Ashland, Kentucky, store, where the Union obtained cards from 21 of the 38 employees by October 5, 1965. The next day, the

And in *General Steel,* an election petitioned for by the Union and won by the employer was set aside by the Board because of the unfair labor practices committed by the employer in the pre-election period.[3]

In each case, the Board's primary response was an order to bargain directed at the employers, despite the absence of an election in *Gissel* and *Heck's* and the employer's victory in *General Steel.* More specifically, the Board found in each case (1) that the Union had obtained

---

assistant store manager told an employee that he knew that the Union had acquired majority status. When the Union requested recognition on October 8, however, the Company refused on the ground that it was not sure whether department heads were included in the bargaining unit—even though the cards represented a majority with or without the department heads. After a second request for recognition and an offer to submit the cards to the employer for verification, respondent again refused, on grounds of uncertainty about the definition of the unit and because a poll taken by the Company showed that a majority of the employees did not want Union representation. Meanwhile, the Company told the employees that an employee of another company store had been fired on the spot for signing a card, warned employees that the Company knew which ones had signed cards, and polled employees about their desire for Union representation without giving them assurances against reprisals.

[3] Throughout the Union's six-month organizational campaign— both before and after its demand for recognition based on possession of cards from 120 of the 207 employees in the appropriate unit— the Company's foremen and supervisors interrogated employees about their Union involvement; threatened them with discharge for engaging in Union activities or voting for the Union; suggested that unionization might hurt business and make new jobs more difficult to obtain; warned that strikes and other dire economic consequences would result (a supervisor informed a group of employees that if the Union came in, "a nigger would be the head of it," and that when the Company put in 10 r~w machines, "the niggers would be the operators of them"); and asserted that, although the Company would have to negotiate with the Union, it could negotiate endlessly and would not have to sign anything.

valid authorization cards [4] from a majority of the employees in the bargaining unit and was thus entitled to represent the employees for collective bargaining purposes; and (2) that the employer's refusal to bargain with the Union in violation of § 8 (a)(5) was motivated, not by a "good faith" doubt of the Union's majority status, but by a desire to gain time to dissipate that status. The Board based its conclusion as to the lack of good faith doubt on the fact that the employers had committed substantial unfair labor practices during their antiunion campaign efforts to resist recognition. Thus, the Board found that all three employers had engaged in restraint and coercion of employees in violation of § 8 (a)(1)—in *Gissel*, for coercively interrogating employees about Union activities, threatening them with discharge, and promising them benefits; in *Heck's*, for coercively interrogating employees, threatening reprisals, creating the appearance of surveillance, and offering benefits for opposing the Union; and in *General Steel*, for coercive interrogation and threats of reprisals, including discharge. In addition, the Board found that the employers in *Gissel* and *Heck's* had wrongfully discharged employees for engaging in Union activities in violation of § 8 (a)(3). And, because the employers had rejected

---

[4] The cards used in all four campaigns in Nos. 573 and 691 and in the one drive in No. 585 unambiguously authorized the Union to represent the signing employee for collective bargaining purposes; there was no reference to elections. Typical of the cards was the one used in the Charleston campaign in *Heck's*, and it stated in relevant part:

"Desiring to become a member of the above Union of the International Brotherhood of Teamsters, Chauffeurs, Warehousemen and Helpers of America, I hereby make application for admission to membership. I hereby authorize you, your agents or representatives to act for me as collective bargaining agent on all matters pertaining to rates of pay, hours, or any other conditions of employment."

the card-based bargaining demand in bad faith, the Board found that all three had refused to recognize the Unions in violation of § 8 (a)(5).

Only in *General Steel* was there any objection by an employer to the validity of the cards and the manner in which they had been solicited, and the doubt raised by the evidence was resolved in the following manner. The customary approach of the Board in dealing with allegations of misrepresentation by the Union and misunderstanding by the employees of the purpose for which the cards were being solicited has been set out in *Cumberland Shoe Corp.*, 144 N. L. R. B. 1268 (1963) and reaffirmed in *Levi Strauss & Co.*, 172 N. L. R. B. No. 57, 68 L. R. R. M. 1338 (1968). Under the *Cumberland Shoe* doctrine, if the card itself is unambiguous (*i. e.*, states on its face that the signer authorizes the Union to represent the employee for collective bargaining purposes and not to seek an election), it will be counted unless it is proved that the employee was told that the card was to be used *solely* for the purpose of obtaining an election. In *General Steel,* the trial examiner considered the allegations of misrepresentation at length and, applying the Board's customary analysis, rejected the claims with findings that were adopted by the Board and are reprinted in the margin.[5]

---

[5] "Accordingly, I reject Respondent's contention 'that if a man is told that his card will be secret, or will be shown only to the Labor Board for the purpose of obtaining election, that this is the absolute equivalent of telling him that it will be used "only" for purposes of obtaining an election.'

.   .   .   .   .

"With respect to the 97 employees named in the attached Appendix B Respondent in its brief contends, in substance, that their cards should be rejected because each of these employees was told *one or more* of the following: (1) that the card would be used to get an election (2) that he had the right to vote either way, even

Consequently, the Board ordered the companies to cease and desist from their unfair labor practices, to offer reinstatement and back pay to the employees who had been discriminatorily discharged, to bargain with the Unions on request, and to post the appropriate notices.

On appeal, the Court of Appeals for the Fourth Circuit, in *per curiam* opinions in each of the three cases (398 F. 2d 336, 337, 339), sustained the Board's findings as to the §§ 8 (a)(1) and (3) violations, but rejected the Board's findings that the employers' refusal to bargain violated § 8 (a)(5) and declined to enforce those portions of the Board's orders directing the respondent companies to bargain in good faith. The court based its § 8 (a)(5) rulings on its 1967 decisions raising the same fundamental issues, *Crawford Mfg. Co.* v. *NLRB*, 386 F. 2d 367, cert. denied, 390 U. S. 1028 (1968); *NLRB* v. *Logan Packing Co.*, 386 F. 2d 562; *NLRB* v. *Sehon Stevenson & Co., Inc.*, 386 F. 2d 551. The court in those cases held that the 1947 Taft-Hartley amendments to the Act, which permitted the Board to resolve representation disputes by certification under § 9 (c) only by secret ballot election, withdrew from the Board the authority to order an employer to bargain under § 8 (a)(5) on the basis of cards, in the absence of NLRB certification, unless the employer knows independently of the cards that there is in fact no representation dispute. The court held that the cards themselves were so inherently unreliable that their use gave an employer virtually an automatic, good faith claim

---

though he signed the card (3) that the card would be kept secret and not shown to anybody except to the Board in order to get an election. For reasons heretofore explicated, I conclude that these statements, singly or jointly, do not foreclose use of the cards for the purpose designated on their face."

that such a dispute existed, for which a secret election was necessary. Thus, these rulings established that a company could not be ordered to bargain unless (1) there was no question about a Union's majority status (either because the employer agreed the cards were valid or had conducted his own poll so indicating), or (2) the employer's §§ 8 (a)(1) and (3) unfair labor practices committed during the representation campaign were so extensive and pervasive that a bargaining order was the only available Board remedy irrespective of a card majority.

Thus based on the earlier decisions, the court's reasoning in these cases was brief, as indicated by the representative holding in *Heck's:*

> "We have recently discussed the unreliability of the cards, in the usual case, in determining whether or not a union has attained a majority status and have concluded that an employer is justified in entertaining a good faith doubt of the union's claims when confronted with a demand for recognition based solely upon union authorization cards. We have also noted that the National Labor Relations Act after the Taft-Hartley amendments provides for an election as the sole basis of a certification and restricts the Board to the use of secret ballots for the resolution of representation questions. This is not one of those extraordinary cases in which a bargaining order might be an appropriate remedy for pervasive violations of § 8 (a)(1). It is controlled by our recent decisions and their reasoning. . . There was not substantial evidence to support the findings of the Board that Heck's, Inc. had no good faith doubt of the unions' claims of majorities." 398 F. 2d, at 338–339.

No. 585.

In No. 585, the factual pattern was quite similar. The petitioner, a producer of mill rolls, wire, and related products at two plants in Holyoke, Massachusetts, was shut down for some three months in 1952 as the result of a strike over contract negotiations with the American Wire Weavers Protective Association, the representative of petitioner's journeymen and apprentice wire weavers from 1933 to 1952. The Company subsequently reopened without a union contract, and its employees remained unrepresented through 1964, when the Company was acquired by an Ohio corporation, with the Company's former president continuing as head of the Holyoke, Massachusetts, division. In July 1965, the International Brotherhood of Teamsters, Local Union No. 404, began an organizing campaign among petitioner's Holyoke employees and by the end of the summer had obtained authorization cards from 11 of the Company's 14 journeymen wire weavers choosing the Union as their bargaining agent. On September 20, the Union notified petitioner that it represented a majority of its wire weavers, requested that the Company bargain with it, and offered to submit the signed cards to a neutral third party for authentication. After petitioner's president declined the Union's request a week later, claiming, *inter alia*, that he had a good faith doubt of majority status because of the cards' inherent unreliability, the Union petitioned, on November 8, for an election that was ultimately set for December 9.

When petitioner's president first learned of the Union's drive in July, he talked with all of his employees in an effort to dissuade them from joining a union. He particularly emphasized the results of the long 1952 strike, which he claimed "almost put our company out of busi-

ness," and expressed worry that the employees were
forgetting the "lessons of the past." He emphasized,
secondly, that the Company was still on "thin ice" financially, that the Union's "only weapon is to strike," and
that a strike "could lead to the closing of the plant," since
the parent company had ample manufacturing facilities
elsewhere. He noted, thirdly, that because of their age
and the limited usefulness of their skills outside their
craft, the employees might not be able to find re-employment if they lost their jobs as a result of a strike. Finally,
he warned those who did not believe that the plant could
go out of business to "look around Holyoke and see a
lot of them out of business." The president sent letters
to the same effect to the employees in early November,
emphasizing that the parent company had no reason to
stay in Massachusetts if profits went down.

During the two or three weeks immediately prior to
the election on December 9, the president sent the employees a pamphlet captioned: "Do you want another
13-week strike?" stating, *inter alia*, that: "We have no
doubt that the Teamsters Union can again close the Wire
Weaving Department and the entire plant by a strike.
We have no hopes that the Teamsters Union Bosses will
not call a strike. . . . The Teamsters Union is a strike
happy outfit." Similar communications followed in late
November, including one stressing the Teamsters' "hood-
lum control." Two days before the election, the Company sent out another pamphlet that was entitled: "Let's
Look at the Record," and that purported to be an obit-
uary of companies in the Holyoke-Springfield, Massachusetts, area that had allegedly gone out of business
because of union demands, eliminating some 3,500 jobs;
the first page carried a large cartoon showing the preparation of a grave for the Sinclair Company and other
headstones containing the names of other plants allegedly
victimized by the unions. Finally, on the day before

the election, the president made another personal appeal
to his employees to reject the Union. He repeated that
the Company's financial condition was precarious; that
a possible strike would jeopardize the continued operation of the plant; and that age and lack of education
would make re-employment difficult. The Union lost
the election 7–6, and then filed both objections to the
election and unfair labor practice charges which were
consolidated for hearing before the trial examiner.

The Board agreed with the trial examiner that the
president's communications with his employees, when
considered as a whole, "reasonably tended to convey to
the employees the belief or impression that selection of
the Union in the forthcoming election could lead [the
Company] to close its plant, or to the transfer of the
weaving production, with the resultant loss of jobs to
the wire weavers." Thus, the Board found that under
the "totality of the circumstances" petitioner's activities
constituted a violation of § 8 (a)(1) of the Act. The
Board further agreed with the trial examiner that petitioner's activities, because they "also interfered with
the exercise of a free and untrammeled choice in the
election," and "tended to foreclose the possibility" of
holding a fair election, required that the election be
set aside. The Board also found that the Union had a
valid card majority (the unambiguous cards, see n. 4,
supra, went unchallenged) when it demanded recognition
initially and that the Company declined recognition,
not because of a good faith doubt as to the majority
status, but, as the § 8 (a)(1) violations indicated, in
order to gain time to dissipate that status—in violation
of § 8 (a)(5). Consequently, the Board set the election
aside, entered a cease-and-desist order, and ordered the
Company to bargain on request.

On appeal, the Court of Appeals for the First Circuit
sustained the Board's findings and conclusions and en-

forced its order in full. 397 F. 2d 157. The court rejected the Company's proposition that the inherent unreliability of authorization cards entitled an employer automatically to insist on an election, noting that the representative status of a union may be shown by means other than an election; the court thus reaffirmed its stance among those circuits disavowing the Fourth Circuit's approach to authorization cards.[6] Because of the conflict among the circuits on the card issues and because of the alleged conflict between First Amendment freedoms and the restrictions placed on employer speech by § 8 (a)(1) in *Sinclair*, No. 585, we granted certiorari to consider both questions. 393 U. S. 997 (1968). For reasons given below, we reverse the decisions of the Court of Appeals for the Fourth Circuit and affirm the ruling of the Court of Appeals for the First Circuit.

II.

In urging us to reverse the Fourth Circuit and to affirm the First Circuit, the National Labor Relations

---

[6] See, *e. g., Joy Silk Mills, Inc.* v. *NLRB*, 87 U. S. App. D. C. 360, 185 F. 2d 732 (1950), cert. denied, 341 U. S. 914 (1951); *NLRB* v. *Gotham Shoe Mfg. Co., Inc.*, 359 F. 2d 684 (C. A. 2d Cir. 1966); *NLRB* v. *Quality Markets, Inc.*, 387 F. 2d 20 (C. A. 3d Cir. 1967); *NLRB* v. *Phil-Modes, Inc.*, 396 F. 2d 131 (C. A. 5th Cir. 1968); *Atlas Engine Works, Inc.* v. *NLRB*, 396 F. 2d 775 (C. A. 6th Cir. 1968), petition for certiorari pending; *NLRB* v. *Clark Products, Inc.*, 385 F. 2d 396 (C. A. 7th Cir. 1967); *NLRB* v. *Ralph Printing & Lithographing Co.*, 379 F. 2d 687 (C. A. 8th Cir. 1967); *NLRB* v. *Luisi Truck Lines*, 384 F. 2d 842 (C. A. 9th Cir. 1967); *Furr's, Inc.* v. *NLRB*, 381 F. 2d 562 (C. A. 10th Cir.), cert. denied, 389 U. S. 840 (1967).

In addition to the First Circuit below, four courts of appeals have subsequently considered the Fourth Circuit's view of the cards and specifically rejected it. *NLRB* v. *United Mineral & Chemical Corp.*, 391 F. 2d 829, 836, n. 10 (C. A 2d Cir. 1968); *NLRB* v. *Goodyear Tire & Rubber Co.*, 394 F. 2d 711, 712–713 (C. A. 5th Cir. 1968); *NLRB* v. *Atco-Surgical Supports*, 394 F. 2d 659, 660 (C. A. 6th Cir. 1968); *NLRB* v. *Ozark Motor Lines*, 403 F. 2d 356 (C. A. 8th Cir. 1968).

Board contends that we should approve its interpretation and administration of the duties and obligations imposed by the Act in authorization card cases. The Board argues (1) that unions have never been limited under § 9 (c) of either the Wagner Act or the 1947 amendments to certified elections as the sole route to attaining representative status. Unions may, the Board contends, impose a duty to bargain on the employer under § 8 (a)(5) by reliance on other evidence of majority employee support, such as authorization cards. Contrary to the Fourth Circuit's holding, the Board asserts, the 1947 amendments did not eliminate the alternative routes to majority status. The Board contends (2) that the cards themselves, when solicited in accordance with Board standards which adequately insure against union misrepresentation, are sufficiently reliable indicators of employee desires to support a bargaining order against an employer who refuses to recognize a card majority in violation of § 8 (a)(5). The Board argues (3) that a bargaining order is the appropriate remedy for the § 8 (a)(5) violation, where the employer commits other unfair labor practices that tend to undermine union support and render a fair election improbable.

Relying on these three assertions, the Board asks us to approve its current practice, which is briefly as follows. When confronted by a recognition demand based on possession of cards allegedly signed by a majority of his employees, an employer need not grant recognition immediately, but may, unless he has knowledge independently of the cards that the union has a majority, decline the union's request and insist on an election, either by requesting the union to file an election petition or by filing such a petition himself under § 9 (c)(1)(B). If, however, the employer commits independent and substantial unfair labor practices disruptive of election conditions, the Board may withhold the election or set it aside, and issue instead a bargaining order as a remedy for the various violations. A bargaining order will not issue, of course, if the union obtained the cards through misrepresentation or coercion or if the employer's unfair labor practices are unrelated generally to the representation campaign. Conversely, the employers in these cases urge us to adopt the views of the Fourth Circuit.

There is more at issue in these cases than the dispute outlined above between the Board and the four employers, however, for the Union, petitioner in No. 691, argues that we should accord a far greater role to cards in the bargaining area than the Board itself seeks in this litigation. In order to understand the differences between the Union and the Board, it is necessary to trace the evolution of the Board's approach to authorization cards from its early practice to the position it takes on oral argument before this Court. Such an analysis requires viewing the Board's treatment of authorization cards in three separate phases: (1) under the *Joy Silk* doctrine, (2) under the rules of the *Aaron Brothers* case, and (3) under the approach announced at oral argument before this Court.

The traditional approach utilized by the Board for many years has been known as the *Joy Silk* doctrine. *Joy Silk Mills, Inc.*, 85 N. L. R. B. 1263 (1949), enforced, 87 ' U. S. App. D. C. 360, 185 F. 2d 732 (1950). Under that rule, an employer could lawfully refuse to bargain with a union claiming representative status through possession of authorization cards if he had a "good faith doubt" as to the union's majority status; instead of bargaining, he could insist that the union seek an election in order to test out his doubts. The Board, then, could find a lack of good faith doubt and enter a bargaining order in one of two ways. It could find (1) that the employer's independent unfair labor practices were evidence of bad faith, showing that the employer was seeking time to dissipate the union's majority. Or the Board could find (2) that the employer had come forward with no reasons for entertaining any doubt and therefore that he must have rejected the bargaining demand in bad faith. An example of the second category was *Snow & Sons*, 134 N. L. R. B. 709 (1961), enforced, 308 F. 2d 687 (C. A. 9th Cir. 1962), where the employer reneged on his agreement to bargain after a third party checked the validity of the card signatures and insisted on an election because he doubted that the employees truly desired representation. The Board entered a bargaining order with very broad language to the effect that an employer could not refuse a bargaining demand and seek an election instead "without a valid ground therefor," 134 N. L. R. B., at 710–711. See also *Dixon Ford Shoe Co., Inc.*, 150 N. L. R. B. 861 (1965); *Kellogg Mills*, 147 N. L. R. B. 342, 346 (1964), enforced, 347 F. 2d 219 (C. A. 9th Cir. 1965).

The leading case codifying modifications to the *Joy Silk* doctrine was *Aaron Brothers*, 158 N. L. R. B. 1077 (1966). There the Board made it clear that it had shifted the burden to the General Counsel to show bad faith and that an employer "will not be held to have violated his bargaining obligation . . . simply because he refuses to rely upon cards, rather than an election, as the method for determining the union's majority." 158 N. L. R. B., at 1078. Two significant consequences were emphasized. The Board noted (1) that not every unfair labor practice would automatically result in a finding of bad faith and therefore a bargaining order; the Board implied that it would find bad faith only if the unfair labor practice was serious enough to have the tendency to dissipate the union's majority. The Board noted (2) that an employer no longer needed to come forward with reasons for rejecting a bargaining demand. The Board pointed out, however, that a bargaining order would issue if it could prove that an employer's "course of conduct" gave indications as to the employer's bad faith. As examples of such a "course of conduct," the Board cited *Snow & Sons, supra; Dixon Ford Shoe Co., Inc., supra,* and *Kellogg Mills, supra,* thereby reaffirming *John P. Serpa, Inc.,* 155 N. L. R. B. 99 (1965), where the Board had limited *Snow & Sons* to its facts.

Although the Board's brief before this Court generally followed the approach as set out in *Aaron Brothers, supra,* the Board announced at oral argument that it had virtually abandoned the *Joy Silk* doctrine altogether. Under the Board's current practice, an employer's good faith doubt is largely irrelevant, and the key to the issuance of a bargaining order is the commission of serious unfair labor practices that interfere with the election processes and tend to preclude the holding of a fair election. Thus, an employer can insist that a union go to an election, regardless of his subjective motivation, so long as he is not guilty of misconduct; he need give no affirmative reasons for rejecting a recognition request, and he can demand an election with a simple "no comment" to the union. The Board pointed out, however, (1) that an employer could not refuse to bargain if he *knew,* through a personal poll for instance, that a majority of his employees supported the union, and (2) that an employer could not refuse recognition initially because of questions as to the appropriateness of the unit and then later claim, as an afterthought, that he doubted the union's strength.

The Union argues here that an employer's right to insist on an election in the absence of unfair labor practices should be more circumscribed, and a union's right to rely on cards correspondingly more expanded, than the Board would have us rule. The Union's contention is that an employer, when confronted with a card-based bargaining demand, can insist on an election only by filing the election petition himself immediately under

§ 9 (c)(1)(B) and not by insisting that the Union file the election petition, whereby the election can be subjected to considerable delay. If the employer does not himself petition for an election, the Union argues, he must recognize the Union regardless of his good or bad faith and regardless of his other unfair labor practices, and should be ordered to bargain if the cards were in fact validly obtained. And if this Court should continue to utilize the good faith doubt rule, the Union contends that at the least we should put the burden on the employer to make an affirmative showing of his reasons for entertaining such doubt.

Because the employers' refusal to bargain in each of these cases was accompanied by independent unfair labor practices which tend to preclude the holding of a fair election, we need not decide whether a bargaining order is ever appropriate in cases where there is no interference with the election processes.

With the Union's arguments aside, the points of difference between the employers and the Board will be considered in the following manner. The validity of the cards under the Act, their intrinsic reliability, and the appropriateness of a bargaining order as a response to violations of § 8 (a)(5) as well as §§ 8 (a)(1) and (3) will be discussed in the next section. The nature of an employer's reaction to an organizational campaign, and particularly the Board's conclusion that the employer's statements in No. 585 contained threats of reprisal and thus constituted restraint and coercion in violation of § 8 (a)(1) and not protected speech, will be covered in the final section.

III.

A.

The first issue facing us is whether a union can establish a bargaining obligation by means other than a Board election and whether the validity of alternate routes to

majority status, such as cards, was affected by the 1947
Taft-Hartley amendments. The most commonly trav-
eled[7] route for a union to obtain recognition as the exclusive bargaining representative of an unorganized
group of employees is through the Board's election and
certification procedures under § 9 (c) of the Act (29
U. S. C. § 159 (c)); it is also, from the Board's
point of view, the preferred route.[8] A union is not
limited to a Board election, however, for, in addition to
§ 9, the present Act provides in § 8 (a)(5) (29 U. S. C.
§ 158 (a)(5)), as did the Wagner Act in § 8 (5), that
"[i]t shall be an unfair labor practice for an employer . . . to refuse to bargain collectively with the
representatives of his employees, subject to the provisions of section 9 (a)." Since § 9 (a), in both the Wagner
Act and the present Act, refers to the representative as
the one "designated or selected" by a majority of the
employees without specifying precisely how that representative is to be chosen, it was early recognized that
an employer had a duty to bargain whenever the union
representative presented "convincing evidence of majority support."[9] Almost from the inception of the Act,

[7] In 1967, for instance, the Board conducted 8,116 elections but
issued only 157 bargaining orders based on a card majority. *Levi
Strauss & Co.*, 172 N. L. R. B. No. 57, 68 L. R. R. M. 1338, 1342,
n. 9 (1968). See also Sheinkman, Recognition of Unions Through
Authorization Cards, 3 Ga. L. Rev. 319 (1969). The number of
card cases that year, however, represents a rather dramatic increase
over previous years, from 12 such cases in 1964, 24 in 1965, and
about 117 in 1966. Browne, Obligation to Bargain on Basis
of Card Majority, 3 Ga. L. Rev. 334, 347 (1969).

[8] See, *e. g.*, *Aaron Brothers*, 158 N. L. R. B. 1077 (1966); cf.,
General Shoe Corp., 77 N. L. R. B. 124 (1948). An employer,
of course, may not, even if he acts in good faith, recognize a
minority union, *Garment Workers' Union* v. *NLRB*, 366 U. S. 731
(1961).

[9] *NLRB* v. *Dahlstrom Metallic Door Co.*, 112 F. 2d 756, 757
(C. A. 2d Cir. 1940).

then, it was recognized that a union did not have to be certified as the winner of a Board election to invoke a bargaining obligation; it could establish majority status by other means under the unfair labor practice provision of § 8 (a)(5)—by showing convincing support, for instance, by a union-called strike or strike vote,[10] or, as here, by possession of cards signed by a majority of the employees authorizing the union to represent them for collective bargaining purposes.[11]

We have consistently accepted this interpretation of the Wagner Act and the present Act, particularly as to the use of authorization cards. See, e. g., NLRB v. Bradford Dyeing Assn., 310 U. S. 318, 339–340 (1940); Franks Bros. Co. v. NLRB, 321 U. S. 702 (1944); United Mine Workers v. Arkansas Flooring Co., 351 U. S. 62 (1956). Thus, in United Mine Workers, supra, we noted that a "Board election is not the only method by which an employer may satisfy itself as to the union's majority status," 351 U. S., at 72, n. 8, since § 9 (a), "which deals expressly with employee representation, says nothing as to how the employees' representative shall be chosen," 351 U. S., at 71. We therefore pointed out in that case, where the union had obtained signed authorization cards from a majority of the employees, that "[i]n the absence of any bona fide dispute[12] as to the existence of the required majority of eligible employees, the employer's denial of recognition of the union would have violated

---

[10] See, e. g., Denver Auto Dealers Assn., 10 N. L. R. B. 1173 (1939); Century Mills, Inc., 5 N. L. R. B. 807 (1938).

[11] The right of an employer lawfully to refuse to bargain if he had a good faith doubt as to the Union's majority status, even if in fact the Union did represent a majority, was recognized early in the administration of the Act, see NLRB v. Remington Rand, Inc., 94 F. 2d 862, 868 (C. A. 2d Cir.), cert. denied, 304 U. S. 576 (1938).

[12] See n. 11, supra.

§ 8 (a)(5) of the Act." 351 U. S., at 69. We see no reason to reject this approach to bargaining obligations now, and we find unpersuasive the Fourth Circuit's view that the 1947 Taft-Hartley amendments, enacted some nine years before our decision in *United Mine Workers, supra*, require us to disregard that case. Indeed, the 1947 amendments weaken rather than strengthen the position taken by the employers here and the Fourth Circuit below. An early version of the bill in the House would have amended § 8 (5) of the Wagner Act to permit the Board to find a refusal-to-bargain violation only where an employer had failed to bargain with a union "currently recognized by the employer or certified as such [through an election] under section 9." Section 8 (a)(5) of H. R. 3020, 80th Cong., 1st Sess. (1947). The proposed change, which would have eliminated the use of cards, was rejected in Conference (H. R. Conf. Rep. No. 510, 80th Cong., 1st Sess., 41 (1947)), however, and we cannot make a similar change in the Act simply because, as the employers assert, Congress did not expressly approve the use of cards in rejecting the House amendment. Nor can we accept the Fourth Circuit's conclusion that the change was wrought when Congress amended § 9 (c) to make election the sole basis for *certification* by eliminating the phrase "any other suitable method to ascertain such representatives," [13] under which the Board had occasionally used cards as a certification basis. A certified union has the benefit of numerous special privileges

---

[13] Section 9 (c) of the Wagner Act had provided:

"Whenever a question affecting commerce arises concerning the representation of employees, the Board may investigate such controversy and certify . . . the name or names of the representatives that have been designated or selected. In any such investigation, the Board . . . may take a secret ballot of employees, or utilize any other suitable method to ascertain such representatives."

which are not accorded unions recognized voluntarily or
under a bargaining order [14] and which, Congress could
determine, should not be dispensed unless a union has
survived the crucible of a secret ballot election.

The employers rely finally on the addition to § 9 (c) of
subparagraph (B), which allows an employer to petition
for an election whenever "one or more individuals or
labor organizations have presented to him a claim [15] to
be recognized as the representative defined in section
9 (a)." That provision was not added, as the employers
assert, to give them an absolute right to an election at
any time, rather, it was intended, as the legislative history indicates, to allow them, after being asked to bargain,
to test out their doubts as to a union's majority in a
secret election which they would then presumably not
cause to be set aside by illegal antiunion activity.[16]   We

---

[14] *E. g.*, protection against the filing of new election petitions by
rival unions or employees seeking decertification for 12 months
(§ 9 (c)(3)), protection for a reasonable period, usually one year,
against any disruption of the bargaining relationship because of
claims that the union no longer represents a majority (see *Brooks* v.
NLRB, 348 U. S. 96 (1954)), protection against recognitional picketing by rival unions (§ 8 (b)(4)(C)), and freedom from the restrictions placed in work assignments disputes by § 8 (b)(4)(D), and on
recognitional and organizational picketing by § 8 (b)(7).

[15] Under the Wagner Act, which did not prescribe who would file
election petitions, the Board had ruled that an employer could seek
an election only when two unions presented conflicting bargaining
requests on the ground that if he were given the same election
petition rights as the union, he could interrupt union drives by
demanding an election before the union had obtained majority
status. The 1947 amendments resolved the difficulty by providing
that an employer could seek an election only after he had been
requested to bargain. See H. R. Rep. No. 245, 80th Cong., 1st
Sess., 35 (1947).

[16] The Senate report stated that the "present Board rules . . .
discriminate against employers who have reasonable grounds for

agree with the Board's assertion here that there is no suggestion that Congress intended § 9 (c)(1)(B) to relieve any employer of his § 8 (a)(5) bargaining obligation where, without good faith, he engaged in unfair labor practices disruptive of the Board's election machinery. And we agree that the policies reflected in § 9 (c)(1)(B) fully support the Board's present administration of the Act (see *supra*, at 591–592); for an employer can insist on a secret ballot election, unless, in the words of the Board, he engages "in contemporaneous unfair labor practices likely to destroy the union's majority and seriously impede the election." Brief for Petitioner, the Board, in No. 573, p. 36.

In short, we hold that the 1947 amendments did not restrict an employer's duty to bargain under § 8 (a)(5) solely to those unions whose representative status is certified after a Board election.[17]

---

believing that labor organizations claiming to represent their employees are really not the choice of the majority." S. Rep. No. 105, 80th Cong., 1st Sess., 10 (1947). Senator Taft stated during the debates:

"Today an employer is faced with this situation. A man comes into his office and says, 'I represent your employees. Sign this agreement, or we strike tomorrow.' . . . The employer has no way in which to determine whether this man really does represent his employees or does not. The bill gives him the right to go to the Board . . . and say, 'I want an election. I want to know who is the bargaining agent for my employees.'" 93 Cong. Rec. 3838 (1947).

[17] As aptly stated in Lesnick, Establishment of Bargaining Rights Without an NLRB Election, 65 Mich. L. Rev. 851, 861–862 (1967):

"Cards have been used under the act for thirty years; [this] Court has repeatedly held that certification is not the only route to representative status; and the 1947 attempt in the House-passed Hartley Bill to amend section 8 (a)(5) . . . was rejected by the conference committee that produced the Taft-Hartley Act. No amount of drum-beating should be permitted to overcome, without legislation, this history."

B.

We next consider the question whether authorization cards are such inherently unreliable indicators of employee desires that, whatever the validity of other alternate routes to representative status, the cards themselves may never be used to determine a union's majority and to support an order to bargain. In this context, the employers urge us to take the step the 1947 amendments and their legislative history indicate Congress did not take, namely, to rule out completely the use of cards in the bargaining arena. Even if we do not unhesitatingly accept the Fourth Circuit's view in the matter, the employers argue, at the very least we should overrule the *Cumberland Shoe* doctrine (see *supra,* at 584) and establish stricter controls over the solicitation of the cards by union representatives.[18]

---

[18] In dealing with the reliability of cards, we should re-emphasize what issues we are not confronting. As pointed out above, we are not here faced with a situation where an employer, with "good" or "bad" subjective motivation, has rejected a card-based bargaining request without good reason and has insisted that the Union go to an election while at the same time refraining from committing unfair labor practices that would tend to disturb the "laboratory conditions" of that election. We thus need not decide whether, absent election interference by an employer's unfair labor practices, he may obtain an election only if he petitions for one himself; whether, if he does not, he must bargain with a card majority if the Union chooses not to seek an election; and whether, in the latter situation, he is bound by the Board's ultimate determination of the card results regardless of his earlier good faith doubts, or whether he can still insist on a Union-sought election if he makes an affirmative showing of his positive reasons for believing there is a representation dispute. In short, a union's right to rely on cards as a freely interchangeable substitute for elections where there has been no election interference is not put in issue here; we need only decide whether the cards are reliable enough to support a bargaining order where a fair election probably could not have been held, or where an election that was held was in fact set aside.

The objections to the use of cards voiced by the employers and the Fourth Circuit boil down to two contentions:[19] (1) that, as contrasted with the election procedure,[20] the cards cannot accurately reflect an employee's wishes, either because an employer has not had a chance to present his views and thus a chance to insure that the employee choice was an informed one, or because the choice was the result of group pressures and not individual decision made in the privacy of a voting booth; and (2) that quite apart from the election comparison, the cards are too often obtained through misrepresentation and coercion which compound the cards' inherent inferiority to the election process. Neither contention is persuasive, and each proves too much. The Board itself has recognized, and continues to do so here, that secret elections are generally the most satisfactory—indeed the preferred—method of ascertaining whether a union has majority support.[21] The acknowledged superiority of the election process, however, does not mean that cards are thereby rendered totally invalid, for where an employer engages in conduct disruptive of the election process, cards may be the most effective—perhaps the only—way of assuring employee choice. As for misrepresentation, in any specific case of

---

[19] The Board's reliance on authorization cards has provoked considerable scholarly controversy. Compare criticism of Board policy, particularly its treatment of ambiguous, dual-purpose cards, in Browne, *supra*, n. 7, and Comment, Union Authorization Cards, 75 Yale L. J. 805 (1966), with defense of Board practice in Lesnick, *supra*, n. 17; Welles, The Obligation to Bargain on the Basis of a Card Majority, 3 Ga. L. Rev. 349 (1969); and Comment, Union Authorization Cards: A Reliable Basis for an NLRB Order To Bargain?, 47 Texas L. Rev. 87 (1968).

[20] For a comparison of the card procedure and the election process, see discussion in *NLRB* v. *Logan Packing Co.*, 386 F. 2d 562, 564–566 (C. A. 4th Cir. 1967).

[21] See nn. 7–8, *supra*.

alleged irregularity in the solicitation of the cards, the proper course is to apply the Board's customary standards (to be discussed more fully below) and rule that there was no majority if the standards were not satisfied. It does not follow that because there are some instances of irregularity, the cards can never be used; otherwise, an employer could put off his bargaining obligation indefinitely through continuing interference with elections.

That the cards, though admittedly inferior to the election process, can adequately reflect employee sentiment when that process has been impeded, needs no extended discussion, for the employers' contentions cannot withstand close examination. The employers argue that their employees cannot make an informed choice because the card drive will be over before the employer has had a chance to present his side of the unionization issues. Normally, however, the union will inform the employer of its organization drive early in order to subject the employer to the unfair labor practice provisions of the Act; the union must be able to show the employer's awareness of the drive in order to prove that his contemporaneous conduct constituted unfair labor practices on which a bargaining order can be based if the drive is ultimately successful. See, e. g., *Hunt Oil Co.*, 157 N. L. R. B. 282 (1966); *Don Swart Trucking Co.*, 154 N. L. R. B. 1345 (1965). Thus, in all of the cases here but the Charleston campaign in *Heck's* the employer, whether informed by the union or not, was aware of the union's organizing drive almost at the outset and began its antiunion campaign at that time; and even in the *Heck's* Charleston case, where the recognition demand came about a week after the solicitation began, the employer was able to deliver a speech before the union obtained a majority. Further, the employers argue that without a secret ballot an employee may, in a card drive, succumb to group pressures or sign simply to get the union "off his back" and then be unable to change his mind as he would be free to do once inside a voting booth. But the same pressures are likely to be equally present in an election, for election cases arise most often with small bargaining units [22] where virtually every voter's sentiments can be carefully and individually canvassed. And no voter, of course, can change his mind after casting a ballot in an election even though he may think better of his choice shortly thereafter.

The employers' second complaint, that the cards are too often obtained through misrepresentation and coercion, must be rejected also in view of the Board's present rules for controlling card solicitation, which we view as adequate to the task where the cards involved state their purpose clearly and unambiguously on their face. We would be closing our eyes to obvious difficulties, of course, if we did not recognize that there have been abuses, primarily arising out of misrepresentations by union organizers as to whether the effect of signing a card was to designate the union to represent the employee for collective bargaining purposes or merely to authorize it to seek an election to determine that issue. And we would be equally blind if we did not recognize that various courts of appeals and commentators [23] have differed significantly as to the effectiveness of the Board's *Cumberland Shoe* doctrine (see *supra,* at 584) to cure such abuses.

Thus, even where the cards are unambiguous on their face, both the Second Circuit (*NLRB* v *S. E. Nichols Co.,* 380 F. 2d 438 (1967)) and the Fifth Circuit (*Engineers & Fabricators, Inc.* v. *NLRB,* 376 F. 2d 482 (1967)) have joined the Fourth Circuit below

[22] See Comment, Union Authorization Cards: A Reliable Basis for an NLRB Order To Bargain?, *supra,* at 94 and n. 32.

[23] See n. 19, *supra.*

in rejecting the Board's rule that the cards will be counted unless the solicitor's statements amounted under the circumstances to an assurance that the cards would be used only for an election, or for no other purpose than an election. And even those circuits which have adopted the Board's approach have criticized the Board for tending too often to apply the *Cumberland* rule too mechanically, declining occasionally to uphold the Board's application of its own rule in a given case. See, *e. g., NLRB* v. *Southbridge Sheet Metal Works, Inc.,* 380 F. 2d 851 (C. A. 1st Cir. 1967); *NLRB* v. *Sandy's Stores, Inc.,* 398 F. 2d 268 (C. A. 1st Cir. 1968); *NLRB* v. *Swan Super Cleaners, Inc.,* 384 F. 2d 609 (C. A. 6th Cir. 1967); *NLRB* v. *Dan Howard Mfg. Co.,* 390 F. 2d 304 (C. A. 7th Cir. 1968); *Furr's, Inc.* v. *NLRB,* 381 F. 2d 562 (C. A. 10th Cir. 1967); *UAW* v. *NLRB,* 129 U. S. App. D. C. 196, 392 F. 2d 801 (1967). Among those which reject the *Cumberland* rule, the Fifth Circuit agrees with the Second Circuit (see *S. E. Nichols Co., supra*), that a card will be vitiated if an employee was left with the impression that he would be able to resolve any lingering doubts and make a final decision in an election, and further requires that the Board probe the subjective intent of each signer, an inquiry expressly avoided by *Cumberland.* See *NLRB* v. *Southland Paint Co.,* 394 F. 2d 717, 728, 730 (C. A. 5th Cir. 1968); *Engineers & Fabricators, Inc.* v. *NLRB, supra.* Where the cards are ambiguous on their face, the Fifth Circuit, joined by the Eighth Circuit (see, *e. g., NLRB* v. *Peterson Bros.,* 342 F. 2d 221 (C. A. 5th Cir. 1965), and *Bauer Welding & Metal Fabricators, Inc.* v. *NLRB,* 358 F. 2d 766 (C. A. 8th Cir. 1966)), departs still further from the Board rule. And there is a conflict among those courts which otherwise follow the Board as to single-purpose cards (compare *NLRB* v. *Lenz Co.,* 396 F. 2d 905, 908 (C. A. 6th Cir. 1968), with *NLRB* v. *C. J. Glasgow Co.,* 356 F. 2d 476, 478 (C. A. 7th Cir. 1966)).

We need make no decision as to the conflicting ap-
proaches used with regard to dual-purpose cards, for in
each of the five organization campaigns in the four cases
before us the cards used were single-purpose cards, stating clearly and unambiguously on their face that the
signer designated the union as his representative.   And
even the view forcefully voiced by the Fourth Circuit
below that unambiguous cards as well present too many
opportunities for misrepresentation comes before us
somewhat weakened in view of the fact that there were
no allegations of irregularities in four of those five campaigns (*Gissel*, the two *Heck's* campaigns,[24] and *Sinclair*).
Only in *General Steel* did the employer challenge the
cards on the basis of misrepresentations.   There, the
trial examiner, after hearing testimony from over 100
employees and applying the traditional Board approach
(see n. 5, *supra*), concluded that "all of these employees
not only intended, but were fully aware, that they were
thereby designating the Union as their representative."
Thus, the sole question before us, raised in only one of
the four cases here, is whether the *Cumberland Shoe*
doctrine is an adequate rule under the Act for assuring
employee free choice.

In resolving the conflict among the circuits in favor
of approving the Board's *Cumberland* rule, we think it
sufficient to point out that employees should be bound
by the clear language of what they sign unless that language is deliberately and clearly canceled by a union
adherent with words calculated to direct the signer to
disregard and forget the language above his signature.
There is nothing inconsistent in handing an employee

---

[24] In the Charleston campaign in *Heck's*, the employees handled
the card drive themselves from beginning to end, contacting the
union, obtaining the blank authorization cards, and soliciting their
fellow employees on that basis; no union agents were involved in
the card signing.

a card that says the signer authorizes the union to represent him and then telling him that the card will probably be used first to get an election. Elections have been, after all, and will continue to be, held in the vast majority of cases; the union will still have to have the signatures of 30% [25] of the employees when an employer rejects a bargaining demand and insists that the union seek an election. We cannot agree with the employers here that employees as a rule are too unsophisticated to be bound by what they sign unless expressly told that their act of signing represents something else. In addition to approving the use of cards, of course, Congress has expressly authorized reliance on employee signatures alone in other areas of labor relations, even where criminal sanctions hang in the balance,[26] and we should not act hastily in disregarding congressional judgments that employees can be counted on to take responsibility for their acts.

We agree, however, with the Board's own warnings in *Levi Strauss & Co.*, 172 N. L. R. B. No. 57, 68 L. R. R. M. 1338, 1341, and n. 7 (1968), that in hearing testimony concerning a card challenge, trial examiners should not neglect their obligation to ensure employee free choice by

---

[25] See 1969 CCH Guidebook to Labor Relations ¶ 402.4.

[26] Criminal sanctions are imposed by § 302 (29 U. S. C. § 186) which makes it unlawful for an employer to pay to and for a union representative to receive "any money or other thing of value." Section 302 (c) (4) (29 U. S. C. § 186 (c) (4)) exempts payments by employers to union representatives of union dues, however, where an employee has executed a "written assignment" of the dues, i. e., a check-off authorization. Signatures are also relied on in § 9 (c) (1) (A) (29 U. S. C. § 159 (c) (1) (A)), which provides for Board processing of representation and decertification petitions when each is supported by a "substantial number of employees" (the basis for the 30% signature requirement, see n. 25, *supra*), and in § 9 (e) which specifically provides for 30% of the signatures in the bargaining unit to empower the Board to hold a union shop de-authorization election.

a too easy mechanical application of the *Cumberland* rule.[27] We also accept the observation that employees are more likely than not, many months after a card drive and in response to questions by company counsel, to give testimony damaging to the union, particularly where company officials have previously threatened reprisals for union activity in violation of § 8 (a)(1).[28] We therefore reject any rule that requires a probe of an employee's subjective motivations as involving an endless and unreliable inquiry. We nevertheless feel that the trial examiner's findings in *General Steel* (see n. 5, *supra*) represent the limits of the *Cumberland* rule's application. We emphasize that the Board should be careful to guard

---

[27] In explaining and reaffirming the *Cumberland Shoe* doctrine in the context of unambiguous cards, the Board stated:

"Thus the fact that employees are told in the course of solicitation that an election is contemplated, or that a purpose of the card is to make an election possible, provides in our view *insufficient* basis in itself for vitiating unambiguously worded authorization cards on the theory of misrepresentation. A different situation is presented, of course, where union organizers solicit cards on the explicit or indirectly expressed representation that they will use such cards *only* for an election and subsequently seek to use them for a different purpose . . . ."

The Board stated further in a footnote:

"The foregoing does not of course imply that a finding of misrepresentation is confined to situations where employees are expressly told in *haec verba* that the 'sole' or 'only' purpose of the cards is to obtain an election. The Board has never suggested such a mechanistic application of the foregoing principles, as some have contended. The Board looks to substance rather than to form. It is not the use or nonuse of certain key or 'magic' words that is controlling, but whether or not the totality of circumstances surrounding the card solicitation is such, as to add up to an assurance to the card signer that his card will be used for no purpose other than to help get an election." 172 N. L. R. B. No. 57, 68 L. R. R. M. 1338, 1341–1342, and n. 7.

[28] See Sheinkman, *supra*, n. 7, at 332–333.

against an approach any more rigid than that in *General Steel*. And we reiterate that nothing we say here indicates our approval of the *Cumberland Shoe* rule when applied to ambiguous, dual-purpose cards.

The employers argue as a final reason for rejecting the use of the cards that they are faced with a Hobson's choice[29] under current Board rules and will almost inevitably come out the loser. They contend that if they do not make an immediate, personal investigation into possible solicitation irregularities to determine whether in fact the union represents an uncoerced majority, they will have unlawfully refused to bargain for failure to have a good faith doubt of the union's majority; and if they do make such an investigation, their efforts at polling and interrogation will constitute an unfair labor practice in violation of § 8 (a)(1) and they will again be ordered to bargain. As we have pointed out, however, an employer is not obligated to accept a card check as proof of majority status, under the Board's current practice, and he is not required to justify his insistence on an election by making his own investigation of employee sentiment and showing affirmative reasons for doubting the majority status. See *Aaron Brothers*, 158 N. L. R. B. 1077, 1078. If he does make an investigation, the Board's recent cases indicate that reasonable polling in this regard will not always be termed violative of § 8 (a)(1) if conducted in accordance with the requirements set out in *Struksnes Construction Co.*, 165 N. L. R. B. No. 102, 65 L. R. R. M. 1385 (1967). And even if an employer's limited interrogation is found violative of the Act, it might not be serious enough to call for a bargaining order. See *Aaron Brothers, supra; Hammond & Irving, Inc.*, 154 N. L. R. B. 1071

---

[29] See Judge Brown's "Scylla and Charybdis" analogy in *NLRB* v. *Dan River Mills*, 274 F. 2d 381, 388 (C. A. 5th Cir. 1960).

(1965).   As noted above, the Board has emphasized that not "any employer conduct found violative of Section 8 (a)(1) of the Act, regardless of its nature or gravity, will necessarily support a refusal-to-bargain finding," *Aaron Brothers, supra,* at 1079.

C.

Remaining before us is the propriety of a bargaining order as a remedy for a § 8 (a)(5) refusal to bargain where an employer has committed independent unfair labor practices which have made the holding of a fair election unlikely or which have in fact undermined a union's majority and caused an election to be set aside. We have long held that the Board is not limited to a cease-and-desist order in such cases, but has the authority to issue a bargaining order without first requiring the union to show that it has been able to maintain its majority status.   See *NLRB* v. *Katz,* 369 U. S. 736, 748, n. 16 (1962); *NLRB* v. *P. Lorillard Co.,* 314 U. S. 512 (1942).   And we have held that the Board has the same authority even where it is clear that the union, which once had possession of cards from a majority of the employees, represents only a minority when the bargaining order is entered.   *Franks Bros. Co.* v. *NLRB,* 321 U. S. 702 (1944).   We see no reason now to withdraw this authority from the Board.   If the Board could enter only a cease-and-desist order and direct an election or a rerun, it would in effect be rewarding the employer and allowing him "to profit from [his] own wrongful refusal to bargain," *Franks Bros., supra,* at 704, while at the same time severely curtailing the employees' right freely to determine whether they desire a representative. The employer could continue to delay or disrupt the election processes and put off indefinitely his obligation to bargain;[30] and any election held under these circumstances would not be likely to demonstrate the employees' true, undistorted desires.[31]

The employers argue that the Board has ample remedies, over and above the cease-and-desist order, to control employer misconduct. The Board can, they assert, direct the companies to mail notices to employees, to read

[30] The Board indicates here that its records show that in the period between January and June 1968, the median time between the filing of an unfair labor practice charge and a Board decision in a contested case was 388 days. But the employer can do more than just put off his bargaining obligation by seeking to slow down the Board's administrative processes. He can also affect the outcome of a rerun election by delaying tactics, for figures show that the longer the time between a tainted election and a rerun, the less are the union's chances of reversing the outcome of the first election. See n. 31, infra.

[31] A study of 20,153 elections held between 1960 and 1962 shows that in the 267 cases where rerun elections were held over 30% were won by the party who caused the election to be set aside. See Pollitt, NLRB Re-Run Elections: A Study, 41 N. C. L. Rev. 209, 212 (1963). The study shows further that certain unfair labor practices are more effective to destroy election conditions for a longer period of time than others. For instance, in cases involving threats to close or transfer plant operations, the union won the rerun only 29% of the time, while threats to eliminate benefits or refuse to deal with the union if elected seemed less irremediable with the union winning the rerun 75% of the time. Id., at 215–216. Finally, time appears to be a factor. The figures suggest that if a rerun is held too soon after the election before the effects of the unfair labor practices have worn off, or too long after the election when interest in the union may have waned, the chances for a changed result occurring are not as good as they are if the rerun is held sometime in between those periods. Thus, the study showed that if the rerun is held within 30 days of the election or over nine months after, the chances that a different result will occur are only one in five; when the rerun is held within 30–60 days after the election, the chances for a changed result are two in five. Id., at 221.

notices to employees during plant time and to give the
union access to employees during working time at the
plant, or it can seek a court injunctive order under
§ 10 (j) (29 U. S. C. § 160 (j)) as a last resort. In
view of the Board's power, they conclude, the bargaining order is an unnecessarily harsh remedy that
needlessly prejudices employees' § 7 rights solely for
the purpose of punishing or restraining an employer.
Such an argument ignores that a bargaining order is
designed as much to remedy past election damage [32] as
it is to deter future misconduct. If an employer has
succeeded in undermining a union's strength and destroy-
ing the laboratory conditions necessary for a fair election,
he may see no need to violate a cease-and-desist order
by further unlawful activity. The damage will have
been done, and perhaps the only fair way to effectuate
employee rights is to re-establish the conditions as they
existed before the employer's unlawful campaign.[33]

[32] The employers argue that the Fourth Circuit correctly observed
that, "in the great majority of cases, a cease and desist order with
the posting of appropriate notices will eliminate any undue influences
upon employees voting in the security of anonymity." NLRB v.
Logan Packing Co., 386 F. 2d, at 570. It is for the Board and not the
courts, however, to make that determination, based on its expert
estimate as to the effects on the election process of unfair labor
practices of varying intensity. In fashioning its remedies under the
broad provisions of § 10 (c) of the Act (29 U. S. C. § 160 (c)),
the Board draws on a fund of knowledge and expertise all its
own, and its choice of remedy must therefore be given special
respect by reviewing courts. See Fibreboard Paper Products Corp.
v. NLRB, 379 U. S. 203 (1964). "[I]t is usually better to minimize
the opportunity for reviewing courts to substitute their discretion for
that of the agency." Consolo v. FMC, 383 U. S. 607, 621 (1966).

[33] It has been pointed out that employee rights are affected
whether or not a bargaining order is entered, for those who desire
representation may not be protected by an inadequate rerun election,
and those who oppose collective bargaining may be prejudiced by
a bargaining order if in fact the union would have lost an election
absent employer coercion. See Lesnick, supra, n. 17, at 862. Any

There is, after all, nothing permanent in a bargaining order, and if, after the effects of the employer's acts have worn off, the employees clearly desire to disavow the union, they can do so by filing a representation petition. For, as we pointed out long ago, in finding that a bargaining order involved no "injustice to employees who may wish to substitute for the particular union some other . . . arrangement," a bargaining relationship "once rightfully established must be permitted to exist and function for a reasonable period in which it can be given a fair chance to succeed," after which the "Board may, . . . upon a proper showing, take steps in recognition of changed situations which might make appropriate changed bargaining relationships." *Frank Bros., supra*, at 705–706.

Before considering whether the bargaining orders were appropriately entered in these cases, we should summarize the factors that go into such a determination. Despite our reversal of the Fourth Circuit below in Nos. 573 and 691 on all major issues, the actual area of disagreement between our position here and that of the Fourth Circuit is not large as a practical matter. While refusing to validate the general use of a bargaining order in reliance on cards, the Fourth Circuit nevertheless left open the possibility of imposing a bargaining order, without need of inquiry into majority status on the basis of cards or otherwise, in "exceptional" cases marked by "outrageous" and "pervasive" unfair labor practices.

---

effect will be minimal at best, however, for there "is every reason for the union to negotiate a contract that will satisfy the majority, for the union will surely realize that it must win the support of the employees, in the face of a hostile employer, in order to survive the threat of a decertification election after a year has passed." Bok, The Regulation of Campaign Tactics in Representation Elections Under the National Labor Relations Act, 78 Harv. L. Rev. 38, 135 (1964).

Such an order would be an appropriate remedy for those practices, the court noted, if they are of "such a nature that their coercive effects cannot be eliminated by the application of traditional remedies, with the result that a fair and reliable election cannot be had." *NLRB* v. *Logan Packing Co.*, 386 F. 2d 562, 570 (C. A. 4th Cir. 1967); see also *NLRB* v. *Heck's, Inc.*, 398 F. 2d 337, 338. The Board itself, we should add, has long had a similar policy of issuing a bargaining order, in the absence of a § 8 (a)(5) violation or even a bargaining demand, when that was the only available, effective remedy for substantial unfair labor practices. See, *e. g.*, *United Steelworkers of America* v. *NLRB*, 126 U. S. App. D. C. 215, 376 F. 2d 770 (1967); *J. C. Penney Co., Inc.* v. *NLRB*, 384 F. 2d 479, 485–486 (C. A. 10th Cir. 1967).

The only effect of our holding here is to approve the Board's use of the bargaining order in less extraordinary cases marked by less pervasive practices which nonetheless still have the tendency to undermine majority strength and impede the election processes. The Board's authority to issue such an order on a lesser showing of employer misconduct is appropriate, we should reemphasize, where there is also a showing that at one point the union had a majority; in such a case, of course, effectuating ascertainable employee free choice becomes as important a goal as deterring employer misbehavior. In fashioning a remedy in the exercise of its discretion, then, the Board can properly take into consideration the extensiveness of an employer's unfair practices in terms of their past effect on election conditions and the likelihood of their recurrence in the future. If the Board finds that the possibility of erasing the effects of past practices and of ensuring a fair election (or a fair rerun) by the use of traditional remedies, though present, is slight and that employee sentiment once expressed through cards would, on balance, be better protected by a bargaining order, then such an order should issue (see n. 32, *supra*).

We emphasize that under the Board's remedial power there is still a third category of minor or less extensive unfair labor practices, which, because of their minimal impact on the election machinery, will not sustain a bargaining order. There is, the Board says, no *per se* rule that the commission of any unfair practice will automatically result in a § 8 (a)(5) violation and the issuance of an order to bargain. See *Aaron Brothers, supra.*

With these considerations in mind, we turn to an examination of the orders in these cases. In *Sinclair*, No. 585, the Board made a finding, left undisturbed by the First Circuit, that the employer's threats of reprisal were so coercive that, even in the absence of a § 8 (a)(5) violation, a bargaining order would have been necessary to repair the unlawful effect of those threats.[34] The Board therefore did not have to make the determination called for in the intermediate situation above that the risks that a fair rerun election might not be possible were too great to disregard the desires of the employees already expressed through the cards. The employer argues, however, that its communications to its employees were protected by the First Amendment and § 8 (c) of the Act (29 U. S. C. § 158 (c)), whatever the effect of those communications on the union's majority or the Board's ability to ensure a fair election; it is to that contention that we shall direct our final attention in the next section.

In the three cases in Nos. 573 and 691 from the Fourth Circuit, on the other hand, the Board did not make a

---

[34] Under the doctrine of *Bernel Foam Products Co.*, 146 N. L. R. B. 1277 (1964), there is nothing inconsistent in the Union's filing an election petition and thereby agreeing that a question of representation exists, and then filing a refusal-to-bargain charge after the election is lost because of the employer's unfair labor practices.

similar finding that a bargaining order would have been
necessary in the absence of an unlawful refusal to bargain. Nor did it make a finding that, even though traditional remedies might be able to ensure a fair election,
there was insufficient indication that an election (or
a rerun in *General Steel*) would definitely be a more
reliable test of the employees' desires than the card count
taken before the unfair labor practices occurred. The
employees argue that such findings would not be warranted, and the court below ruled in *General Steel* that
available remedies short of a bargaining order could
guarantee a fair election. 398 F. 2d 339, 340, n. 3. We
think it possible that the requisite findings were implicit
in the Board's decisions below to issue bargaining orders
(and to set aside the election in *General Steel*); and we
think it clearly inappropriate for the court below to make
any contrary finding on its own (see n. 32, *supra*). Because the Board's current practice at the time required
it to phrase its findings in terms of an employer's good
or bad faith doubts (see Part II, *supra*), however, the
precise analysis the Board now puts forth was not employed below, and we therefore remand these cases for
proper findings.

IV.

We consider finally petitioner Sinclair's First Amendment challenge to the holding of the Board and the
Court of Appeals for the First Circuit. At the outset
we note that the question raised here most often arises
in the context of a nascent union organizational drive,
where employers must be careful in waging their antiunion campaign. As to conduct generally, the above-
noted gradations of unfair labor practices, with their
varying consequences, create certain hazards for employers when they seek to estimate or resist unionization
efforts. But so long as the differences involve conduct
easily avoided, such as discharge, surveillance, and coer-

cive interrogation, we do not think that employers can complain that the distinctions are unreasonably difficult to follow. Where an employer's antiunion efforts consist of speech alone, however, the difficulties raised are not so easily resolved. The Board has eliminated some of the problem areas by no longer requiring an employer to show affirmative reasons for insisting on an election and by permitting him to make reasonable inquiries. We do not decide, of course, whether these allowances· are mandatory. But we do note that an employer's free speech right to communicate his views to his employees is firmly established and cannot be infringed by a union or the Board. Thus, § 8 (c) (29 U. S. C. § 158 (c)) merely implements the First Amendment by requiring that the expression of "any views, argument, or opinion" shall not be "evidence of an unfair labor practice," so long as such expression contains "no threat of reprisal or force or promise of benefit" in violation of § 8 (a)(1). Section 8 (a)(1) in turn, prohibits interference, restraint or coercion of employees in the exercise of their right to self-organization.

Any assessment of the precise scope of employer expression, of course, must be made in the context of its labor relations setting. Thus, an employer's rights cannot outweigh the equal rights of the employees to associate freely, as those rights are embodied in § 7 and protected by § 8 (a)(1) and the proviso to § 8 (c). And any balancing of those rights must take into account the economic dependence of the employees on their employers, and the necessary tendency of the former, because of that relationship, to pick up intended implications of the latter that might be more readily dismissed by a more disinterested ear. Stating these obvious principles is but another way of recognizing that what is basically at stake is the establishment of a nonpermanent, limited relationship between the employer, his economically dependent employee and his union agent, not the election of legislators or the enactment of legislation whereby that relationship is ultimately defined and where the independent voter may be freer to listen more objectively and employers as a class freer to talk. Cf. *New York Times Co.* v. *Sullivan,* 376 U. S. 254 (1964).

Within this framework, we must reject the Company's challenge to the decision below and the findings of the Board on which it was based. The standards used below for evaluating the impact of an employer's statements are not seriously questioned by petitioner and we see no need to tamper with them here. Thus, an employer is free to communicate to his employees any of his general views about unionism or any of his specific views about a particular union, so long as the communications do not contain a "threat of reprisal or force or promise of benefit." He may even make a prediction as to the precise effects he believes unionization will have on his company. In such a case, however, the prediction must be carefully phrased on the basis of objective fact to convey an employer's belief as to demonstrably probable consequences beyond his control or to convey a management decision already arrived at to close the plant in case of unionization. See *Textile Workers* v. *Darlington Mfg. Co.,* 380 U. S. 263, 274, n. 20 (1965). If there is any implication that an employer may or may not take action solely on his own initiative for reasons unrelated to economic necessities and known only to him, the statement is no longer a reasonable prediction based on available facts but a threat of retaliation based on misrepresentation and coercion, and as such without the protection of the First Amendment. We therefore agree with the court below that "[c]onveyance of the employer's belief, even though sincere, that unionization will or may result in the closing of the plant is not a statement of fact unless, which is most improbable, the eventuality of closing is capable of proof." 397 F. 2d 157, 160. As stated elsewhere, an employer is free only to tell "what he reasonably believes will be the likely economic consequences of unionization that are outside his control," and not "threats of economic reprisal to be taken solely on his own volition." *NLRB* v. *River Togs, Inc.*, 382 F. 2d 198, 202 (C. A. 2d Cir. 1967).

Equally valid was the finding by the court and the Board that petitioner's statements and communications were not cast as a prediction of "demonstrable 'economic consequences,'" 397 F. 2d, at 160, but rather as a threat of retaliatory action. The Board found that petitioner's speeches, pamphlets, leaflets, and letters conveyed the following message: that the company was in a precarious financial condition; that the "strike-happy" union would in all likelihood have to obtain its potentially unreasonable demands by striking, the probable result of which would be a plant shutdown, as the past history of labor relations in the area indicated; and that the employees in such a case would have great difficulty finding employment elsewhere. In carrying out its duty to focus on the question: "[W]hat did the speaker intend and the listener understand?" (A. Cox, Law and the National Labor Policy 44 (1960)), the Board could reasonably conclude that the intended and understood import of that message was not to predict that unionization would inevitably cause the plant to close but to threaten to throw employees out of work regardless of the economic realities. In this connection, we need go no further than to point out (1) that petitioner had no support for its basic assumption that the union, which had not yet even presented any demands, would have to strike to be heard, and that it admitted at the hearing that it had no basis for attributing other plant closings in the area to unionism; and (2) that the Board has often found that employees, who are particularly sensitive to rumors of plant closings,[35] take such hints as coercive threats rather than honest forecasts.[36]

Petitioner argues that the line between so-called permitted predictions and proscribed threats is too vague to stand up under traditional First Amendment analysis and that the Board's discretion to curtail free speech rights is correspondingly too uncontrolled. It is true that a reviewing court must recognize the Board's competence in the first instance to judge the impact of utterances made in the context of the employer-employee relationship, see *NLRB* v. *Virginia Electric & Power Co.*, 314 U. S. 469, 479 (1941). But an employer, who has control over that relationship and therefore knows it best, cannot be heard to complain that he is without an adequate guide for his behavior. He can easily make his views known without engaging in " 'brinkmanship' " when it becomes all too easy to "overstep and tumble [over] the brink," *Wausau Steel Corp.* v. *NLRB*, 377 F. 2d 369, 372 (C. A. 7th Cir. 1967). At the least he can avoid coercive speech simply by avoiding conscious overstatements he has reason to believe will mislead his employees.

For the foregoing reasons, we affirm the judgment of the Court of Appeals for the First Circuit in No. 585, and we reverse the judgments of the Court of Appeals for the Fourth Circuit in Nos. 573 and 691 insofar as they decline enforcement of the Board's orders to bargain and remand those cases to that court with directions to remand to the Board for further proceedings in conformity with this opinion.

It is so ordered.

---

[35] See Bok, *supra*, n. 33, at 77; n. 31, *supra*.

[36] See. *e. g.*, *Kolmar Laboratories, Inc.*, 159 N. L. R. B. 805, 807–810, and cases (relied on by the trial examiner here) cited at 809, n. 3, enforced, 387 F. 2d 833 (C. A. 7th Cir. 1967); *Surprenant Mfg. Co.*, 144 N. L. R. B. 507, 510–511, enforced, 341 F. 2d 756, 761 (C. A. 6th Cir. 1965).

APPENDIX G

POST-GISSEL BARGAINING ORDERS

Name of Case	Unfair Labor Practices Held To Warrant A Bargaining Order
World Carpets, Inc., 176 NLRB No. 138, 71 LRRM 1353 (1969)	Promises of benefits and threats of job loss.
Nat Harrison Associates, Inc., 177 NLRB No. 24, 71 LRRM 1473 (1969)	Interrogating employees, promising benefits, threatening discharges and the closure of the plant, and discharging two employees.
V & H Indus. Inc., 177 NLRB No. 118, 71 LRRM 1549 (1969)	Threats to close the plant to one employee and of loss of benefits to two employees, interrogating an employee and laying off four employees.
General Stencils, Inc., 178 NLRB No. 18, 71 LRRM 1652 (1969)	Creating the impression of surveillance, interrogating employees and threatening employees with loss of privileges and possible layoffs.
Zolan Sale of Kansas, Inc., 178 NLRB No. 42, 73 LRRM 1059 (1969)	Threatening employees with job loss, creating the impression of surveillance and interrogating an employee.
Marie Phillips, Inc., 178 NLRB No. 53, 72 LRRM 1103 (1969)	Threatening loss of wages and the closing of the plant, promising benefits and discharging an employee.
Texaco Inc., 178 NLRB No. 72, 72 LRRM 1146 (1969)	Promising and granting benefits, interrogating employees, and soliciting and adjusting employee grievances.
May & Bigley, Inc., 178 NLRB No. 102, 72 LRRM 1268 (1969)	Not allowing employees to work on a holiday, stating that the company would never recognize a union, threatening surveillance and discharging an employee.

Name of Case	Unfair Labor Practices Held To Warrant A Bargaining Order
Centac Corp., 179 NLRB No. 46, 73 LRRM 1461 (1969)	Illegal assistance to union, threatening and discharging employees.
J. P. Stevens Inc. (Gulistan Div.), 179 NLRB No. 47, 75 LRRM 1375 (1969)	Interrogating employees, threatening plant closure or a work cutback, discharging employees, refusing to hire a woman because related to union adherent, promising and granting benefits, creating the impression of surveillance, and putting into effect an invalid no-solicitation rule.
Morrison Cafeteria Co., 179 NLRB No. 97, 74 LRRM 1064 (1969)	Interrogating employees, threatening to close, to fire employees and the loss of benefits, promising a benefit to an employee, discharging an employee, and requesting two employees to report to management about the union.
Diamond Standard Fuel Corp., 179 NLRB No. 117, 72 LRRM 1501 (1969)	Threatening plant closure and firing of employees, interrogating employees, soliciting an employee to report about the union and laying off employees.
Brescome Disb. Corp., 179 NLRB No. 137, 72 LRRM 1590 (1969)	Illegal assistance and domination of employee's association, interrogation and threats to employees, and grant of benefits.
M. H. Brown Co., 179 NLRB No. 155, 72 LRRM 1560 (1969)	Interrogating employees, granting a general increase and discharging employees.
Atlanta Daily World, 179 NLRB No. 166, 72 LRRM 1407 (1969)	Soliciting employees to discourage others from supporting the union, threatening loss of work, promising benefits, orally giving the impression that the selection of a bargaining representative would be futile, and interrogating employees.
Triggs-Miner Corp., 180 NLRB No. 39, 73 LRRM 1085 (1969)	Granting a general wage increase, interrogating employees, threatening work loss and promising benefits.
W. T. Grant Co., 180 NLRB No. 45, 73 LRRM 1047 (1969)	Interrogating and threatening employees, and denying present benefits.

Name of Case	Unfair Labor Practices Held To Warrant A Bargaining Order
Howard Mfg. Co., 180 NLRB No. 47, 75 LRRM 1515 (1969)	Creating an atmosphere of fear, interrogating employees, engaging in surveillance, and deterring employees from accepting union literature.
Vars Buick Corp., 180 NLRB No. 101, 73 LRRM 1110 (1970)	Interrogation and discharge of two employees.
Wilson Furniture & Co., 181 NLRB No. 14, 74 LRRM 1015 (1970)	Interrogating employees, threatening discharge and loss of privileges, giving the impression of and engaging in surveillance, and discharging an employee.
Copps Corp., 181 NLRB No. 52, 73 LRRM 1413 (1970)	Interrogating, threatening to reduce working hours, promising benefits, soliciting employees for surveillance of union and discharging three employees.
Transport Inc., 181 NLRB No. 69, 73 LRRM 1612 (1970)	Interrogating, threatening loss of benefits and discharge, and discharging an employee.
American Door Co., 181 NLRB No. 11, 73 LRRM 1305 (1970)	Threatening to close plant, reduce overtime, engaging in surveillance and discharging two employees.
Clark Sprague, Inc., 181 NLRB No. 91, 73 LRRM 1425 (1970)	Promising benefits to abandon the union.
Merritt Motor Co., 181 NLRB No. 172, 74 LRRM 1032 (1970)	Threatening to eliminate overtime, offering wage and fringe benefit increases.
Mr. Wicke, Ltd., 182 NLRB No. 10, 74 LRRM 1074 (1970)	Threatening that a strike was inevitable and increasing wages after the union filed objections to the election.
Reed Seismic Co., 182 NLRB No. 21, 76 LRRM 1514 (1970)	Granting wage increases and using undercover agents for surveillance.
Arbie Mineral Feed Co., 182 NLRB No. 24, 74 LRRM 1062 (1970)	Interrogating, threatening loss of overtime, and discharging employees.
Broad Street Hosp. & Medical Center, 182 NLRB No. 44, 74 LRRM 1207 (1970)	Employer had independent knowledge of majority status based on a card check and changed terms and conditions of employment.

Name of Case	Unfair Labor Practices Held To Warrant A Bargaining Order
Pacific Abrasive Supply Co., 182 NLRB No. 48, 74 LRRM 1113 (1970)	Employer had knowledge of union's majority because he questioned all employees.
Tower Enterprises, Inc., 182 NLRB No. 56, 74 LRRM 1141 (1970)	Granting wage increases.
Beverages, Inc., 182 NLRB No. 136, 74 LRRM 1604 (1970)	Threatening to discharge and discharging an employee.
Juniata Packing Co., 182 NLRB No. 140, 74 LRRM 1241 (1970)	Interrogating, threatening loss of benefits, plant closure and delay of planned wage increases, and discharging an employee.
Waters Distrib. Co., 182 NLRB No. 141, 74 LRRM 1222 (1970)	Impliedly threatening loss of benefits, and instituting a health plan while objections to election were pending.
Hilltop Van & Storage, 182 NLRB No. 145, 76 LRRM 1517 (1970)	Discharging employees.
Martin Electronics, Inc., 183 NLRB No. 4, 76 LRRM 1872 (1970)	Threatening, interrogating and increasing production quotas.
Dawson Metal Prods., Inc., 183 NLRB No. 25, 74 LRRM 1268 (1970)	Interrogating and threatening employees, promising benefits and refusing to hire applicants because of union affiliation.
C & M Sportswear Mfg. Corp., 183 NLRB No. 29, 74 LRRM 1535 (1970)	Interrogating, threatening, promising benefits and warning employees not to talk about the union.
Breezway Foods, Inc., 183 NLRB No. 92, 75 LRRM 1144 (1970)	Interrogating, polling and threatening employees and discharging an employee.
Great Plains Steel Corp., 183 NLRB No. 96, 76 LRRM 1876 (1970)	Threatening plant closure, withholding wage increases because of the union, promising benefits and granting increases after the union lost the election.
Walker Co., 183 NLRB No. 136, 74 LRRM 1409 (1970)	Interrogating and discharging employees.

Name of Case	Unfair Labor Practices Held To Warrant A Bargaining Order
Acker Indus. Inc., 184 NLRB No. 51, 74 LRRM 1640 (1970)	Threatening plant closure and discharge, and discharging an employee.
Hickman Garment Co., 184 NLRB No. 99, 74 LRRM 1657 (1970)	Previous unfair labor practice findings and threats of reprisal and loss of work or pay, interrogating, promising benefits, and creating the impression of surveillance.
Skaggs Transfer, Inc., 185 NLRB No. 91, 75 LRRM 1174 (1970)	Increasing wages and hours, interrogating, threatening and discharging an employee.
Zink's Foods, Inc., 185 NLRB No. 109, 75 LRRM 1211 (1970)	Interrogating, threatening to close store, to discharge and to reduce hours, discharging an employee, promising better wages and granting increases after union lost election.
Tri-State Stores, Inc., 185 NLRB No. 117, 75 LRRM 1268 (1970)	Interrogating, threatening plant closure, granting wage increases, reducing work week, discharging an employee, and assisting employees to repudiate the union.
Sayer Printing Co., 185 NLRB No. 120, 75 LRRM 1276 (1970)	Threatening plant closure, loss of benefits and discharge, and interrogating and discharging employees.
Dixiesteel Bldgs., Inc., 186 NLRB No. 25, 76 LRRM 1855 (1970)	Interrogating, threatening refusal to bargain and discharge of employees, and promising benefits.
Riviera Manor Nursing Home, Inc., 186 NLRB No. 113, 76 LRRM 1832 (1970)	Threatening, interrogating, and promising wage, insurance and holiday benefits.
State Elec. Supply Co., 187 NLRB No. 9, 75 LRRM 1575 (1970)	Interrogating, threatening plant closure and ordering employees to abandon union.
Medley Distilling Co., 187 NLRB No. 12, 76 LRRM 1103 (1970)	Interrogating, threatening discharge and discharging employees.
The Denham Co., 187 NLRB No. 53, 76 LRRM 1141 (1970)	Promising benefits and changing wages and conditions of employment.

Name of Case	Unfair Labor Practices Held To Warrant A Bargaining Order
Texas Transp., 187 NLRB No. 78, 76 LRRM 1057 (1970)	Threatening discharge, interrogating, and offering employees wage increases.
Kaiser Agricultural Chems., 187 NLRB No. 95, 76 LRRM 1188 (1970)	Interrogating, threatening loss of benefits, and engaging in surveillance.
Serbert Distrib. Co., 187 NLRB No. 108, 76 LRRM 1473 (1971)	Discharging four employees.
Central Distrib. Co., 187 NLRB No. 121, 76 LRRM 1472 (1971)	Interrogating and threatening an employee, changing wages and discharging two employees.
United Packing Co., 187 NLRB No. 132, 76 LRRM 1156 (1971)	Threatening job losses and plant closure, promising benefits and granting benefits after the union lost the election.
Colonial Knitting Corp., 187 NLRB No. 134, 76 LRRM 1244 (1971)	Interrogating, granting wage increases and denying increases to other employees because of the union.
Atlantic Steamers Supply Co., 188 NLRB No. 40, 76 LRRM 1828 (1971)	Interrogating, threatening and discharging an employee.
George J. Roberts & Sons, 188 NLRB No. 51, 76 LRRM 1337 (1971)	Interrogating, threatening, laying off, discharging employees and refusing to hire a friend of a union adherent.
The Dalf Corp., 188 NLRB No. 57, 76 LRRM 1845 (1971)	Interrogating, threatening discharge and changing working conditions.
Essex Wire Corp., 188 NLRB No. 59, 77 LRRM 1016 (1971)	Threats of reprisals and loss of jobs and benefits, interrogations as to wearing of union buttons by employees and as to how they would vote, and misrepresenting facts in a handbill.
Ship Shape Maintenance Co., 189 NLRB No. 58, 77 LRRM 1137 (1971)	Transferring eligible voters so that they could not vote in election.
Zurmuhler & Associate, 189 NLRB No. 63, 77 LRRM 1192 (1971)	Interrogating, threatening loss of work, and discharging employees.

Name of Case	Unfair Labor Practices Held To Warrant A Bargaining Order
Escondido Ready-Mix Concrete, Inc., 189 NLRB No. 69, 77 LRRM 1045 (1971)	Granting wage increases day before election.
Moric Precision Machining Co., 190 NLRB No. 25, 77 LRRM 1102 (1971)	Interrogating, threatening reprisals and discharge, creating the impression of surveillance and laying off employees.
Lexington Convalescent & Nursing Home, Inc., 190 NLRB No. 30, 77 LRRM 1189 (1971)	Threats, interrogation and discharge of employees.
WKRG-TV, Inc., 190 NLRB No. 34, 77 LRRM 1078 (1971)	Promising and granting benefits, soliciting employee grievances, threatening loss of benefits and maintaining an invalid no-solicitation rule.
Air Transp. Equip., Inc., 190 NLRB No. 69, 77 LRRM 1431 (1971)	Interrogating, threatening plant closure, promising a cafeteria, a bonus and the promotion of five employees, and laying off employees.
D. H. Overmyer Co., 190 NLRB No. 71, 77 LRRM 1591 (1971)	Interrogating, threatening employees with physical harm and with discharge, withdrawing privileges and promising benefits.
Mansion House Center Mgt. Corp., 190 NLRB No. 18, 77 LRRM 1052 (1971)	Discharging eight employees.
Starward Fabrics, Inc., 190 NLRB No. 97, 77 LRRM 1233 (1971)	Interrogating employees, granting a raise to an employee and threatening to move and eliminate overtime.
Paschall Truck Lines, Inc., 190 NLRB No. 108, 77 LRRM 1292 (1971)	Interrogating, threatening discharge, creating the impression of surveillance and discharging employees.
E. L. Jones Dodge, Inc., 190 NLRB No. 136, 77 LRRM 1297 (1971)	Threatening closure, creating the impression of surveillance and laying off employees.
Fresno Macaroni Mfg. Co., Inc. d/b/a Perfection Macaroni Co., 191 NLRB No. 21, 77 LRRM 1696 (1971)	Promising benefits, stating the company would never bargain, threatening reorganization to evade duty to bargain, suggesting promotion to employee if he abandoned union.

Name of Case	Unfair Labor Practices Held To Warrant A Bargaining Order
City & County Elec. Sanitary Sewer Service, Inc., 191 NLRB No. 27, 77 LRRM 1615 (1971)	Creating the impression of surveillance, threatening reprisals, interrogating employees, promising improved working conditions.
City Welding & Mfg. Co., 191 NLRB No. 30, 77 LRRM 1901 (1971)	Creating the impression of surveillance, threatening to close the plant and loss of employment, interrogating employees, asking employees for authorization cards, granting a wage increase.
American Enterprises, 191 NLRB No. 118, 77 LRRM 1586 (1971)	Interrogating employees, threatening employees with discharge, threatening to close the plant, forbidding employees to discuss the union.
K. Wm. Beach Mfg. Co., 192 NLRB No. 47, 77 LRRM 1716 (1971)	Employer discharged all employees day after recognition demand.
Scoler's Inc., 192 NLRB No. 49, 77 LRRM 1858 (1971)	Interrogating employees, threatening reprisals, implying wage increase would be granted if asked, promising favored treatment to those opposed to union.
Bell Mfg. Div., Di Giorgio Leisure Prod., Inc., 192 NLRB No. 77, 77 LRRM 1907 (1971)	Interrogating employees, giving and promising wage increases and threatening reprisals.
Pure Chem. Corp., 192 NLRB No. 88, 77 LRRM 1923 (1971)	Interrogating employees, promising benefits and threatening economic retaliation.
Ace Foods, Inc., 192 NLRB No. 180, 78 LRRM 1154 (1971)	Interrogating employees, threatening layoffs, creating impression of surveillance, creating impression unionization would be futile, and promising benefits.
Sutton Tank Co., 193 NLRB No. 32, 78 LRRM 1226 (1971)	Interrogating employees, promising benefits and threatening reprisals.
Wisconsin Bearing Co., 193 NLRB No. 35, 78 LRRM 1301 (1971)	Interrogating employees, threatening reprisals, engaging in surveillance, threatening layoffs and plant closure, promising transfers instead of layoffs to non-union employees, withholding wage increases to union adherents, stating would not hire union adherents.

Name of Case	Unfair Labor Practices Held To Warrant A Bargaining Order
Mallow Plating Works, 193 NLRB No. 96, 78 LRRM 1329 (1971)	Threatening employees, threatening to close the plant, interrogating employees, prohibiting discussion of the union and discriminatory layoffs.
Short Shop, Inc., 193 NLRB No. 107, 78 LRRM 1571 (1971)	Interrogating employees, creating an impression of surveillance, threatening discharge.
Almaden Volkswagen, 193 NLRB No. 110, 78 LRRM 1371 (1971)	Interrogating employees, discriminatory discharge of union leader, threatening employees, and promising benefits when employees resigned from union.
Isaac Putterman d/b/a Rockville Nursing Center, 193 NLRB No. 149, 78 LRRM 1519 (1971)	Threatening discharge and reprisals, requiring employees to sign union cards.
Tri-County Tube, Inc., 194 NLRB No. 5, 78 LRRM 1530 (1971)	Threatening reprisals, promising benefits.
Leslie Metal Arts Co., 194 NLRB No. 20, 78 LRRM 1567 (1971)	Threatening employees with more unfavorable job conditions.
Dodson's Market, Inc., 194 NLRB No. 22, 78 LRRM 1628 (1971)	Employer altered its operations, transferred an employee in retaliation for union activity, threatened to withhold increases, reduced work hours of two union supporters, and caused constructive discharge of union supporter.
M. J. Pirolli & Sons, Inc., 194 NLRB No. 37, 78 LRRM 1631 (1971)	Threatening reprisals, interrogating employees, and discharge of union supporters.
Mid Missouri Motors, 194 NLRB No. 79, 78 LRRM 1709 (1971)	Threatening reprisals, interrogating and discharging employees, warning strikers of discharge unless they abandon the strike.
United Elec. Co., 194 NLRB No. 105, 79 LRRM 1051 (1972)	Interrogating and discharging employees.
Overland Distribution Centers, Inc., 194 NLRB No. 113, 79 LRRM 1188 (1972)	Illegally assisting an inside union, sponsoring the ballots and insisting on an election for officers in inside union.

APPENDIX H

BOARD-APPROVED EMPLOYER SPEECHES

LORD BALTIMORE PRESS *

"I want to apologize for the fact that I am going to have to read my remarks this afternoon. I would like nothing better than to talk with all of you informally and straight from the shoulders —with no prepared written material. Unfortunately, I am going to read my talk because under the circumstances that exist here in San Leandro this week, I would not want to have my thoughts incorrectly referred to later on.

"Before getting into the principal subject of this meeting—the rerun election next Tuesday—even though it is to some extent repetitive of my remarks at the big meeting this afternoon—I would like to take a few minutes to review again the extremely competitive situation in which our Company has found itself for the past 12 to 18 months. I want to spend a little more time talking about competition because I cannot over-emphasize the importance of this subject to all of us. The real basis for economic security and growth for this plant, and LBP as a whole— or any company for that matter, rests on how well we meet our competition head-on.

"As I have said on numerous occasions, to folks in all of our plants, it is a basic fact of economic life that no business can survive, let alone prosper and grow, if it cannot meet and do better than its competitors. To the extent that Lord Baltimore

300

Press can do better in providing quality cartons, at competitive price levels, when our customers require them, then we will be doing better than our competition. These three things; quality, service and competitive cost are what determines how well we can meet competition. And unless we can meet and do better than our competitors the kind of security we all want just will not exist.

"The kind of real economic security that we all want for ourselves and our families can only be secured by continuous full employment of our plants. And the only way to keep any plant operating is by being able to secure enough sales, at reasonable prices, to keep our equipment busy. I know of no Union or Union contract that provides work for this plant, or any other plant.

"If a Union imposes uncompetitive conditions on an employer it can make it almost impossible for the Company to secure enough sales to provide full and regular employment. Some companies have even been forced out of business because they could not survive as a result of competitive disadvantage. There have been several recent cases in our own industry.

"I know you are familiar with the closing of the Weyerhaeuser plant at Rochester, New York, where the ALA had a contract. The current ALA strike going on at the KVP-Sutherland Company in Kalamazoo, Michigan which began August 27th of last year is another example of what can happen to the economic security of a large group of people and their company. The ALA members at KVP-Sutherland have not received a pay check in 10 months. And, right here in San Francisco, I understand that three shops under contract to the ALA have closed down since the first of the year.

"To repeat—No Union or Union contract can provide what this or any company needs to be successful—the ability to secure enough sales to keep its people and equipment busy. On the other hand, irresponsible Union leadership or uncompetitive conditions can make it practically impossible for a company to do this. Competition then—or rather a company's ability to beat its competitors—is really the key to job security for all of us.

. . .

"I am not going to repeat all of the arguments and statements which have been previously made to you regarding our opposition to the ALA. Let me make one thing absolutely clear however, the Company's opposition to the ALA is not based on any admiration for the Printing Specialties Union.

"As I said before, no Union, in my opinion, can deliver job security. It is fundamentally the Company and its employees, working together as a team, that secures sales, and provides the plants and equipment which create and maintain jobs for all of us. No outside third party provides the money for the continuous growth and development that enables a company to increase its competitive position.

. . .

"Before making up your mind, give careful consideration to the effect of your vote on you and your families. Give careful attention to the record of the ALA here in the Bay Area and ask yourself if they have really done a good job for their members— and what kind of a job they can do for you. Ask yourself—will ALA representation really be better for me as an employee of the Lord Baltimore Litho Department?

"Ask yourself why the employees of the Fibreboard Corporation voted to decertify the ALA after the ALA had been their representative for only one year.

"In a recent letter to you the ALA said that 'you are entitled to as much as any lithographer in Local 17 shops.' Well, that might be worth saying if Local 17 lithographers had done so well. Let me remind you of some of the things that the ALA has gotten for Local 17 members in the past several years—like a 10 week strike—like a three year contract that contained no wage adjustment in the first year and only $1.00 increased welfare benefits—like substantial unemployment in the local—like special dues assessments to finance a legal battle (which was part of the reason for the 10 week strike) over contract language drafted by their Eastern lawyers, part of which has been ruled illegal.

"Contrast this with the substantially improved position we have enjoyed in San Leandro and what it has meant in the way of steady work for the employees of this plant. The good teamwork here has enabled us to have a level of work which has made it possible to minimize layoffs, short work weeks and reclassifications. Your steadily improving productivity and quality have given the sales force a good product to sell. This is the way real job security is built—by a cooperative effort of a team of skilled people—skilled craftsmen—skilled salesmen and skilled managers.

"I sincerely believe that we have the basis for a good long term growth and development at San Leandro. Certainly the tremendous growth and expansion of the entire West Coast will benefit our industry. And I'm convinced we can get our fair share of this potential by continuing to work closely and well. In my opinion, there is no reason to interrupt this excellent relationship by permitting the ALA to enter our affairs with what I consider to be an unrealistic approach to the carton industry and our special problems.

"Let me conclude my remarks by asking you to give us—and yourself—and Fred Commerford the opportunity to really show what this plant can accomplish.

"When you go to the polls on next Tuesday, think about your vote very carefully. It is important to your future and that of your family. And if you agree that there is not need here for the ALA—then I know you will vote against the ALA.

"I want to thank you for your patience. I will be home on Tuesday evening awaiting a telephone call to tell me the results with complete faith and confidence because of your good judgment."

BABCOCK & WILCOX CO.**

"During the past week, Widenhouse has called for help and the Union has sent in more organizers. It is making its last desperate effort to fool you men and women to vote for the union. From the stand that you people are taking, they know that they must turn on the heat to win. So, they've made a lot of wild statements. The closer the voting day the wilder the statements seem to get. They've told deliberate lies to try and deceive you; they've made threats and have done a lot of mud-slinging. Why? Because when the going gets rough—that is all that they know how to do. They lost two elections up at Cheraw and they know that they are licked here. That's why they are so desperately trying to stir up trouble and hate.

"I know that they are not fooling many of you with that kind of talk, but so that we may all keep the record straight, I want to answer some of those wild statements. I want to answer them plainly and straight from the shoulder.

"The union would have you believe that the Company is afraid that a union may force us to do more for you than we are now doing. They claim that is the reason why we are fighting to keep it out. That is a lie. The union is the one doing the fighting; making the threats; doing the mud-slinging. It is the union that started all this; not the Company and not you people. You did not ask them to come, they were sent down from the North. Most of you, today, wish that they had left you and us alone.

"We owe it to you, though, to tell you what we think. We believe that the reason the union is after you is to collect money from you for something that you already have; for something that you can get anyway—without any union. We know and we promise you that the union cannot force the Company to do any more than it has done in the past and will do in the future.

"We know, and you know, that in trying to use force, unions have shut plants down. We don't want to see that happen here, because of some men who don't even work here and who would not lose anything while you were out on strike.

"We want to keep the unity, friendship and cooperation that we have had here. The union claims to want the same thing, but they are already threatening many of you who are opposed to them. What do you think of that? Let me tell you—here and now—that so long as Babcock & Wilcox operates in Augusta, no union will make good any threat against any of you. You do not and will not have to join any union to work here.

"The union would have you believe that Babcock came to Augusta because wages were low here. You know, even before I tell you, that is not true. It shows that the union organizers either know nothing about our business, or have no regard for the truth. You all know that the main thing we use in making our brick is kaolin—the chalk that comes from Hephzibah, only a few miles from here. That's why we are here. The kaolin we need is in Georgia. This is a sample of the kind of talk the union has been handing out. Can you have any trust in a man who is either so dumb about your business, or deliberately hides the facts?

"You may have heard that the union has guaranteed to get you a raise. That is another wild statement that they cannot make good. Who is going to back up that statement? When Babcock tells you something you know you can believe it. When a union organizer tells you something, how can you depend on it? The union does not pay wages—they collect dues. We are paying top wages in Augusta now—we have always paid good wages and no union can get a raise for you that the Company will not give you anyway, without a union. The CIO hasn't been needed to get you raises in the past and won't be needed to get you raises in the future.

"Unions do not pay wages, but by making unreasonable demands they can and do force strikes. That can happen right here. If it does, everybody loses, but most of all you people and your families will lose. The Union and the Company can stand something like that a whole lot better and a lot longer than you can. That's what is going on in Detroit and Pittsburgh, and the other places where the CIO is. Many of those people have lost almost three months' pay. And what are they getting for it? They walk up and down in front of closed plants in the snow and the cold and the rain, and maybe they get a sandwich and a cup of coffee. Maybe they'll get some more pay when the CIO gets tired of it and lets them go back to work. But it is going to take them two and maybe three years of hard work to make up for what they've already lost.

"While I am talking about wages, let me tell you that we have checked one of the plants here in Georgia where this particular union has organized the workers. We found that after about two years of paying union dues, the workers in that plant are not making as much money as you people here.

"The union would have you believe that the Company is a foreign organization—that they have no interest in you or the community in which you live. That it is a greedy monster taking everything and giving nothing. That, too, is a lie. This Company is the largest and oldest American boiler company. This plant, during the past 17 years has been a pretty good thing for you. By its coming here many of you are better off. A great many of you have seen it start from almost nothing; in fact, many of you helped to put up the buildings and new equipment as the plant grew from year to year. . . . Many of you have bought homes and raised your children on what you earned here.

"The Company has contributed many thousands of dollars to worthwhile community activities such as the hospital, Paine College, the Y. M. and Y. W. C. A. . . . and many others. It pays a lot of money in taxes to Richmond County to support the schools, the roads and the local Government. And yet, Widenhouse-Scott & Co. say that we are Public Enemy No. 1.   Who are they to say such things?

"The union would have you believe that your bosses and the officials of this Company are your enemies.   You know that is not true.   You know that men like Mr. Carmichael, Mr. Happy and others who have been here all their lives, have always taken care of you.   You know these men and what they can and will do for you, but you don't know what the CIO man can do for you. . . .

"The nearer we come to the time to vote the more desperate the union will get—the more lies they will tell about us and the more they will promise you.   Don't be fooled by that sort of talk.   Look at the record of what this Company has done.   Compare what you have here now with what your friends and neighbors are getting any place in Augusta.   Remember, too . . . all of us enjoy many privileges under our present way of doing things. We don't want you to get hurt and do something that you will feel sorry for later on.

"Remember, Babcock owns this plant—not the union.   Babcock will continue to run this plant—not the union. . . .   To vote against the CIO vote on the right side of the ballot."

* 145 NLRB 888, 890-93, 55 LRRM 1068 (1964).

** 77 NLRB 577, 22 LRRM 1057 (1948).

APPENDIX I

UNION RECOGNITION
UNDER SPECIAL CIRCUMSTANCES

The following discussion is not intended to be all inclusive, but merely to acquaint the practitioner with other methods by which unions obtain recognition, and some of the problems involved.

1. Voluntary Recognition of a Minority Union

This is the case of the willing employer and the willing union. Colloquially, it is called the top-down deal. An employer may be convinced of the inevitability of becoming organized and desires a union which will not be too demanding. The union and this employer make a "deal." A collective bargaining agreement is signed. The agreement may allege that the union represents a majority of the employer's employees. This representation is not true. The employer has embraced a union without the assent of the employees. The ensuing contractual relationship, understandably, is referred to as a "sweetheart contract." It is unlawful.[1] State and federal agencies have sought to deter and eradicate this type of activity.[2]

An employer sometimes invites an "easy-to-live-with" union to represent his employees upon learning that they are being organized by what he considers to be a more militant union. Paradoxically, a so-called militant union in one employer's eye may be considered passive by another employer. It is ironic that

308

one employer may "invite in" the same union his neighbor actively seeks to avoid.

Employers who engage in this type of activity are deceiving themselves. A contract signed with the "invitee" is vulnerable to attack from the employees themselves or the union whose position was usurped.[3]

A contract entered into under these circumstances violates Section 8(a)(1) and Section 8(a)(2) of the Act. If the contract provides for compulsory union membership, Section 8(a)(3) of the Act also is violated.[4] The employer may not be exculpated by a defense of mistaken belief in the union's majority status.[5]

A minority union which enters into a contract with an employer is equally guilty of a violation of the Act. It violates Section 8(b)(1), a union unfair labor practice, because it undertakes to "restrain or coerce employees in the exercise of the rights guaranteed in Section 7" of the Act to choose their own representatives.[6]

The employer may be held liable for the financial losses incurred by his employees in their forced payment of union dues and initiation fees. The Board may spare the union the obligation to return the monies it has actually received, and put the burden of reimbursement solely upon the employer. The union thus remains enriched.[7]

2. Voluntary Recognition by Accretion

Some employers, to be sure, like to have all their eggs in one basket. Unions prefer it too. They are spared the task and expense of organizing the employees in new or added facilities. Accordingly, they sometimes successfully persuade employers to agree in a contract covering presently existing units that the union will be automatically recognized for new facilities not then existing. This agreement is referred to as an accretion clause.

An employer who agrees to an accretion clause takes the risk that the legality of his action may be challenged by another union or by the employees themselves at the new location. They may assert that the new unit is not an accretion to the old because of geographic separation or dissimilarity of benefits, personnel policies or working conditions. There are many Board decisions resolving such challenges after extended proceedings.[8]

3. Involuntary Recognition Resulting from Picketing

Occasionally, a union will seek to coerce an employer into recognizing it by picketing his place of business. Should the employer succumb, its recognition of the union will be involuntary, and without employee assent.

(a) filing an unfair labor practice charge

An employer confronted with recognition picketing may file an unfair labor practice charge against the union alleging a violation of Section 8(b)(7) of the Act. The Board is required to proceed forthwith to investigate the charge, giving it priority over all other cases.[9]

The statute is violated only when an object of the picketing is to organize the employees or to force the employer to recognize or bargain with the union. Counsel therefore must support the unfair labor practice charge with affidavits proving this allegation. Such proof may consist of a conversation between the employer and the union representatives in which the representative directly or obliquely asked for recognition.

It may consist of a picture of the signs carried by the pickets stating "no contract—no work," or similar slogans, evidencing the purpose of the picketing.[10] Taking such a picture for the purposes of preparation for litigation is permissible.[11]

Employees of the employer confronted by picketing also are subjected to the pressures brought on by fear of loss of access to their place of work, or cessation of work for lack of product and loss of customers. The employer should therefore speak to his employees promptly. They should be told of their rights and the consequences of the union's actions. The employees should be urged to report threats or incidents of harrassment and physical injury, directed not only to themselves, but also to passersby, delivery men, fellow employees and customers. If ever the union's tactics result in an election proceeding, the employer will have many telling points for later discussion.

The employer and counsel should keep a complete log of incidents, in aid of further Board proceedings. Where mass picketing, blocking of entrances, physical attacks, or other criminal or tortious conduct take place, this log of evidence, pictorial and parol, will be most helpful in applying for injunctive relief in the civil courts.

(b) absence of an election petition as a condition

The picketing is proscribed where it is conducted by the union *without a petition being filed* within a "reasonable" time, not exceeding thirty days from the commencement of such picketing.[12]

(c) the union may file a petition

The union can avoid the consequences of an unfair labor practice charge by filing a petition for an election within thirty days after it commences picketing. This will cause the regional director to stay the unfair labor practice investigation, and direct an expedited election. The regional director is under instruction to by-pass the usual formalities of the election procedure, such as the requirement of a 30% showing of interest by the union, and a determination of the appropriate unit through a formal hearing.[13]

(d) the Employer may file a petition

The filing of an employer petition often is met by the union's filing of an unfair labor practice charge against the employer to block his petition.   Spurious or not, the charge must be investigated.   The result: the employer's petition is held in abeyance, while the picketing continues.

(e) picketing after losing an election

The employer's objective in filing a petition is to obtain an expedited election and a certification by the regional director that a majority of employees have rejected the union.   If the union continues to picket after having lost an election, the employer may then utilize Section 8(b)(7)(B) and charge the union with picketing for recognition where a valid election has been held.

(f) injunctive relief

When a charge is filed under Section 8(b)(7)(B) as described in (e) above, or under 8(b)(7)(C) as described in (b) above, the Board's regional attorney will, if he believes the charge has merit, seek an injunction against the picketing from the United States District Court.[14]

Obviously, while these procedures are being followed, often taking many weeks and sometimes several months, the employer's business is being strangled.   If he can hold out long enough, he will one day receive the relief intended by Congress when it passed this law.

4. Employer Successorship

A new owner of a going business sometimes succeeds to the union of his predecessor.[15]   Under certain circumstances, he may be required to assume and honor the collective bargaining agreement of the union representing the employees of the seller.[16] The factual circumstances of each sale, transfer or merger must be studied to determine whether the new owner can reasonably be said to be a successor.   It is not a *per se* conclusion.[17]

When involved in the purchase of a business, merger or consolidation, counsel should carefully research the labor relations facets of the company to be acquired. The state of the vendor's industrial relations may be as important as the items appearing on its balance sheet and profit and loss statements. As elsewhere, *caveat emptor.*

5. Union Successorship—The Take Over of an Independent Union

An "independent union" is a generic term applied to a union which is not affiliated with the AFL–CIO. When the United Mine Workers and the International Brotherhood of Teamsters withdrew from the AFL–CIO, they thereby became "independent."

We are speaking in a narrower sense. The term, as used here, refers to a union representing the employees of one company. Such a union has no connection with any other organization. Often, the union bears the name of the company whose employees it represents. Many of these "company unions" [18] had their genesis at the time of the enactment of the National Labor Relations Act. Their formation grew out of a desire to avoid organization by affiliated unions.

From the very earliest days of the Act, affiliated unions coveted the membership of such unions. The affiliated union's *modus operandi* was to file charges with the Board alleging that the independent was a company-dominated or supported union. It would seek to show that the employer had provided the independent union with free use of company premises, duplicating machines, secretarial service, post office address, telephone, bulletin board, committee meeting rooms or the payment of the officers and grievance committee for time spent on union business. If company domination was proven, the NLRB ordered the union disestablished and forbade employer recognition.[19] When this happened, the charging union moved in and enfolded the employees under its banner. Hundreds of present-day affiliated local unions had their origins as independents.

Today, affiliated unions continue to eye the remaining independents, using a different approach. Instead of seeking the disestablishment of the independent, they now seek to capture it intact. Typically, the procedure is as follows:

(1) An officer of the independent union contacts, or is contacted by, representatives of the affiliated union. The affiliated union's representatives promise that, as a more experienced and aggressive union, it can do more for the employees than the independent.

(2) The independent's officers are given authorization cards for distribution among the membership, designating the affiliated union as the bargaining agent.

(3) A membership meeting is held by the independent to discuss the possibility of affiliation. The affiliated union's representatives are invited to speak. They point out the claimed advantages which would result from affiliation. A resolution of affiliation is proposed and another meeting its scheduled to vote on the affiliation question. If necessary, proposals are voted upon to amend the independent's constitution and by-laws, which often prohibit affiliation.[20]

(4) Notices are posted to advise employees of the scheduled affiliation vote. The issue is discussed. The cases reflect that often debate is limited to those who speak favorably on the issue. It is not uncommon that a standing vote is used instead of a secret ballot.

(5) If the affiliation is approved, a vote may be taken to re-elect the present union's officers as officers of the "new" affiliated local. Thereafter, the independent union may transfer its assets and official union records into the affiliated union's control in order to complete the transition.

(6) If the vote is in favor of affiliation, the employer is notified that the independent membership has voted to affiliate with an international union, which is now the appropriate representative of his employees. He may also be advised to substitute the

name of the affiliated union in the pertinent provisions of the contract. Finally, he is requested to recognize the new union as the bargaining representative of the employees.

(7) If the employer refuses to recognize the affiliated union, the union files a "petition for amendment of certification" with the Board in which it seeks to substitute itself for the independent as the employees' representative.[21]

(8) A hearing is held to determine if the independent union is a functioning, viable entity and whether the change in representative reflected a true majority view. If the Board finds that the independent no longer exists and that an uncoerced majority of those attending the union meeting voted for the affiliation, it will amend the certification. If the employer refuses to honor the amendment to the certification, the affiliated union can file unfair labor practice charges against the company and the Board will order it to bargain.[22]

In most cases, the Board has permitted the amendment on the theory that the formerly certified independent union is no longer a separate functioning entity, but has been transformed chameleon-like into the affiliated union.[23]

However, recently Board Chairman Miller has questioned this fiction:

> I agree with the result reached by my colleagues in this case, for the reason that it appears to conform with such precedent as we have in this area. That precedent, however, rests upon a rather thin premise, i.e., that the now affiliated local is the same entity as the former independent union. . . .
>
> [T]his case raises a serious question as to whether such a finding here is no more than a legal fiction.
>
> Members of locals affiliated with large international unions enjoy the benefits of, and are subject to the

restrictions imposed by the constitutions, bylaws and practices of those sophisticated and highly institutionalized nationwide organizations. They are of a quite different character from a totally local, 'homegrown' and autonomous independent union. Few realists in the world of industrial relations would assert that a local of the Auto Workers or the Steelworkers is the 'same union' as the autonomous predecessor independent. A Board claiming expertise in this area of social and economic life should not close its eyes to these realities.

What we are really doing in these cases, therefore, is to permit certification of a new and different bargaining agent during the life of a contract, contrary to our usual contract-bar rules, although we place a limitation on the normal right of a new agent to engage in fresh bargaining, holding that it must instead administer the existing contract. . . .

. . . We now certify this new bargaining agent without having ourselves supervised the procedures by which the employees have determined to change agents. Instead, we content ourselves with the 'internal' procedures of the employee group, provided they meet certain minimum safeguards of due process, which admittedly generally fall short of the carefully supervised and controlled procedures which apply when we are petitioned to conduct an election under Section 9 of our Act.

The rather incongruous result is that if the officers of an independent union were to secure the signatures of an overwhelming majority of the total work force on cards indicating a desire to abandon the independent, authorizing representation by a newly chartered local of an affiliated union and petitioning us to conduct an election to determine by secret ballot whether a change in employee choice had indeed occurred, we would summarily dismiss the petition on contract-bar principles. But if the same officers call an 'affiliation' meeting and secure even a slim majority vote for affiliation by members present and voting in a procedure occuring outside our regulated procedures, we routinely issue our certificate to the same newly chartered local.

I would prefer, if we are to continue to reach the result here, that we adopt an appropriate modification of our contract-bar principles and permit, under appropriate circumstances, a mid-contract Board election to determine whether a different agent should administer the agreement for its duration. I believe we should face up to the facts in this manner, rather than to continue to rely on elections conducted under varying privately adopted rules.[24]

Thus, from an employer's vantage point, it can be seen that living with an independent union is precarious. The threat of affiliation is ever present. Many an employer has rued the day that he encouraged such collective action.

NOTES TO APPENDIX I

1. Marin Chatmar, Inc., 188 NLRB No. 8, 76 LRRM 1252 (1971).

2. For a summary of the efforts of the New York State Labor Relations Board, see Kramer, *SLRB: An Evolutionary Instrument For Social Justice, Economic Progress*, N.Y. Law Journal, July 6, 1971, at 10-11. For a graphic portrayal of how a union seduces an employer into this illicit arrangement, see NLRB v. Amalgamated Local 355, __ F. Supp. __, 77 LRRM 2989 (E.D.N.Y., No. 69 C 1569, decided Oct. 23, 1970).

3. Sturgeon Elec. Co., 166 NLRB 210, 65 LRRM 1530 (1967), *enf'd in part & remanded in part*, 419 F.2d 51 (10th Cir. 1969), *reaff'd*, 181 NLRB No. 30, 73 LRRM 1320 (1970).

4. Western Bldg. Maintenance Co., 162 NLRB 778, 64 LRRM 1120 (1968), *enf'd*, 402 F.2d 775 (9th Cir. 1968).

5. ILGWU v. NLRB, 366 U.S. 731 (1961), *affirming* 280 F.2d 616 (D.C. Cir. 1960), *enforcing* Bernhard-Altmann Texas Corp., 122 NLRB 1289, 43 LRRM 1283 (1959).

6. In *Western Bldg. Maintenance Co., supra* note 4, the Board also held that the union violated Section 8(b)(2).

7. Virginia Elec. & Power Co. v. NLRB, 319 U.S. 533 (1943), *affirming* 132 F.2d 390 (4th Cir. 1942), *enforcing* 44 NLRB 404, 11 LRRM 64 (1942).

8. No accretion: Essex Wire Corp., 130 NLRB 450, 47 LRRM 1369 (1961). Accretion: Continental Can Co., 127 NLRB 286, 46 LRRM 1014 (1960).

9. LMRA § 101.10(1), 29 U.S.C. § 160(1) (1964).

10. Island Coal & Lumber Corp., 159 NLRB 895, 62 LRRM 1443 (1966), *enf'd,* 387 F.2d 170 (2d Cir. 1967).

11. This is not to say that an employer may under all circumstances photograph picketing and distribution of literature. *See,* Gen. Eng'r, Inc., 131 NLRB 901, 48 LRRM 1153 (1961); Hudson Hosiery Co., 109 NLRB 1410, 34 LRRM 1574 (1954).
52 LRRM 1426 (1963); Local 239, Teamsters, 127 NLRB 958, 46 LRRM

12. For a dicussion of whether the Board need wait the full 30 days before seeking an injunction, see District 65, RWDSU, 141 NLRB 991, 1123 (1960), *enf'd,* 289 F.2d 41 (2d Cir. 1961). *See also,* Katz, *Expedited Representation Elections Under Section 8(b)(7)(C),* Symposium On LMRDA 988 (R. Slovenko ed. 1961).

13. Local 1265, RCIA v. Brown, 284 F.2d 619 (9th Cir. 1960), *cert. denied,* 366 U.S. 934 (1961).

14. Vincent v. Local 294, Teamsters, __ F. Supp. __, 76 LRRM 2858 (N.D. N.Y., No. 70-CV-244, decided August 17, 1970); Hoffman v. San Francisco Joint Board, __ F. Supp. __, 66 LRRM 2653 (N.D. Cal., No. 48187, decided Nov. 24, 1967).

15. John Wiley & Sons, Inc. v. Livingston, 376 U.S. 543 (1964), *affirming* 313 F.2d 52 (2d Cir. 1963), *rev'g* 203 F. Supp. 171 (S.D. N.Y. 1962); Overnite Transp. Co., 157 NLRB 1185, 61 LRRM 1520 (1966), *enf'd,* 372 F.2d 765 (4th Cir. 1967).

16. Ranch-Way, Inc., 183 NLRB No. 116, 74 LRRM 1389 (1970), *enf'd,* 445 F.2d 625, 77 LRRM 2689 (10th Cir. 1971); Burns Int'l. Detective Agency, Inc., 182 NLRB No. 50, 74 LRRM 1098 (1970), *enf'd in part,* 441 F.2d 263 (2d Cir. 1971), *cert. granted* __ U.S. __, 78 LRRM 2463 (Nos. 71-123 and 71-128, decided Oct. 12, 1971); Hackney Iron & Steel Co., 167 NLRB 613, 66 LRRM 1139 (1967), *enf'd in part,* 404 F.2d 556 (D.C. Cir. 1968).

17. Builders Realty & Mortgage Co., d/b/a Ramada Inn, 186 NLRB No. 87, 76 LRRM 1210 (1970); Southland Mfg. Corp., 186 NLRB No. 111, 76 LRRM 1204 (1970), *supplementing* 157 NLRB 1356, 61 LRRM 1552 (1966).

18. The term "company union" also is used to describe a union which is company dominated. H.S. Roberts, *Dictionary of Industrial Relations* 63-64 (1966).

19. Divigard Baking Co., 153 NLRB 363, 59 LRRM 1477 (1965), *enf'd,* 367 F.2d 389 (2d Cir. 1966); Aluminum Extrusions, Inc., 148 NLRB 1662, 57 LRRM 1219 (1964).

20. East Dayton Tool & Die Co., 190 NLRB No. 115, 77 LRRM 1274, 1275 (1971).

21. See Chapter V, *infra* pages 88-89.

22. U.S. Steel Corp., 189 NLRB No. 25, 76 LRRM 1570 (1970); New England Foundry Corp., 192 NLRB No. 115, 78 LRRM 1112 (1971).

23. East Dayton Tool & Die Co., *supra* note 20, at 77 LRRM 1277; U.S. Steel Corp., 185 NLRB No. 98, 75 LRRM 1203 (1970).

24. Hamilton Tool Co., 190 NLRB No. 114, 77 LRRM 1257, 1261-262 (1971) (Miller, C., concurring opinion).

APPENDIX J

NLRB JURISDICTIONAL STANDARDS

The Board's jurisdictional standards are based upon minimum amounts of annual business volume.

(a) *Retail businesses:* gross sales volume of $500,000 per annum.[1]

(b) *Non-retail*[2]: $50,000 inflow or outflow, direct or indirect, as herein defined:

> *Direct inflow:* goods or services furnished directly to the employer from outside the state in which he is located.
>
> *Indirect inflow:* goods or services which the employer purchased from a seller or supplier within the state who received them directly from outside the state.[3]
>
> *Direct outflow:* goods shipped or services furnished by the employer outside his home state.
>
> *Indirect outflow:* goods or services furnished to customers within the state who themselves meet a jurisdictional standard other than "indirect outflow" or "indirect inflow."

Direct and indirect inflow may be combined, as may direct and indirect outflow. Inflow and outflow, however, may not be combined.[4] The standard for an employer engaged in a combined retail and wholesale business is that of the non-retailer.[5]

320

(c) *Miscellaneous businesses*—annual volume.

Office building	$100,000 [6]
Instrumentalities of interstate commerce	50,000 [7]
Public utilities	250,000 [8]
Transit systems	250,000 [9]
Taxicabs	500,000 [10]
Newspapers	200,000 [11]
Radio and Television	100,000 [12]
Telephone and Telegraph	100,000 [13]
National defense	Finding of Substantial Impact Required [14]
Hotels and Motels	500,000 [15]
Proprietary hospitals	250,000 [16]
Proprietary nursing homes	100,000 [17]
Colleges and Universities	1,000,000 [18]
Trade associations	50,000 of one member or of more than one member combined [19]

Other non-profit institutions [20]

Sports [21]

NOTES TO APPENDIX J

1. Carolina Supplies & Cement Co., 122 NLRB 88, 43 LRRM 1060 (1958).

2. Siemons Mailing Serv., 122 NLRB 81, 43 LRRM 1056 (1958).

3. 23 NLRB Ann. Rep. 8 (1958).

4. *Id.*

5. Siemons Mailing Serv., *supra* note 2.

6. Gross revenue of $100,000, of which $25,000 must be derived from organizations that meet any of the Board's standards exclusive of indirect outflow or indirect inflow. Mistletoe Operating Co., 122 NLRB 1534, 43 LRRM 1333 (1958).

7. HPO Serv., Inc., 122 NLRB 394, 43 LRRM 1127 (1958).

8. $250,000 gross volume or $50,000 outflow or inflow, direct or indirect. Sioux Valley Empire Elec. Ass'n., 122 NLRB 92, 43 LRRM 1061 (1958).

9. Charleston Transit Co., 123 NLRB 1296, 44 LRRM 1123 (1959).

10. Red & White Airway Cab Co., 123 NLRB 83, 43 LRRM 1392 (1959).

11. Belleville Employing Printers, 122 NLRB 350, 43 LRRM 1125 (1958).

12. Raritan Valley Broadcasting Co., 122 NLRB 90, 43 LRRM 1062 (1958).

13. *Id.*

14. Ready Mixed Concrete & Materials, Inc., 122 NLRB 318, 43 LRRM 1115 (1958).

15. It no longer matters whether the hotel is residential or transient. Penn-Keystone Realty Corp., 191 NLRB No. 105, 77 LRRM 1600 (1971).

16. Butte Medical Properties, d/b/a Medical Center Hosp., 168 NLRB 266, 66 LRRM 1259 (1967); 33 NLRB Ann. Rep. 29 (1968).

17. Univ. Nursing Home, Inc., 168 NLRB 263, 66 LRRM 1263 (1967).

18. Cornell Univ., 183 NLRB No. 41, 74 LRRM 1269 (1970); NLRB Rules & Regulations § 103.1, 35 Fed. Reg. 18370 (1970).

19. Siemons Mailing Serv., *supra* note 2.

20. Children's Village, 186 NLRB No. 137, 76 LRRM 1383 (1970); Drexel Home, 182 NLRB No. 151, 74 LRRM 1232 (1970); Woods Hole Oceanographic Institution, 143 NLRB 568, 53 LRRM 1296 (1963).

21. American League, 180 NLRB No. 30, 72 LRRM 1545 (1969).

APPENDIX K

NOTICE OF DESIGNATION OF REPRESENTATIVE FOR SERVICE

National Labor Relations Board

NOTICE OF DESIGNATION OF REPRESENTATIVE
AS AGENT FOR SERVICE OF DOCUMENTS
IN REPRESENTATION PROCEEDING

CASE NO.

TO: Regional Director,

I, the undersigned party, hereby designate my representative, whose name and address appears below and who has entered an appearance on my behalf in this proceeding, as my agent to receive exclusive service of all documents and written communications relating to this proceeding, excepting only decisions directing an election, notices of an election, and subpoenas, and authorize the National Labor Relations Board to serve all such documents only on said representative. This designation shall remain valid until a written revocation of it signed by me is filed with the Board.

Signature of party (please sign in ink)	Representative's name, address, zip code (print or type)	
Date		
	Area Code	Telephone Number

323

TABLE OF CASES

INDEX

339

A